CREATING YOUR OWN WEB PAGES SECOND EDITION

CREATING YOUR OWN WEB PAGES

SECOND EDITION

Written by Andy Shafran

Creating Your Own Web Pages, Second Edition

Library of Congress Catalog No.: 97-66488

ISBN: 0-7897-1232-6

99 98 97   6 5 4 3 2 1

Interpretation of the printing code: the rightmost double-digit number is the year of the book's printing; the rightmost single-digit number, the number of the book's printing. For example, a printing code of 97-1 shows that the first printing of the book occurred in 1997.

Screen reproductions in this book were created with Collage Plus from Inner Media, Inc., Hollis, NH.

Credits

PRESIDENT
Roland Elgey

PUBLISHER
Stacy Hiquet

DIRECTOR OF MARKETING
Lynn E. Zingraf

PUBLISHING MANAGER
Jim Minatel

EDITORIAL SERVICES DIRECTOR
Elizabeth Keaffaber

ACQUISITIONS MANAGER
Cheryl D. Willoughby

ACQUISITIONS EDITOR
Jane K. Brownlow

PRODUCT DIRECTOR
Stephen L. Miller

PRODUCTION EDITOR
Jim Bowie

PRODUCT MARKETING MANAGER
Kristine Ankney

ASSISTANT PRODUCT MARKETING MANAGERS
Karen Hagen
Christy M. Miller

STRATEGIC MARKETING MANAGER
Barry Pruett

TECHNICAL EDITOR
Tony Schafer

TECHNICAL SUPPORT SPECIALIST
Nadeem Muhammed

SOFTWARE RELATIONS COORDINATOR
Susan D. Gallagher

EDITORIAL ASSISTANT
Andrea Duvall

BOOK DESIGNER
Ruth Harvey

COVER DESIGNERS
Ruth Harvey
Kim Scott

PRODUCTION TEAM
Michael Beaty
Jessica Ford
Tony McDonald
Julie Searls

INDEXER
Eric Brinkman

Composed in *Century Old Style* and *ITC Franklin Gothic* by Que Corporation.

About the Author

Andy Shafran has been writing computer books for several years. He actually enjoys working with the Internet, World Wide Web, and related information technologies, such as Lotus Notes. Born in Columbus, Ohio, Andy recently graduated from Ohio State University with a degree in Computer Science Engineering. He now lives in Cincinnati, the Queen City, and is an avid Reds and baseball fan.

He has written several other computer books, including *Creating Your Own Netscape Web Pages*; *Enhancing Netscape Web Pages*; *Creating Your Own Web Graphics*; and *Creating and Enhancing Netscape Web Pages, Bestseller Edition*.

When he's not writing he enjoys live theater, particularly Broadway shows. He also loves traveling abroad and is constantly making excuses to buy yet another plane ticket to a foreign country. You can talk to Andy via e-mail at **andy@shafran.com** or visit his WWW page at **http://www.shafran.com**.

Acknowledgments

Although I wrote this book, many, many people put in significant effort to make it a reality. Most importantly, I'd like to acknowledge my wife Liz, who is busy herself in grad school, but found the time to edit, research, and help me out on this project.

I'd also like to thank the hundreds of people who've sent me e-mail on the previous edition. Without their help, this book wouldn't exist. They really helped me focus this book to the right audience and put together a cohesive, usable, and entertaining book on creating Web pages that anyone can understand and everyone can use.

Additionally, there are several individuals at Que who I'd like to thank individually. Jim Minatel has been in on this entire project from the beginning. Jane Brownlow has been a good partner and consistently came through for this entire project. Stephen Miller collaborated with me on several important aspects. I'd also like to thank Laddie Irvin and Jim Bowie. As usual, the team over at Que has been great to work with.

Finally, I'd like to thank Mark Braunwart for providing advice and an ear to chew on when discussing various aspects of HTML, the WWW, and creating Web pages.

We'd Like to Hear from You!

As part of our continuing effort to produce books of the highest possible quality, Que would like to hear your comments. To stay competitive, we *really* want you, as a computer book reader and user, to let us know what you like or dislike most about this book or other Que products.

You can mail comments, ideas, or suggestions for improving future editions to the address below, or send us a fax at (317) 581-4663. For the online inclined, Macmillan Computer Publishing has a forum on CompuServe (type **GO QUEBOOKS** at any prompt) through which our staff and authors are available for questions and comments. The address of our Internet site is **http://www.quecorp.com** (World Wide Web).

In addition to exploring our forum, please feel free to contact me personally to discuss your opinions of this book: I'm **76103,1334** on CompuServe, and **smiller@que.mcp.com** on the Internet.

Thanks in advance—your comments will help us to continue publishing the best books available on computer topics in today's market.

Stephen L. Miller
Product Development Specialist
Que Corporation
201 W. 103rd Street
Indianapolis, Indiana 46290
USA

Contents at a Glance

Introduction   1

I | Planning Your Web Page

1   A Web Crawler's Beginning   9
2   Weaving Your Own Web   29

II | Creating a Basic Web Page

3   Web Page Basics   51
4   Adding Style to Your Text   67
5   Adding Lists and Tables   83

III | Spicing Up Your Web Page

6   Using Graphics to Excite Your Page   107
7   Linking Your Web Pages   137

IV | Advanced Web Page Publishing

8   Image Map Education   155
9   Customizing Your Web Page   175
10   Making Your Web Page Multimedia   195

V | Final Touches

11   Important Design Considerations   213
12   Publicizing Your Web Page   231
13   Using HTML Editors and Other Web Tools   251

VI | Appendix

A   What's on the CD-ROM   265

Index   275

Bonus Appendixes on the CD-ROM

B   Home Page Final Checklist
C   References Used in This Book
D   Legal Issues with Web Pages

Table of Contents

Introduction   1

What You'll Learn in This Book   2

Practicality Is Its Own Virtue   2

Who Is This Book for?   3

What This Book Isn't   3

How This Book Helps You Create Your Home Page   3

What's on the CD-ROM?   6

Conventions Used in This Book   6

Keeping the Book's Content Current   7

I   Planning Your Web Page

1   A Web Crawler's Beginning   9

What Is the World Wide Web?   10

    Multimedia   10

    Hypertext Links   11

    HTML   13

    Internet Protocols   14

    Interaction to a New Level   15

How the Web Works   16

    Client/Server-Based   16

    SLIP/PPP Modem Connection Required   17

    A Brief History of the Web   18

    Future Web Directions   19

Getting to Know Popular WWW Browsers   21

    Netscape Communicator   21

    Internet Explorer   21

    Other Web Browsers   23

What Is HTML and What Are the Standards?   24

HTML 3.2—the Current Standard   25

    HTML Extensions   26

    The High End of HTML   26

2 Weaving Your Own Web   29

What's a Home Page?   30

Why Create a Home Page?   30
Personal Pages   31
Business Pages   32

Gathering Ideas and Constructing a Blueprint   34
Short but Sweet: John's Page   34
Intermediate Level: My Personal Page   35
Classy Web Page: The Crime Scene   35
Excellent Commercial Site: ESPN SportsZone   37
Fantastic Commercial Site: Coca-Cola   37
Organizing Your Home Page   38
Sketching Your Page Out   39

Writing HTML   40
Creating HTML Files   41
Using an HTML Editor   42

Connecting to a Web Provider   43
What You are Looking for   44
Expected Costs   44
Web Provider Listings   45
Geocities   46
Forman Interactive   47
Online Services   47
One Alternative: Running Your Own Web Server   49

Uploading Your Web Pages   50

II | Creating a Basic Web Page

3 Web Page Basics   51

Using the Standard Home Page Template   52

Important HTML Tags   52
<HTML> and *</HTML>*   53
<HEAD> and *</HEAD>*   53
<BODY> and *</BODY>*   54
<ADDRESS> and *</ADDRESS>*   54

Titling Your Home Page   55

Creating Headings   56

Adding Text and Information   58

Breaking Text into Readable Chunks   59
    Paragraph Tag   60
    Line Break Tag   60
    Horizontal Rules   61
    Line Extensions   62
    Preformatted Text   66

4   Adding Style to Your Text   67

Updating Text Appearance   68
    Centering   68
    Bold Text   68
    Italic   69
    Blinking   69
    Strikethrough   70
    Underline   70
    Making Your Text Slightly Larger or Smaller   70
    Subscript and Superscript   72

Working with the *FONT* Tag   72
    Setting Actual Font Size   73
    Setting Relative Font Sizes   73
    Embedding *<FONT>* Tags   74
    Font Faces   75

Controlling Text Color   78
    Coloring by *FONT*   78
    Other Ways to Change Text Color   79
    Color by Hexadecimal   79

Adding Special Characters   81

5   Adding Lists and Tables   83

What Are Lists and Tables?   84

What Lists Help You Accomplish   84
    Organize with Lists   84
    Simplify Large Amounts of Information   85
    Describe a Step-By-Step Process   86

Add a List to Your Page   87

Unordered (Bulleted) List   88
Ordered (Numbered) List   89
Definition List   91

Lists Within Lists   93

Tabling Your Home Page   94

Add a Table   95

Using Advanced Table Features   98
Lines Spanning Multiple Rows   98
Spanning Multiple Columns   99
Embedding Lists into Tables   100
Setting Your Text Alignment   101
Table Colors   102

Table Alternatives   104
Lists Can Replace Tables   104
Preformatted Text   104

III | Spicing Up Your Web Page

6 Using Graphics to Excite Your Page   107

Pros and Cons of Web Page Graphics   108

Where You Can Find Graphics, Images, and Pictures   109
On the Enclosed CD-ROM   109
Borrow from Other Pages   110
Other Existing Images   113
Create Your Own   113
Using PaintShop Pro   114
Current Scanner Quality and Detail   115

Adding an Image to Your Home Page   116
Using the Proper Image File Types   116
Adding the Image   117
Image File Size Guidelines   120

Manipulating Your Home Page Images   122
Providing Alternative Text   122
Aligning Your Image   123
Sizing Your Image   125

Adding Icons to Your Home Page   126
   Lines and Bars   127
   Bullets   127
   New Icons   128
   Construction Icons   128
   Navigation Icons   128

Give Your Home Page Some Background   129
   Adding Background Colors   129
   Using Background Images   130
   Background Problems   131

Creating Transparent GIFs   131
   How Web Browsers Treat Transparent GIFs   132
   Making Transparent GIFs   133
   Creating a Transparent GIF from Scratch   133

Overlaying Images   135

7   Linking Your Web Pages   137

Understanding Hypertext Links   138

Anatomy of a Link   138

Creating a Link   139
   Linking to Local Web Pages   140
   Linking Elsewhere on the WWW   141
   Link Color   144

Using Images as Links   144

Using Anchors on Your Home Page   146
   Creating and Naming an Anchor   148
   Linking to an Anchor   149

Organize Your Links with Lists   150

Useful Linking Tips   151
   Don't Over Link   151
   Link Specific/Descriptive Words   152
   Describe Large Links   153
   Keep Your Links Current   153

IV | Advanced Web Page Publishing

8 Image Map Education 155

How Do Image Maps Work? 156
   Image Maps Are Not New Technology 157
   Differences Between Server-Side and Client-Side
   Image Maps 158

Creating an Image Map 159
   Finding a Good Image 159
   Planning the Map 161
   Adding the Image to Your Web Page 162
   Mapping Your Image 162

Understanding the Image Map Shapes 167
   Rectangles 168
   Circles 169
   Polygons 169
   How Do Overlapping Regions Work? 170
   Adding a Default Link 171

Test the Image Map with a Browser 172

Providing a Textual Alternative 172

Image Map Design Tips 173

9 Customizing Your Web Page 175

Expanding Your Web Page into a Web Site 176
   Why Split Up Your Home Page 176
   Design Your Home Site Correctly 177
   Splitting Your Page 179
   Linking Your Pages 181
   Web Site Management 182

Tracking How Many People Visit Your Home Page 183
   Adding the Simple Counter 183
   More Advanced Counters 186

Getting Feedback from Visitors with a Quick Guestbook 186

Linking to Other Internet Resources 189
   FTP 189
   News 191
   Gopher 192
   E-Mail 193

10 Making Your Web Page Multimedia 195

A Sampling of Multimedia Sites 196
    Politically Correct Bedtime Stories 196
    Great Multimedia Example—Independence Day 196

Understanding and Using Audio Clips 198
    Explain Audio File Types and Formats 198
    Where You Can Find Audio Clips 199

Adding Audio Clips to Your Web Page 201
    Adding Sounds via Hypertext Links 201
    Embedding Sound with Netscape 202
    Embedding Sounds with Internet Explorer 204

Understanding and Using Video Clips 204
    Explaining Video File Types and Formats 205
    Where You Can Find Video Clips 206

Adding Video Clips to Your Home Page 209
    Adding Video Clips via Hypertext Links 209
    Embedding Video with Netscape 210
    Embedding Video with IE 211

Mixing Multimedia 211

V Final Touches

11 Important Design Considerations 213

Home Page Design Tips 214
    Measure Your Page's Consistency 214
    Brevity Is a Virtue 214
    Don't Overdo Your Web Page with Glitz 216
    Keep Your Web Page Alive 216

Be Aware of Creeping Featurism 218
    Don't Hide Links and Features 219
    Explore Other Sites—Borrow Design Concepts 221

Improving Your HTML Code 221
    Make It Readable 222
    Comment Your HTML 224

Test Your Web Page 225
    Preview Your Page 225

Use Another Browser   227
Test and Validate Your HTML Document   227

12   Publicizing Your Web Page   231

Attracting Visitors to Your Web Page   232
Why Publicize Your Web Page?   232
Set Reasonable Expectations   233

Using WWW Catalogs and Announcement Services   234
Announcement Services   234
WWW Directories   237
Searching the WWW   241
Submit It!—16 WWW Catalogs in One   243

Using UseNet Newsgroups   244
comp.infosystems.www.announce   244
Personal Newsgroup Interests   246

Other Ways to Advertise Your Home Page   247
Resumes and Business Cards   247
Signing Your Mail and News Postings   247
Ask Other WWW Sites to Link to You   247

WWW Advertisements   248

13   Using HTML Editors and Other Web Tools   251

Choosing Your Web Publishing Tools   252
Using HotDog Pro   252
CoffeeCup   256
HoTMetaL Free and HoTMetaL Pro   257
Netscape Composer   258
HTML Tools for Microsoft Users   259

Other Programs Useful for Building Web Pages   260
PaintShop Pro   260
GIF Construction Set   262

Staying Current   263

VI | Appendix

A   What's on the CD-ROM   265

Programs and Examples Used in This Book   266
CoffeeCup HTML Editor   266

HotDog HTML Editor   266

MapTHIS!   266

Collections of Images and Graphics   267

Sound Clips   267

Video Clips   267

Example Files   268

References Used in This Book   268

A Complete Listing of Software on the CD-ROM   268

Index   275

Bonus Appendixes on the CD-ROM

B   Home Page Final Checklist

C   References Used in This Book

D   Legal Issues with Web Pages

Introduction

Welcome to *Creating Your Own Web Pages, Second Edition*. This book is the complete easy-to-use reference that steps you through building a fantastic Web page from start to finish.

This book is a completely revised and updated version of the previous best-selling edition. Each chapter has been rewritten and carefully thought out to incorporate new changes that affect individuals when creating Web pages. Also, we've completely retooled the CD-ROM so that it has literally one of the most useful sets of tools on the market—you will be impressed.

In this introduction, I'll talk about all of the important information you'll need to remember while reading through this book. I'll describe who this book is written for, what kind of information you can find inside, what assumptions I've made, and even summarize each chapter for quick reference. You'll learn why this book is the best—and only—book about Web pages you'll need. ■

What You'll Learn in This Book

As you start reading this book, you'll learn a lot of new information that can help create your Web page. Whether it's understanding HTML or incorporating basic design considerations, I've carefully written this book to bring you through the entire process of creating a new Web page in the easiest possible method.

Specifically, you'll learn how to:

- Plan your home page.
- Choose a Web provider and upload your page to the Internet.
- Understand the ins and outs of HTML.
- Organize information with lists and tables.
- Link your home page to others throughout the world.
- Incorporate other Internet resources, such as FTP and Gopher, into your home page.
- Embed pictures, audio clips, and video clips into your home page.
- Maintain your home page to keep it current, interesting, and fun.
- Attract visitors from around the world to your home page.
- Build interactive image maps on your Web site.

Practicality Is Its Own Virtue

This book is written from a very specific point of view—trying to answer: "How can I create my Web page?" In a practical and easy-to-understand manner, I'll answer that question thoroughly so that by the end of this book, you'll have a solid handle on what the Web is and how you can be a part of this exciting new technology.

I'm going to take you through the real-life issues that you face while creating your Web page. You'll have to decide what kind of information to put on your page, how to organize it, which links you should include, and how to keep your page up to date.

Web pages are written in HyperText Markup Language (HTML). While HTML is not overly difficult, some concepts can be hard to understand and work with. I'll trailblaze the path through the multitude of HTML tags and teach you what you need to know to build your Web pages.

I'm not going to waste much of your time writing about the intricacies of HTML, arguing over Internet bandwidth, or other issues that probably don't interest you. Instead, you'll find a step-by-step guide to help you accomplish all your home page objectives. You'll find that I mix real-life Web pages with contrived examples to show how HTML works when building Web pages.

Who Is This Book for?

Anyone who has experienced the World Wide Web, and wants to create his or her own unique home page, will be interested in this book. In general, the beginner and average-level World Wide Web surfer and Internet user will find this book a suitable and complete tool for creating home pages.

I made several assumptions about you—the reader—when writing this book:

- **You've seen the Web**—It's important that you understand what the World Wide Web is and have a rudimentary understanding of how it works (I'll go over this in more detail in the first chapter). You should know the difference between Netscape (a WWW browser) and Microsoft Excel (not a browser). You don't have to be an Internet guru, but familiarity helps. You should also have a current WWW browser (Netscape or Internet Explorer) installed and available to use.

- **You have an Internet SLIP/PPP connection**—This book doesn't cover how to get up and running with an Internet connection that lets you access the World Wide Web. It does, however, talk about special places on the Internet to put your home page if you don't know where to place it. A general Internet reference book (such as Que's *Special Edition Using the Internet, Third Edition*) will help you get up and running with the Web very quickly. Alternatively, an ISDN or direct Internet connection (read Que's *Special Edition Using ISDN, Second Edition*) is just as fine for using the Web (such as at your place of employment).

- **You're ready to build your part of the Web**—This book has been carefully laid out and planned in the way I think is most useful and efficient. Creating a Web page can be fun, interesting, and occasionally challenging.

What This Book Isn't

No book can be everything. Technology is constantly changing; books don't often have 2,500 pages; and you, the reader, don't need to worry about every Web detail that exists.

I've tried to include the information that you would find most valuable when trying to create your own Web pages. Although I try to cover new technology, the World Wide Web is an evolving project and new enhancements are constantly introduced. In this book, you'll find some of the most popular and useful techniques and tools that exist. But you won't find a comprehensive list of all the HTML tags, nor will you find a comprehensive and dry reference. Instead, it is a casual set of lessons for building Web pages.

How This Book Helps You Create Your Home Page

Although meant to be read in order, you'll probably find that each chapter is structured so that you can read them individually. Each chapter is broken down into edible chunks of information that make it easy to digest the process of creating a home page. Think of each chapter as a new lesson in the learning process.

Here is a brief summary of what you'll find in this book and how it is organized.

Part I: Planning Your Web Page

This part includes the first two chapters of the book, which detail the first few steps in building a great Web site. Chapter 1, "A Web Crawler's Beginning," gives a basic introduction to the World Wide Web and contains important information detailing how the Web works. You'll also learn what a home page is.

In Chapter 2, "Weaving Your Own Web," you'll see how to plan and organize your home page, and you'll see several different example Web pages that already exist on the WWW. You'll be introduced to HTML and to a Web provider—a vendor who stores your home page on the Internet for a monthly charge. I'll show you what to look for and how much to pay when choosing a Web provider of your own.

Part II: Creating a Basic Web Page

Read through this part to get up to speed on the basics of creating a Web page. You'll learn all of the important basic concepts that you need to be familiar with when building Web pages and how to control the way text looks in a browser. Chapter 3, "Web Page Basics," overviews how to add text, break up blocks of text, and what elements of HTML every Web page should have.

Next, Chapter 4, "Adding Style to Your Text," details how text attributes can be used to add text-formatting features to your home page while keeping the information easy to read, colorful, and exciting.

Chapter 5, "Adding Lists and Tables," explains how to use and include tables and lists in your home page. This chapter not only explains how to use lists and tables effectively, but also helps you decide when to use and customize them for your personal preferences.

Part III: Spicing Up Your Web Page

Part III helps you add some personality and liveliness to your home page by using two critical WWW features—links and graphics. Chapter 6, "Using Graphics to Excite Your Page," teaches you how to integrate graphics and pictures into your Web page. You'll learn how to use some of the images from the included CD-ROM (or use your own pictures) as important parts of your page.

In Chapter 7, "Linking Web Pages," you'll see how to add and organize hypertext links. You'll learn how to link your document to any other spot on the Web. In addition, you'll see how to use graphics as hotlinks and how to sort and organize links without overwhelming people that browse your page.

Part IV: Advanced Web Page Publishing

Part IV covers some more advanced issues that you'll want to use in your Web sites to add special effects and interactivity to visitors. In Chapter 8, "Image Map Education," you'll learn how you can build your own clickable image maps. Image maps are Web graphics that let visitors go to different places on the WWW, depending on which part of the image they click.

Chapter 9, "Customizing Your Web Page," is where I'll demonstrate advanced ways to coordinate and build your pages. You'll learn how to incorporate additional World Wide Web features by tracking the number of visitors who stop by and browse, by adding a simple guestbook so that visitors can sign in when they stop by, and by using other Internet resources (such as FTP and Usenet newsgroups) as part of your Web page experience.

The last chapter in this section, Chapter 10, "Making Your Web Page Multimedia," explains the basics of using multimedia (audio and video) in your Web page. You'll learn how to add sound bites and cool video clips to your home page for a dazzling effect.

Part V: Final Touches

Once you are familiar with HTML, this section explains several other issues that Web creators can use to touch up their site.

Chapter 11, "Important Design Considerations," helps tie all of your Web knowledge together. I focus on important design issues you need to know when making Web pages. I'll step you through many common items you should look for when putting together your Web page. You'll even learn how to officially validate your HTML code to make sure it follows HTML standards.

Chapter 12, "Publicizing Your Web Page," teaches you how to let other WWW users know that your home page exists—after all, what good is a home page if no one ever visits? You'll learn the proper publicity channels and where to announce to the Internet that you're ready for visitors to stop by and see the fruits of your labor.

Chapter 13, "Using HTML Editors and Other Web Tools," is one of my favorite chapters in the book. You'll learn that many tools exist to help you in the Web authoring process. I introduce HTML editors and several other tools found on the included CD-ROM that you'll use when developing pages.

Appendixes

Several appendixes are provided for your benefit. Use them as references for the book while you're creating your home page. Appendixes B – D are located on the CD-ROM.

Appendix A, "What's on the CD-ROM," provides a comprehensive listing of the files, tools, and utilities that are included on the enclosed CD-ROM. I've spent a great deal of time putting together many of the samples and examples used in this book so you can see them work on your own computer. Explore the CD to see these files in action.

Appendix B, "Home Page Final Checklist," contains a simple checklist to make sure you've caught most of the common mistakes made by new home-page creators. I've summarized some of the common tips and tricks.

Appendix C, "References Used in This Book," lists all referenced URLs and additional sites on the Web to help you create cool home pages. A live version of this appendix can also be found on the CD-ROM that accompanies this book.

Appendix D, "Legal Issues with Web Pages," is an introduction on some of the complex legal issues that can arise when creating your own Web pages. Copyright and global legality issues are discussed so that you can be informed of the legal world around us.

Additionally, there are many sample graphics, sound files, and video clips that you can use on your Web page. In fact, the CD-ROM is almost full—that's hundreds of megs of stuff for you to use with your Web page. For more information, see the next section.

What's on the CD-ROM?

Included in the back of this book is a CD-ROM full of important and useful files for enhancing Web pages. On this CD-ROM you'll find dozens of useful programs, samples, graphics, and multimedia clips.

Specifically, on the CD-ROM you'll find the following:

- Dozens of useful images and graphics for your personal use
- Many useful HTML editors and tools for creating Web pages
- Hotlists, references, and templates discussed in this book
- Multimedia clips and demonstrations that work with Web browsers
- Netscape plug-ins and helper applications

Conventions Used in This Book

As you're reading through the book, I use several different conventions that highlight specific types of information that you'll want to keep an eye out for:

- All HTML codes and tags will appear in `FULL MONOSPACE CAPS`. That's so you can tell the difference between text that appears onscreen and text that tells your browser what to do. Netscape and Internet Explorer don't care whether your HTML tags are in full caps.
- In addition, all URLs are displayed in **boldface**. You can type them directly into your browser Location window and go directly to the site.

Besides these standard textual conventions, I also use several different icons throughout this book.

On the CD-ROM

This icon indicates that the specific files, tools, references, and examples are on the CD-ROM enclosed in the back of this book. Check out Appendix A for more information on exactly where the file is located on the CD-ROM.

TIP Text formatted in this manner offers extra information that is related to the issue being discussed. You'll find personal anecdotes and experiences, specific design techniques, and general information extras in these boxes.

CAUTION

This feature alerts you to actions and commands that could make permanent changes or potentially cause future problems. You will also be alerted to possible security concerns. Make sure you read this text carefully; it could have important information that directly affects your Web page.

N O T E Notes present interesting or useful information that isn't necessarily essential to the discussion. A note provides additional information that might help you avoid problems. They also offer advice that relates to the topic. ■

Keeping the Book's Content Current

Keeping information current and relevant can be difficult when dealing with something that evolves as quickly as the World Wide Web. Features are constantly being updated, changed, and released. I have learned this lesson—particularly when working on new editions of my books. Over half of my original links and references are now old, obsolete, or relocated—that's quite a few.

Realizing this, I've devoted a significant amount of time to building and maintaining a comprehensive Web site that keeps you, the reader of this book, informed and current. On this Web site, I'll post corrections to the book, keep a list of new and important references that are useful to readers, and add new information that is so cutting edge that it wasn't available at the time of this printing.

You'll also be able to leave your comments about the book and how you liked it. I'll keep this site current, and you might want to visit it often. I think you'll find it an excellent additional value that you get when purchasing this book. My job as the author doesn't stop when this book is published; it's continuously evolving.

Stop by the book's home page at **http://www.shafran.com/create**. Or if you'd like to send some e-mail directly, I'd love to hear from you. Your input and comments are critical to making sure that this book covers all the right information in an easy-to-use manner. Send e-mail to **andy@shafran.com**. ●

A Web Crawler's Beginning

A new chain of stores is popping up around the nation. These stores carry video and sound equipment, a fully stocked inventory of albums, CDs, and software, as well as a complete bookstore. They are true "multimedia" stores—more like warehouses, actually. Now, let's take that same concept and make it available electronically. What do you have? The World Wide Web. But, there's much more to know about the Web than this. The Web is an important communications and informational tool that is accessible to just about anyone with a computer.

By the time you've picked up this book and decided to create your own Web page, you will have spent several hours "surfing" the Internet and exploring the World Wide Web. In this chapter, I introduce and explain important concepts about the Web, and make sure you understand several details before creating your own home page. ■

What is the World Wide Web?

You'll understand what makes up this complex Web of computers talking to one another around the world.

How the Web works

Look here to learn how computers use special communications methods and protocols to make up the backbone of the Internet and WWW.

The history and future of the Web

Learn about the original WWW and how it has evolved over the past few years.

How browsers fit into the big Web picture

Look here to learn more about this ubiquitous software—the Web browser.

HTML (HyperText Markup Language)

Discover the special markup language that defines every single Web page.

What Is the World Wide Web?

Have you noticed that when you watch television, a lot of the advertisers now include their World Wide Web (WWW) address in the commercials? Everyone from Toyota (**http://www.toyota.com**) to Magnavox (**http://www.magnavox.com**) is jumping on the Web page bandwagon. Most of them use the exact same features that you can have in your Web pages—cool graphics, lots of information, and multimedia clips. You also might have noticed people putting their URL on résumés and business cards. It seems as if everyone is going "http://crazy."

As you may have gathered, there's a reason for the increased popularity in the Web. Like you, millions of people are becoming more familiar with the Internet and online services every year, and the number of WWW users is growing at an astronomical clip.

Nowadays, there's an estimated 25 million people with access to the World Wide Web (for more information on these statistics, check out **http://www.cc.gatech.edu/gvu/user_surveys/**). After three years of unprecedented growth, the World Wide Web is still expanding and reinventing itself. Internet access has become so ubiquitous that Congress has even started to evaluate whether it should be regulated as a public service—like the telephone and gas companies.

What is it about the Web that makes everybody want to use it? Businesses like it, individuals like it, even the government has its act together and maintains several great WWW sites. The answer is really quite simple, people have become enraptured with the unique and interactive combination of text, images, audio, and video that's available at their fingertips. You've already become addicted; that's why you bought this book—to become part of this electronic revolution. Simply put, the *World Wide Web* is a graphical way of retrieving information from the Internet.

In this section, you'll see a more complete description of what the WWW is and how it works. A textbook definition of the Web might be: "an interactive multimedia, hypertext environment using a markup language that supports multiple Internet protocols." That's a good definition of the WWW if you completely understand what it means. Let me break down that sentence for you, just in case.

Multimedia

While most of the information found on the Internet is in straight-text format, sometimes a picture is worth a thousand words (or more). One of the main features of the WWW is the ability to view images and text alike on the same screen. That makes using the Web graphical, fun, and exciting. In fact, not only does the Web allow you to mix graphics and text together, but audio and video clips are also part of the whole multimedia experience. Figure 1.1 shows a multimedia Web site for the special-effects-movie bonanza, *Dante's Peak*, which shows text, graphics, movie clips, and sound integrated on a single site.

FIG. 1.1
An example of multimedia is the home page for *Dante's Peak*, which can be found at **http://www. dantespeak.com**.

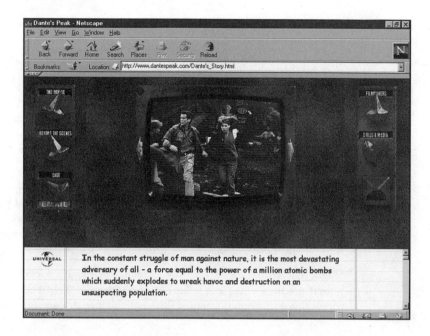

Besides pictures and images, audio bites or video clips are also a cornerstone of the Web. Any site on the Web can integrate all four types of media into a single WWW page.

Movie studios regularly take advantage of the multimedia facets of the Web. On one screen you can read a movie review, see a picture of the movie poster, hear an actor recount his experience, and even see a preview of the movie at the same site.

Hypertext Links

The Web is what's called a "hypertext" environment. Hypertext means that certain information that you see is "linked" to other pieces of information. For instance, when you use the Help feature in Windows software such as Word or Excel, there are highlighted words that, by clicking them, take you to help for that word. Similarly, by clicking your mouse on a hypertext link, you automatically bring up the linked information as a separate document.

These hypertext links are the basic building blocks of the Web. Every document is comprised of links that take you to other Web sites, pictures, sound files, and other related information. You've probably used these links extensively when exploring on your own through the WWW.

On the Web, these different places and links are called *Uniform Resource Locators* (URLs). Every document and file on the Internet has its own unique URL that allows it to be linked to other documents easily. You can think of these URLs as addresses. While URLs might seem complicated, they're really easy to understand once you break them apart. Each address has three basic elements:

- *URL Type*: The beginning of each URL identifies the type of link it is. For instance, **http://** indicates a Web link; **Gopher://** indicates a Gopher link; **FTP://** indicates a link to an FTP site; **file://** points to a specific file on your computer, and so on.

- *Domain*: Following the URL type is the actual *Domain Name*, or address, of the URL. For instance, Microsoft's Web address is **www.microsoft.com**, so their URL would be **http://www.microsoft.com/**. My domain name is **www.shafran.com** so the URL to my Web page is **http://www.shafran.com**.

- *Directory or Document*: If a link is going to a particular document or directory, this would be attached to the end of the URL. For example, on my Web site, I have a subdirectory named **create** that I made especially for this book. In that subdirectory, the main HTML page is called **index.htm**. So my URL to the file in that subdirectory is **http://www.shafran.com/create/index.htm**.

Similarly, Microsoft has a Web page on their Web site in a document called **ShortCuts.htm**. This file is in the **/Misc** directory of their Web site. So if you wanted to access this document, the entire URL would be **http://www.microsoft.com/Misc/ShortCuts.htm**.

Let's say you were looking at a Web page of a fictitious circus, as shown in Figure 1.2. From this screen you can link to other pages that show you more information about each of the attractions, animals, and performers. The links to other places are usually underlined or appear in a different color so they're easy to identify.

FIG. 1.2

The circus home page is only the beginning of my quest for elephant knowledge.

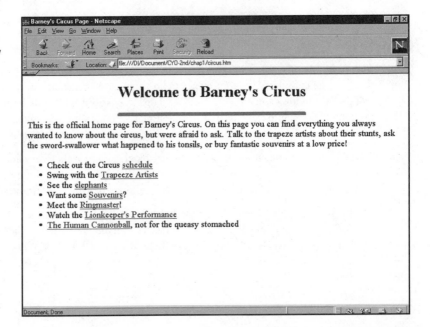

If you select the link to the elephants, you'll be brought to the circus elephant home page (see Figure 1.3). You can see a description of the elephant performances, and even a few neat pictures. There are also additional links that bring you to other elephant-related resources on the Web. These links have nothing to do with the circus, but are interesting to people who like elephants. You can follow links to zoos or African Savannahs, or maybe even learn about an elephant graveyard.

FIG. 1.3
This page links to all the elephant pages in the circus as well as other WWW pages.

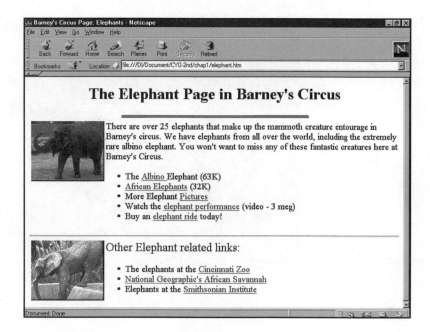

That's how the Web works. Related information is linked together in any way you choose. It's extremely flexible and friendly to use hypertext. From this single screen you can visit sites all over the world. You can see the Cincinnati Zoo Web page, *National Geographic* online, or the Smithsonian Institute all with a single click.

HTML

The World Wide Web is based on a programming language called *HyperText Markup Language (HTML)*. HTML is a subset of an existing, more complicated language named SGML (but we won't go into that here).

A markup language uses tags that are inserted into textual documents that explain how information should be formatted onscreen. All HTML documents are purely text-based. Web browsers, such as Netscape, read the HTML documents and determine how to display that information onscreen. For example, the following line lists a simple sentence with two pairs of HTML tags specifying how some of the text should look:

```
<B>This is <I>my</I> home page</B>
```

would bold the entire line as well as display "my" in italics.

Tags determine which text should appear larger (as headlines), how paragraphs are formatted, where graphics should be placed, and how to link to other WWW pages (as in the example in Figure 1.4). You'll learn all about the proper use of tags as you read through this book. Figure 1.4 uses the View, Source (View, Page Source in Netscape) command from your browser to bring up the HTML text that determines how information and graphics should appear on the screen.

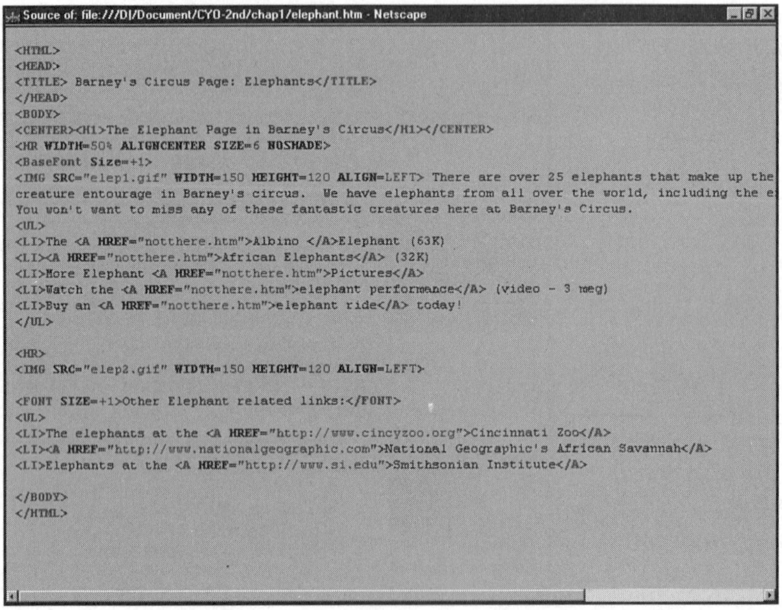

FIG. 1.4

Here's the same elephant home page in HTML format. Quite a difference!

```
Source of: file:///D|/Document/CYO-2nd/chap1/elephant.htm - Netscape

<HTML>
<HEAD>
<TITLE> Barney's Circus Page: Elephants</TITLE>
</HEAD>
<BODY>
<CENTER><H1>The Elephant Page in Barney's Circus</H1></CENTER>
<HR WIDTH=50% ALIGN=CENTER SIZE=6 NOSHADE>
<BaseFont Size=+1>
<IMG SRC="elep1.gif" WIDTH=150 HEIGHT=120 ALIGN=LEFT> There are over 25 elephants that make up the
creature entourage in Barney's circus.  We have elephants from all over the world, including the e
You won't want to miss any of these fantastic creatures here at Barney's Circus.
<UL>
<LI>The <A HREF="notthere.htm">Albino </A>Elephant (63K)
<LI><A HREF="notthere.htm">African Elephants</A> (32K)
<LI>More Elephant <A HREF="notthere.htm">Pictures</A>
<LI>Watch the <A HREF="notthere.htm">elephant performance</A> (video - 3 meg)
<LI>Buy an <A HREF="notthere.htm">elephant ride</A> today!
</UL>

<HR>
<IMG SRC="elep2.gif" WIDTH=150 HEIGHT=120 ALIGN=LEFT>

<FONT SIZE=+1>Other Elephant related links:</FONT>
<UL>
<LI>The elephants at the <A HREF="http://www.cincyzoo.org">Cincinnati Zoo</A>
<LI><A HREF="http://www.nationalgeographic.com">National Geographic's African Savannah</A>
<LI>Elephants at the <A HREF="http://www.si.edu">Smithsonian Institute</A>

</BODY>
</HTML>
```

Internet Protocols

There's a lot more to the Web than simply hyperlinking thousands of different documents together. The Web uses its own communications method, the HTTP protocol, to send and receive pages back and forth across the Internet. *HTTP* (which stands for *HyperText Transfer Protocol*) is an Internet protocol that allows two computers to talk to each other in a specified format. A protocol is just a set of standards that two computers use to talk with each other and to exchange information between them.

While it is the most popular protocol in use today, HTTP is not the only Internet protocol supported by the WWW.

Using the Web and HTML, you can integrate the following Internet applications into your Web pages:

■ *UseNet*—For access to newsgroups around the world.

■ *FTP*—Used for uploading and downloading files by using File Transfer Protocol.

- *Gopher*—A menu-based, "low-level" version of the Web, which links different resources on the Internet.
- *WAIS* (*Wide Area Information Service*)—Provides a way to search a variety of different databases.
- *Telnet*—Allows you to directly connect to other computers on the Internet.
- *E-mail*—For sending messages across the world electronically.

The Web gives you convenient access to all of these different Internet services together in one place.

N O T E   Understanding how files are sent back and forth between your computer and the Internet is important because it shows how your computer works when it connects to the Internet. When your browser visits a Web site, it sends an URL request for a particular site—like say **http://www.quecorp.com**. When the URL is sent, the computer on the receiving end automatically knows how to interpret the request. Once the two computers begin this communication, a "connection" is established. The computer on the Internet figures out which text and graphics files to send back to you and then closes the "connection."

Each time you visit a particular site on the Internet, both computers establish a new connection and figure out which files to send each other. So visiting **http://www.shafran.com** and **http://www.shafran.com/create** is two separate connections.

What does all this mean to you? It explains why sometimes you have a short delay when visiting Web pages while other times you have to wait several moments before the page comes up. Each page you visit requires creating a new connection with the Web server. Sometimes, the Web server is available, so that creating a connection is instantaneous, but often servers place URL requests in a line, so you have to wait to connect to the Web server. ■

Interaction to a New Level

Unlike television, the WWW is a truly interactive experience. Users control which Internet sites they visit, how long they look at information, and where they go next. Visiting a different Web page is only a single click away.

In addition, Web pages often interact with the visitors, making it fun and exciting for people to "experience" different pages. For example, the Warner Brothers Web page, shown in Figure 1.5, lets you explore current movies, television shows, comic books, musical artists, and more. You can listen to songs, watch sample video clips, and even send e-mail to movie stars and their fan clubs all from your comfortable browser window.

No longer do you have to sit down on the couch and choose from a few television stations. With the WWW, you can visit *any* site *anytime* and see what they have to offer.

FIG. 1.5

Stopping by Warner Brothers Online (**http:// www.warnerbros.com**) is quite an interactive experience.

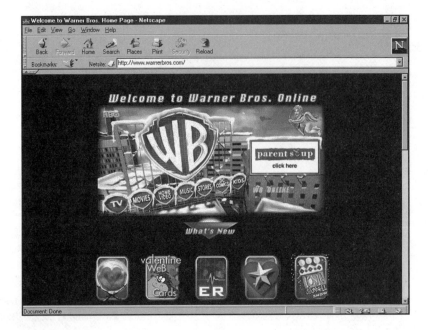

How the Web Works

This is the only section in these introductory few chapters where you are going to go into more technical detail about the underlying way the World Wide Web works. As you explore the Web and start creating your own home page, you'll find it useful to understand the different pieces that comprise the Web and how they all fit together.

Additionally, I'll throw in some informational details which describe the history and evolution of the Web to its present point today.

Client/Server-Based

The Web is a "client/server" application. Client/server means that somewhere there exists a computer running Web server software, and many different users (like you and me) are clients using Web browsers, accessing information from the Web server.

Web servers help send information back and forth to users across the world; they maintain connections with other Web servers, and they keep track of important usage statistics, such as the number of visitors to a specific Web page. Currently, there are nearly 150,000 Web servers on the Internet that are constantly talking to one another.

Perhaps, you can think of it this way. Each Web server contains all of the protocols and information available on a particular site. Where the documents are, whether there are executable programs that can be accessed, and more are all contained on the Web server. When you use Netscape to then access that Web site, the server jumps into action by providing the information that Netscape is requesting.

To use a previous example, when you tell browsers to "go" to **http://www.microsoft.com/Misc/ShortCuts.htm**, Microsoft's Web server first interprets your request from Netscape, then finds the **/Misc** directory, locates the **ShortCuts.htm** document and "serves" the contents of that document to your computer. Finally, Netscape takes that information, and translates the code in the file into a viewable document.

> **N O T E**   Since the Web is a distributed system with servers across the globe, there is no central main Web server that controls the others. Thus, if a particular Web server becomes inactive, all of the other servers operate fine in its absence. If there were one central computer that ran into problems, 25 million Web surfers would be out of luck. ■

SLIP/PPP Modem Connection Required

Access to the Web requires a special Internet connection that is client/server-based. *SLIP (Serial Line Internet Protocol)* and *PPP (Point-to-Point Protocol)* connections allow Internet users to download useful information to their computers so they can retrieve it quicker the next time they need that information. SLIP and PPP connections also allow you to perform several tasks at one time. You can browse the Web, download e-mail, and read news all at once.

Without these connections, you cannot use Netscape, Internet Explorer, and many of the other cool resources on the Internet. The opposite of a SLIP or PPP connection is a simple shell account that will only allow you to use a textual interface to the Internet. Therefore, it's important to make sure that you request SLIP or PPP access from your *Internet Service Provider (ISP)*.

Once you have such a connection, you will also need software that will allow your computer to "talk" in these protocols. Many ISPs provide this software with their service. On a PC, a WinSock (Windows Socket) client such as Trumpet WinSock is often used. You can download an undated WinSock client at **http://www.shareware.com**.

Oftentimes you might have a direct connection to the Internet, not requiring a modem at all. You can find these direct connections most often in corporate and educational environments. Direct Internet connections are often significantly faster than using a modem—10–20 times faster! Also, they don't require a SLIP or PPP connection because you are already talking to the Internet full-time.

> **CAUTION**
>
> Since you will be using your SLIP or PPP connection to transfer a lot of data (graphics, audio, and other resources take up a lot of room), you also will want to make sure you have a high-speed modem. A 14.4 modem is sufficient, but using a 28.8 will deliver better performance and is recommended. Newer model modems now support up to 57.6 baud—if your Internet Provider can go that fast. (Visit **http://www.usr.com** for more info on these speedy modems!) Another option is getting an ISDN card in your computer, along with an ISDN connection with your local phone company. Since this option isn't available everywhere, contact your local phone company to see if you can do it or check out Que's *Special Edition Using ISDN*,

continues

continued

> *Second Edition,* a complete reference on understanding this new technology. If you plan on spending a lot of time online, it's worth it—ISDN connections can deliver speeds up to 128,000 baud!

A Brief History of the Web

The Web has been around since early 1989, when a group of research scientists at *CERN (The European Laboratory for Particle Physics),* in Switzerland, came up with the concept of how the Web would work. They released their work in 1991 and started generating interest in it. The scientists were significant in the setup of the *W3 Consortium* (**http://www.w3.org**), the powers that dictate the next generation of HTML and the Web (shown in Figure 1.6).

FIG. 1.6

This is where the Web started.

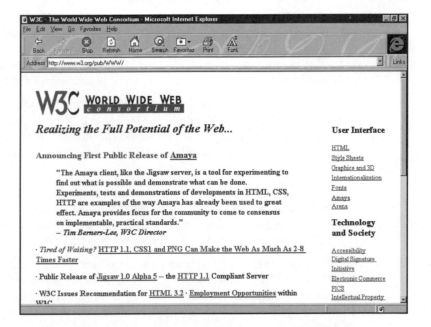

After being used sparingly for about a year, *Mosaic,* the first extremely popular Web browser, was released and received rave reviews. Mosaic was easy to use, available on the UNIX, PC, and Macintosh platforms, and distributed freely. Not long after, the original developer of Mosaic partnered with a Silicon Graphics founder to create Netscape (**http://www.netscape. com**), today's reigning browser software. It is estimated that as much as 80 percent of all Web traffic worldwide comes from people using Netscape, which has been one of the leading pioneers in developing new Web technologies. A shareware version of Netscape can be downloaded by home users for free.

Lately, a new browser entered the market, Internet Explorer by Microsoft (**http://www. microsoft.com/ie**) and has quickly become accepted by the Internet community.

One way to think of the WWW's popularity is to remember how Microsoft Windows became such an amazing success. Before Windows, DOS was a text-only byzantine operating system that required decent training and knowledge to used successfully. Windows changed all that. Windows allows you to do virtually everything DOS did, except now you have a graphical and intuitive interface. Copying files is no longer a challenge of remembering the right command, now you drag a file from one window to another. Similarly, the graphical nature of the WWW has catapulted the Internet and electronic communication into the spotlight. Before the WWW existed, the Internet required knowing a motley set of commands, but now you can navigate all across the world, collecting files and learning information, with a few clicks of your mouse.

Future Web Directions

Now that you know the history of the Web, let's turn our eyes to some future enhancements that we'll see soon. Probably the most noticeable and immediate change will be continued enhancements to HTML, the simple-to-use markup language that controls how information appears in browsers on your computer. Over the past few years, HTML has passed through several incarnations and recently HTML version 3.2 was approved and recommended by the Web Consortium (**http:/www.w3.org**), an international standards organization which controls Web standards and related issues. You will continue to see more enhancements to HTML that allow for easier integration with multimedia files, such as audio and video clips, and more flexibility of page layout and design.

Additionally, another new extension to HTML that is just beginning to be used today is the concept of *cascading style sheets* (CSS for short). Style sheets allow you to control certain font attributes to text on your Web page and allow for significantly more design and layout control over the appearance of information. Figure 1.7 shows a sample page that uses cascading style sheets on the Web Consortium's site.

Along the same lines, Virtual Reality Modeling Language (VRML) is also making its way into the WWW limelight. VRML allows Web creators to make interactive, three-dimensional worlds that visitors can literally walk through and see. These three-dimensional worlds have been around for a couple of years, but with new standards and easier tools to create them, VRML is increasingly found on more pages across the world.

Figure 1.8 shows a Virtual Reality Toy Brick (remarkably similar to Legos) world built with VRML (**http://trailhead.mit.edu/~toybrick/**).

FIG. 1.7

Style Sheets make entire page layout and text control a snap.

FIG. 1.8

Three-dimensional toy bricks are easy to create with VRML.

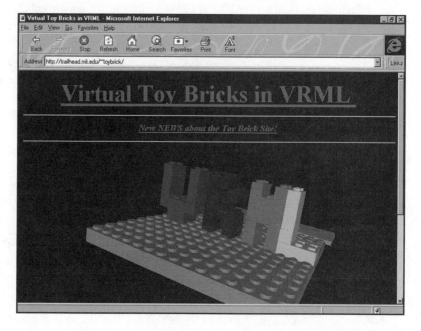

Getting to Know Popular WWW Browsers

Web browsers are the software installed on your personal computer that allows you to surf, or visit Web pages across the world. Browsers know how to interpret text and HTML tags sent across the Internet and display them properly on the screen. Browsers come for virtually every type of computer that exists and are relatively easy to install and use. Browsers understand and can interpret HTML. They know that <B>Hello</B> means to write the word hello on the screen and to make it appear in boldface.

This section talks about the two popular browsers in use today—Netscape Communicator (previously known as Netscape Navigator) and Microsoft Internet Explorer. I'll introduce each of these two browsers, show you how to download them, and try to differentiate between them.

Besides the two heavyweights, browsers come in all shapes and sizes. There are several specialized browsers that may come in handy when browsing Web pages or that you might run across. I'll try to give you a lowdown on some of the other browsers in use today.

Netscape Communicator

Netscape is by far the most popular and widely used browser in the world. Netscape revolutionized the Internet and WWW by making a fantastically easy-to-use program available for free to individual users everywhere.

Through the years, Netscape has evolved into a complete Internet communications tool, including a browser, authoring tool, mail program, and newsreader (among others). This entire suite is called Netscape Communicator, though in this book I often just refer to it colloquially as *Netscape*.

If you only had one browser you ever wanted to use, Netscape is the one to download and install. Stop by the Netscape Home page at **http://home.netscape.com** (see Figure 1.9) and follow the instructions for downloading their browser.

Netscape is the market leader because it has a very wide support of HTML and other important Web technology. Netscape has a very open architecture, which means it runs with Java, the Internet-focused language developed by Sun Microsystems, plug-ins, special enhancements for Web developers to use, and JavaScript, a scripting language which Web creators can use to add logic to their Web pages.

These advanced features make Netscape the premier choice, as well as its availability on virtually every platform, including Windows 3.1, Windows 95, Macintosh, OS/2, and many versions of UNIX.

Internet Explorer

The most notable competition to Netscape is Microsoft's Internet Explorer. Internet Explorer is another state-of-the-art browser that supports many of the new features introduced by Netscape and several technological advancements of its own. IE supports all levels of HTML and has a very friendly and familiar interface for users who are already familiar with Microsoft's other products.

FIG. 1.9

Netscape is the center of all things Web.

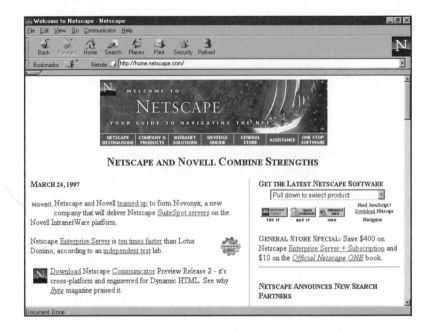

Figure 1.10 shows the Microsoft Web page where you can download the latest version of the Internet Explorer (**http://www.microsoft.com/ie/default.asp**).

FIG. 1.10

Microsoft's Internet Explorer is the best alternative if you decide not to use Netscape all the time.

On the CD

Internet Explorer is a very good Web browser and has virtually all of the same functionality as Netscape. In fact, millions of users prefer IE because it comes with the ability to screen Web sites for certain types of content, support for dynamic ActiveX programs which provide special interaction with Web servers, and Microsoft's integration of IE with the Windows operating systems. Internet Explorer is becoming an integral part of Windows NT and Windows 95. I included Internet Explorer on the CD-ROM that came with this book.

In reality, you can't go too wrong with either Web browser. Although each has some special features that the other is missing, both are commonly accepted throughout the world. Nearly every HTML command and feature described in this book is supported by both Netscape and IE (don't worry, I'll point out features that aren't supported by both). And, if you're like many discerning Web users (including me), you'll download and install both Web browsers and use them each interchangeably.

Other Web Browsers

Table 1.1 shows a brief list of several other browsers that you might run into, and where you might find them on the WWW. For a complete list of all Web browsers available, stop by BrowserWatch at **http://www.browserwatch.com**.

Table 1.1	Other WWW Browsers
Browser	**URL and Description**
Accent	**http://www.accentsoft.com**
	A multilingual browser that lets you create and view Web pages in dozens of different languages. This is a good choice for making information available for global visitors.
Mosaic	**http://www.ncsa.uiuc.edu/SDG/Software/Mosaic/ NCSAMosaicHome.html**
	This is the browser that started it all. Mosaic started as an educational project to graphically manipulate the Web and became wildly popular. Mosaic is free and has been licensed to several other companies around the world, so it will remain in use for quite some time.
Amaya	**http://www.w3.org/pub/WWW/Amaya/**
	An experimental browser which always supports the latest and greatest HTML features discussed by the Web Consortium. A great choice if you run a flavor of UNIX, but not available for Windows or Macintosh users.

What Is HTML and What Are the Standards?

HTML stands for *HyperText Markup Language*. It is the standard by which documents on the Web are presented in browsers like Netscape. As the name implies, HTML is a method for taking standard text and marking it up in such a way that the browser interprets specific tags and displays information in specially formatted ways. Tags can be added to encompass fonts, styles, and special effects on standard text. This allows you to create a standard text file which can be interpreted and provide a fun and graphical interface when displaying text.

In addition to text styles, HTML is also responsible for telling the browser when text on the page should be considered a link, where to insert graphical elements, and when to insert special elements like image maps, background graphics, mail-to commands, and other special features on the page. Figure 1.11 shows the behind-the-scenes HTML code for a sample Web page.

FIG. 1.11

The plain-text HTML codes behind a typical Web page.

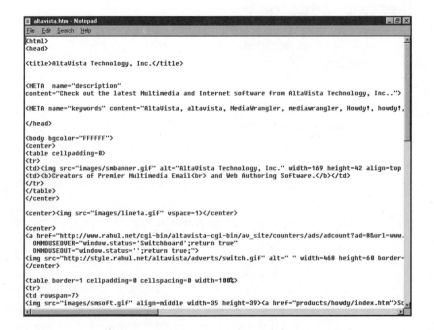

Now take a look at Figure 1.12, the same page of text, only interpreted by a browser.

In Figure 1.11, you might have noticed that HTML is all ASCII text. It is interpreted by the browser into formatted text and links. It is your browser's full-time job to recognize and understand all sorts of innovative HTML tags and display them properly for Web visitors around the world.

FIG. 1.12
There's quite a difference, isn't there?

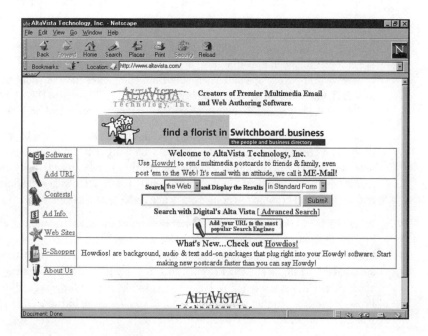

HTML 3.2—the Current Standard

HTML is a special set of textual tags that tell programs such as Netscape and Internet Explorer how to display information on a computer screen.

Not quite a programming language, HTML has a very specific format that must be followed in order to properly mark up text accordingly. This format is set and is a community standard so that everyone in world recognizes how HTML tags should be used and formatted. This community standard is known as the *Document Type Definition*, or *DTD*.

The first DTD of HTML was release 1.0, which introduced HTML to the Internet. Not long afterwards, HTML version 2.0 was created. HTML 2.0 was more robust and well thought-out to better handle some of the issues that were affecting the WWW. HTML 2.0 introduced many new types of tags and supported all of the original 1.0 tags as well.

Recently, discussion has finished for HTML version 3.2 (version 3.0 was never released). HTML 3.2 includes advanced tags which let you control text better within the browser and add multimedia clips quicker.

HTML is a revolving standard and is continually updated and revised. Anyone can participate in the discussion over new HTML tags and standards. Go to the Web Consortium's home page at **http://www.w3.org** for more information.

This book covers HTML version 3.2. I talk about several new features that are only supported by the latest browsers and will make your Web page look spectacular.

HTML Extensions

Although HTML is a worldwide-accepted standard for coding and creating Web pages, there are several enhancements that have been proposed by the two big heavyweights in the browser world—Netscape and Microsoft. Both companies have introduced special extensions to HTML that build on the functionality in version 3.2. These new HTML extensions allow for additional flexibility, multimedia support, and text and font control on Web pages.

Netscape, which holds an estimated 70 percent market share among browsers is the pioneer in these HTML extensions. HTML features like blinking text and centered paragraphs are often confused for HTML 3.2 standard elements, but they're not. In fact, many of the HTML elements commonly found on the Web today—like different font sizes, flexible numbered lists, and background graphics—require Netscape or Netscape-compatible browsers to view.

In today's world, most major Web browsers support the HTML standard set of tags and most popular extensions introduced by Microsoft and Netscape. There are, however, a handful of tags, such as scrolling marquees, multimedia effects, and certain formatting tags that are only supported by a single specific browser. In general, you'll want to stay away from these nonstandard HTML tags so your Web site is accessible by everyone, regardless of which Web browser they use. In this section of the book, you'll only be introduced to standard HTML tags which are supported by all common browsers.

The High End of HTML

At its most extreme, HTML becomes a programming language—or, at least, it invites programming languages into the fray. With HTML we can also create forms for getting user responses, allow users to search our site by using keywords and search fields, or even conduct transactions over the Web—accepting credit card numbers or similar payment information in exchange for products or services.

Once the user fills in a form and sends it to your Web server to be processed, things are accomplished through what are known as CGI (Common Gateway Interface) scripts. Forms are simple extensions of HTML, which are simple to use and create. On the backside, CGI scripts accept data entered online in forms and process the information. CGI scripts can be written in Perl, C, and other popular programming languages. Fortunately, many examples exist allowing you to reuse existing CGI scripts for many common purposes instead of reinventing the wheel. Regardless, some knowledge of scripting or programming languages is required to use some of these advanced HTML features. Figure 1.13 shows a sample HTML page which includes a game built exclusively for the Web. Stop by **http://www.zoop.com** to see what's happening and to play for a while.

FIG. 1.13
Zoop is an exciting game built with advanced HTML and WWW programming.

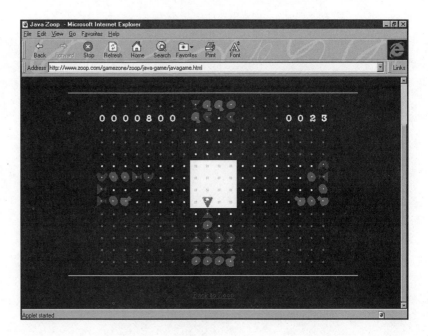

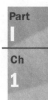

Part
I

Ch
1

Weaving Your Own Web

In the last chapter, you saw an overview of the World Wide Web, which included a brief explanation of a home page. Now, you're ready to start learning how to create your own personal Web page, and make it available for the millions of people on the Internet to check out.

You'll step through the process of planning your Web site, and see how to explore existing pages to figure out exactly what your pages should look like. You'll investigate several different types of Web sites and then develop a plan for your personal Web pages.

In addition, you'll see the important process of selecting a Web provider, or host, for your Web pages. You'll learn what features to look for and how to find an affordable or free Web provider. ■

How to put together your Web page

It is your job to figure out the kind of information you want to put on your home/Web page.

How you might want your Web page to look

Look here to figure out how to organize and design your Web page once the content has been decided.

Understand how to build HTML files

Making Web pages can be done in several ways, with or without special programs. Learn the differences and strategies behind making HTML files.

Internet connections for establishing a Web page

These techniques show you how to send a completed Web page to the Internet.

What's a Home Page?

Think of a large city. There are commercial buildings, industrial buildings, and residences. Every building has its own unique identity, from large skyscrapers to fast-food restaurants. They all have their own atmosphere and flavor. When you buy your own house, you get the opportunity to decorate and landscape it however you like. You can keep your house prim and proper with all the shrubs trimmed, or let weeds overtake your lawn.

Creating your own home page is a similar concept. There are thousands of home pages out there for businesses, organizations, and individuals. You're learning how to create your own home page, or "residence," on the World Wide Web. You get to choose what type of information and/or graphics to make available, how it looks when people stop by for a visit, and how to keep it properly maintained. A Web page that looks like garbage to you may be another's personal treasure trove.

There are no home-page police that will stop by and make sure that everything is designed so that it's easy to use, or make sure the information on it is current. Your only restrictions are following the laws of your country (most notably, copyright, pornography, and privacy laws). It takes some effort to create an attractive and innovative home page that people will want to visit time and time again.

Read through this chapter to learn more about what the World Wide Web is and how it works. I'll step you through what terms you should be familiar with and make sure you are familiar with how to build and make your own home page available.

Why Create a Home Page?

There are more than 30,000,000 Web pages out there already, and you are getting ready to mark your own corner of the Internet. Before you do, it's a good idea to decide why you want your own home page.

Home pages come in all different shapes and sizes. Some are merely personalized Internet vanity plates, while others offer unique information found nowhere else (such as the floating fish cam page—a home page that takes snapshots of an aquarium periodically through the day). Many people offer their services or sell products directly through their home pages.

Some people have Web pages just for fun; others just heard about the Web and thought a home page would be cool. You've got to decide your own reason for having a Web page.

N O T E Personally, I think everyone should have their own Web page, so they can create their own unique environment that reflects their personality. My Web page reflects my interests and lets others with the same interests interact with me.

I don't have a Web page to sell my services or promote my products (although you can certainly find that information on there). Instead, I want that information to be freely available to whomever might want it. ■

Once you've decided why you want a Web page, your next decision is what information should appear on it. Having an established Web-page goal will make it tremendously easier for you to design and create your Web page.

Personal Pages

The vast majority of Web pages out there are personal home pages, created by individuals just like you. Ironically, personal pages are the ones you are least likely to visit because:

- There are so many of them, and they aren't easily indexed by category.
- They generally aren't as cool as some of the more impressive, commercial sites.

However, personal home pages offer you your own customized place on the WWW and allow you to share information with your friends, family, and other Internet denizens. Figure 2.1 shows a sample personal page that's on the Web.

FIG. 2.1

This personal page (**http://www.geocities.com/TimesSquare/4810/**) is pretty standard of what you'll find when browsing around.

Most of the information in this book is geared towards helping you create snazzy-looking personal Web pages. Here's a list of information that commonly appears on a personal Web page:

- Contact information
- Hobbies
- Interests
- Occupation
- Personal background

- Self-picture
- Publications
- Links to other neat Web pages

 T I P Many people create home pages and then put their URL on their business cards and resumes (I do). Not only does this demonstrate that they are technically savvy, but it also gives them a chance to let their true personality shine because a home page is a true reflection of your interests, hobbies, and personality.

Business Pages

As more and more individuals are jumping onto the WWW, an increasing amount of businesses are also taking the plunge. Virtually every day a new large company or corporation is announcing their brand new site on the Web, and scores of smaller companies make their appearance as well.

Asked why they want to be on the Web, practically every company will answer the same thing: "It's a fantastic and complete marketing tool." The WWW offers an unprecedented opportunity for businesses and companies to get publicity and market their products and services for a relatively cheap price.

Support   Companies such as Microsoft, Lotus, and IBM have recognized the potential to offer technical support to their customers via the WWW. Microsoft offers technical knowledge (see Figure 2.2) and Lotus has its internal "white papers," all available through the Web.

FIG. 2.2
Here's a sample of Microsoft's support site (**http://www. microsoft.com/ Support/**).

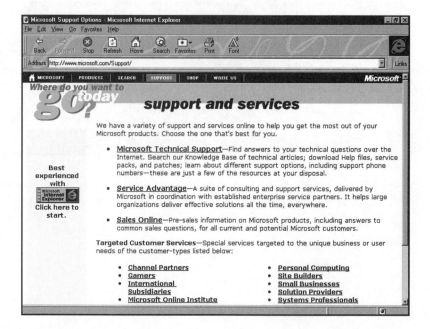

Supporting customers on the Web has evolved into an effective and affordable medium and more and more companies offer support over the Web every day.

Sell Products   Nowadays, you can buy virtually anything on the WWW. Whether you want an antique rocking chair, or clothing from the latest fashion, you'll find it on the Web (see Figure 2.3). WWW commerce is still a relatively new industry. Only recently have technological innovations made it possible to securely send credit card numbers across the Internet—and even then, only certain WWW sites support this new technology.

Part

I

Ch

2

Apparently, selling products on the Web is quite lucrative. Several companies have announced that their sales have gone up significantly since they've had a presence on the WWW. The more you browse on the Web, the more you'll find an opportunity to spend money and buy items from the comfort of your own computer. (You can even order a pizza through the Web in some places.)

FIG. 2.3

Here's a good place to see how companies are selling their wares over the Web (**http://www. amazon.com**).

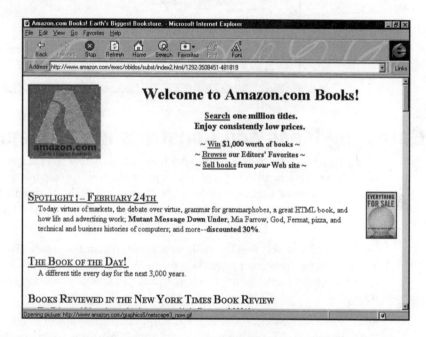

Advertising   Another reason many sites have been developed is purely for advertising. For example, the LensCrafters Web site (**http://www.lenscrafters.com**, Figure 2.4) doesn't sell products, nor does it offer support for people with glasses. It is simply an advertisement for this company.

FIG. 2.4
This page is geared for people who wear glasses.

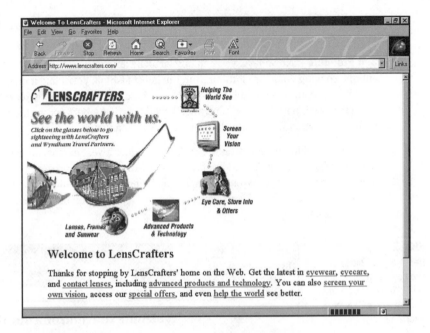

Gathering Ideas and Constructing a Blueprint

There are two aspects to evaluating every home page: content and presentation. First, you have to decide what information to put on your home page. Some people (like me) put personal information such as pictures and hobbies on their pages, while others only list their technical interests. You get to decide how much and what type of information you make available on the Web.

Don't worry if you can't decide exactly what to put on your home page. There are no wrong answers. Simply create your page, put it on the WWW, and see what other people think. The response you get from your original page will likely motivate you for updating it in various ways.

Read this section to learn about different ways of organizing and presenting your home page. You'll see several different home pages that actually exist, and some suggestions for how you can make your page top-notch. While I won't tell you what exactly to put on your home page, I will make some suggestions and show you some examples to help you along the way. As I do, I'll point out some of the good things you may want to include and some of the bad things you may want to avoid.

Short but Sweet: John's Page

This page is an example of how even an extremely simple home page can easily fit your needs, represent yourself adequately, and not take an overwhelming amount of time designing, planning, and maintaining.

Take a look at John's page (see Figure 2.5). He lists a few things about himself and his background, including his recent theatrical credits. There isn't too much information here, but it is well organized, and easy to read.

Stop by and visit him at **http://home.sprynet.com/sprynet/johnbeatty/**.

FIG. 2.5
John's page is easy to take care of, but there's not a lot of meat there (yet).

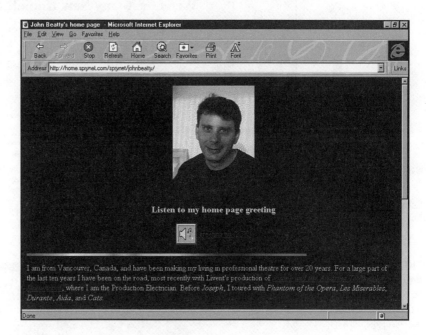

Intermediate Level: My Personal Page

Here's my own personal home page (see Figure 2.6). You might be surprised that it doesn't have thousands of graphics, tons of links, and use every HTML feature listed in this book. I have spent a lot of time organizing my page to make it easy to use. I've also discovered that most pages that have an abundance of graphics are often too confusing to even use.

That said, my page is the next level up from John's in difficulty, design, and presentation. It took me a while to put together, but it isn't that difficult to keep current or add new information. My URL is **http://www.shafran.com**.

Classy Web Page: The Crime Scene

This is one of my favorite sites on the WWW. This is the home page for an ongoing investigation regarding a murder that occurred in Mississippi (everything is fictional—honest).

This site uses a nice combination of text, graphics, and organizational techniques for an all-around superb site. Exploring this site, you'll find video clips, audio bites, and several images, all related to the case.

Visit **http://www.quest.net/crime/** to see if you can crack the case (see Figure 2.7)!

FIG. 2.6

My page represents an organized home page without adding too many z's to pizzazz.

FIG. 2.7

The Crime Scene Evidence File is probably a precursor to how investigators might work in the future!

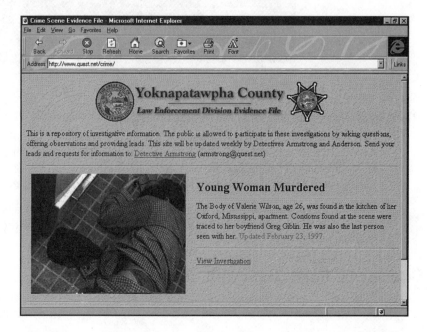

Excellent Commercial Site: ESPN SportsZone

Here are a couple of commercial sites so you can see what other types of pages look like. Commercial pages tend to be more impressive because they have more financial backing than individual home pages.

This site is ESPN's home page, entitled SportsZone (see Figure 2.8). Every time you link to this page you find the newest and latest sports information. That makes you want to come back again and again.

Although their page design is relatively simple, the large amount of information that constantly hits this page makes it one of the hottest spots on the Internet. Stop by and see for yourself at **http://espnet.sportszone.com/**.

FIG. 2.8
ESPN's SportsZone talks about teams, trades, and tribulations affecting major league sports.

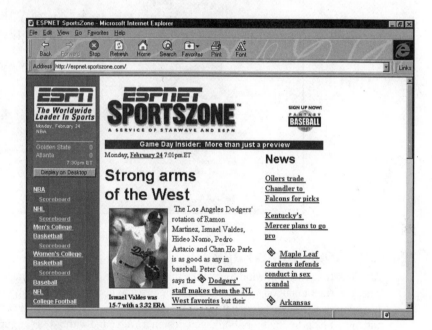

Fantastic Commercial Site: Coca-Cola

This is the place to stop by for a cool and interactive Web experience. One stop here and you know you're in for a treat (see Figure 2.9).

This site takes advantage of some of the most complicated features of Web publishing. Geared towards the latest in browser technology, the site uses clickable graphics (where different spots of a graphic take you to different Web pages), forms, and practices good design techniques.

One drawback to creating a site like Coca-Cola is the amount of work it takes to maintain the Web site. Updates constantly have to be created and the information always needs to stay current. In addition, creating the maps and forms used can be a difficult process even for programmers. But when you're a company as wealthy as Coca-Cola, you can afford it. Quench your thirst at **http://www.cocacola.com/**.

FIG. 2.9

It's fun looking at sites like this, but maintaining it would be a nightmare.

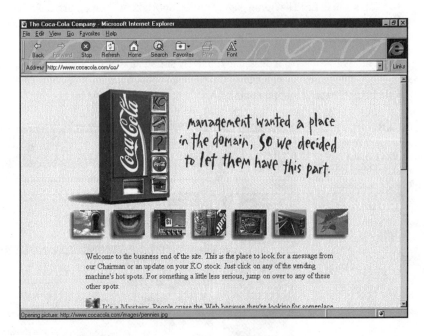

Organizing Your Home Page

After finishing the whirlwind tour of the above Web sites, you probably have lots of ideas for what you want to put on your home page. Before you dive in, though, you may want to take a few minutes to think about what you're going to include. Just as an architect doesn't build without a blueprint, neither should you design a Web page without first figuring out what belongs where.

The first step is organizing the information you want to put on your page. I recommend organizing your home page into three different categories—personal, professional, and miscellaneous. After all, your goal is probably to put useful information about yourself on the WWW.

Now, when visitors stop by your home page, they know where to look for information. Friends can go to the personal section, potential employers know that the professional section is what they want, and everyone can explore your miscellaneous section. If everything was just listed together, visitors would have to read through your entire page before they find what they're looking for.

Then you'll need to break down each section even further. Decide whether you want to make your address and phone number available. Do you want to include a picture of yourself? What kinds of hobbies do you have? Visit my home page to see how I dealt with those issues. Feel free to "borrow" design ideas from my page or any other page that you like on the Internet. Remember though that "borrowing" design ideas is not the same as taking images and information from another Web site and placing it on your own. Walt Disney wouldn't mind if you checked out their HTML code to figure out why their Web pages are so cool, but you'd be breaking the law to snag a picture of Mickey Mouse for your Web page. For more information on copyright issues, see Appendix C, "Legal Issues with Web Pages."

 TIP Remember that you don't have to put *everything* on your home page on the first try. Spend your time putting a good but simple (John's) page up there first. From there you can increase your page's complexity.

Sketching Your Page Out

Once you've started organizing your information, take some time sketching out how you want your home page to look. Just because the WWW is on a computer doesn't mean that good old pencil and paper can't help you out.

Draw your ideal page. Put your images, lines of text, and headlines all on your sheet of paper. I've found that drawing out Web pages (called prototyping in the business world) helps me think through the whole process. I know how big I want to make my images, how much text to type (approximately), what colors (if any) to use, and what kind of tables and lists I need to use (you'll learn more about these in Chapter 5, "Adding Lists and Tables"). Don't be afraid to draw several sketches, even if they are very different (see Figure 2.10).

By adding this step to your Web page process, you're bound to have put more thought into what information makes sense on a home page and how you want to present it.

FIG. 2.10

Here are a few sketches of how I thought my home page could look.

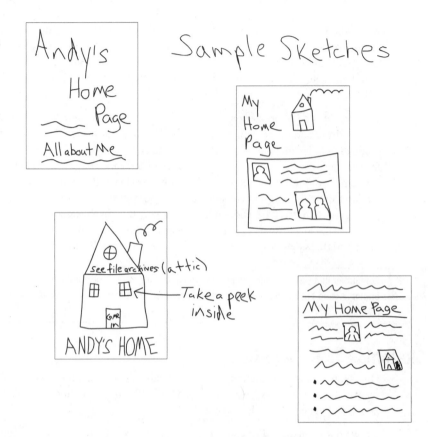

Writing HTML

As I discussed in Chapter 1, "A Web Crawler's Beginning," HTML documents are text-based files that have special codes, called markup tags, within them. These markup tags instruct WWW browsers on how to interpret and display text and graphics.

HTML files look like regular word-processed documents, except that they have tags strewn throughout them. The key to understanding HTML files is knowing how to create them. When you look through an HTML file, you might notice codes like `<B>`, `<IMG SRC="graphic.gif">`, `<A HREF="link.htm">`, `</UL>`, and many more sporadically placed. The subsequent chapters in this book will explain exactly what all those tags mean, but you need to know where to type them in, and how to save a file specifically in HTML.

Creating HTML Files

Since HTML documents are completely text, virtually any word processor or text editor from Windows Notepad to Microsoft Word can be used to create a home page.

When you use one of these simple text editors, you are required to know each and every HTML tag, and then type it into your file. Then, you must save the file onto your computer and preview it with a Web browser. Only by looking at the HTML file in a browser do you know whether you made any mistakes, or exactly how the Web page will appear.

Figure 2.11 shows the use of the simplest of all text editors—Windows 95 Notepad to create an HTML file.

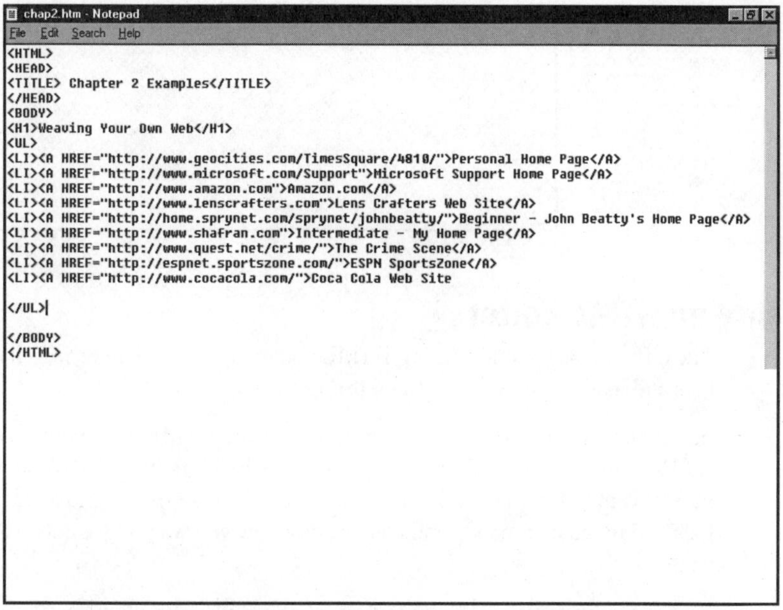

FIG. 2.11

Here's a simple HTML file made with the simplest text editor.

```
chap2.htm - Notepad
File  Edit  Search  Help
<HTML>
<HEAD>
<TITLE> Chapter 2 Examples</TITLE>
</HEAD>
<BODY>
<H1>Weaving Your Own Web</H1>
<UL>
<LI><A HREF="http://www.geocities.com/TimesSquare/4810/">Personal Home Page</A>
<LI><A HREF="http://www.microsoft.com/Support">Microsoft Support Home Page</A>
<LI><A HREF="http://www.amazon.com">Amazon.com</A>
<LI><A HREF="http://www.lenscrafters.com">Lens Crafters Web Site</A>
<LI><A HREF="http://home.sprynet.com/sprynet/johnbeatty/">Beginner - John Beatty's Home Page</A>
<LI><A HREF="http://www.shafran.com">Intermediate - My Home Page</A>
<LI><A HREF="http://www.quest.net/crime/">The Crime Scene</A>
<LI><A HREF="http://espnet.sportszone.com/">ESPN SportsZone</A>
<LI><A HREF="http://www.cocacola.com/">Coca Cola Web Site

</UL>

</BODY>
</HTML>
```

There are several important things to notice about this example. First, carefully inspect the text on the screen. You'll notice that it more or less makes sense to be read, but that there are probably a few lines that are confusing. Now, take a look at the file name (in the title bar at the top of the screen). Notice how it ends with the **.HTM** extension. All HTML files should be saved with the **.HTM** or **.HTML** file extension. This helps your computer know that this isn't an ordinary text file, but one that has special HTML codes embedded within it.

Now, look at Figure 2.12. This is how a Web browser (Internet Explorer) interprets the previous HTML file. Try to compare which text appears on the screen with the text in my HTML file.

FIG. 2.12
My HTML file is brought
to life by a Web browser.

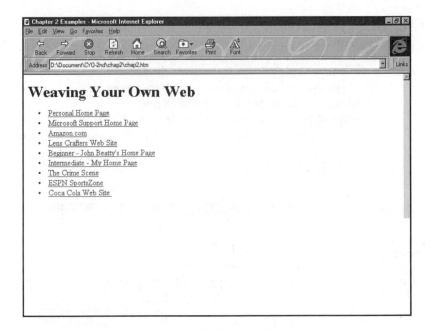

Using an HTML Editor

The difficult part about creating HTML documents is remembering all the specific markup tags and learning how to use them properly.

Several programs exist to make it easier to create HTML documents. These programs, called *HTML editors*, are specifically geared towards building the HTML codes for you, so you don't have to remember them. HTML Editors allow you to type in text, and then, using special buttons and menu commands, indicate exactly how you want that information to appear on a Web page.

As you can imagine, HTML editors are very popular and often easy to use. Their whole goal in life is to make knowing every HTML command by heart a thing of the past. Unfortunately, many HTML editors are expensive and often overkill for the majority of individuals who want to create simple and practical Web pages. Good HTML editors start around $99.95 and offer extreme flexibility, including the latest HTML tags, advanced programming, and more. Also, if you only use an HTML editor, you might find it difficult to make detailed and intricate changes to your Web page. Figure 2.13 shows a good HTML Editor called HotDog Pro (**http://www. sausage.com**) being used to edit a Web page.

In this book, you are introduced to the basics of HTML, so you can understand how to build your own Web page from scratch. In Chapter 13, "Using HTML Editors and Other Web Tools," you are introduced to several very popular HTML editors and tools. Once you understand how to use basic HTML commands, you'll likely find these tools and editors powerful enhancements in the Web creation process.

FIG. 2.13
HotDog Pro is the best of breed for simple HTML editors.

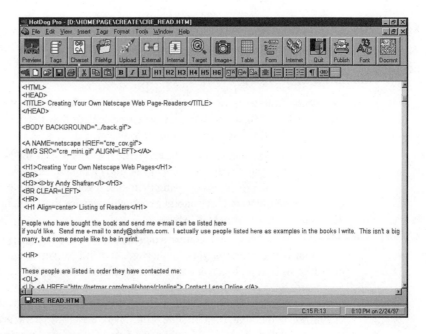

Part

I

Ch

2

Connecting to a Web Provider

Once you have your browser in place and you know how to create an HTML file, the last piece of "equipment" you'll need to create your own home page is a spot on the Internet.

A *Web provider* is an organization that rents space on its computer connected to the Internet for a monthly fee. For this small charge, you can put your own customized home page on the Internet and let it be available to anyone across the world anytime they wish to stop by.

You probably already have an Internet provider if you're already browsing the Web. Many Internet providers double as Web providers and allow you to put your home page up. However, some Internet providers don't offer this type of access and others charge an arm and a leg.

The main difference between an Internet provider and Web provider is the kind of service they offer. Internet providers rent you accounts that let you dial and connect with the Internet and then check your e-mail, browse the WWW, and so on. Web providers offer a simpler service. They provide disk space on a computer that is connected to the Internet 24 hours a day, seven days a week, which runs special software called a Web server.

This section describes the ideal characteristics of a Web provider and even offers some pointers to finding your own low cost spot on the Internet.

What You are Looking for

Web providers come in all different shapes and sizes. Some of them are friendly and affordable, while others charge outrageous fees and add hidden costs at every turn. Here is a list of characteristics of a good Web provider:

- **Freedom**—You can have anything you want on your home page (assuming it doesn't break any laws). Some providers try to censor content they deem inappropriate. This may or may not influence your choice of a Web provider.

- **Reliability**—Your home page is useless if the provider's Web site is unreliable. Stop by their home page several times during peak (day) and nonpeak (evening) hours to make sure you have no problems accessing their site. If you regularly get "Site not found" errors, you might want to try another company because that often indicates their connection to the Internet isn't stable.

- **Affordability**—After doing comparison shopping, you're being ripped off if you pay more than $10 a month for your home page. In fact, I've even found several sites that offer free Web pages to anyone who asks (read on for those). Be careful of hidden costs. Some sites have low costs as long as few people stop by your Web page, but charge incrementally depending on the number of visitors who surf on by. Just like any time you buy or rent something, read the fine print. There are always a few scam artists out there to make a buck from those of us not paying close attention. If your provider seems to have many "possible" costs and "access charges" you might as well switch to a free or low cost one that I mention here.

- **Support**—Web page publishing can be difficult if no one is there to answer your questions. This book should guide you through most of your basic HTML questions, but you're bound to have more. Look for a Web provider who you can call with questions, or will answer your e-mail within 24 to 48 hours.

- **Creativity**—The more people who visit your Web provider's site, the more people who could stop by your home page. Your Web provider's home page is often an accurate gauge for how well they know HTML and how creative they are.

Expected Costs

As mentioned above, you can find a good Web provider that will charge you less than $10 a month for storing a decent-sized Web page at its Internet site.

Several other costs can be accrued when creating a new Web site. Most of these can be avoided, but be aware that these extra costs can nickel and dime you until you're in the poorhouse—if you're not careful.

- **Startup Costs**—Ranging from $0 to $150, Web providers often charge a one-time fee to set up and install your personal Web page. After buying this book, you shouldn't need to pay anyone a dime for setting up a Web page—you'll know almost as much as they do.

- **Maintenance Charges**—A good Web page will have information updated often. Some Web providers let you update your page for free, others charge as much as $50 for ongoing maintenance. I try to stick only with the free ones, but keep your eyes peeled for all sorts of ways a Web provider can nickel and dime you. There should be very few maintenance charges (if any) that a personal home page creator should ever have to pay. Sometimes though, you may want a larger Web provider if you are creating a site for a business; that way you pay them to maintain your site.

- **Consulting Charges**—Most Web providers also offer customized Web consulting to create advanced Web pages for businesses and companies. If advanced and complicated HTML publishing is what you need (like the Coca-Cola page seen earlier this chapter), expect to pay at least $50 an hour.

Web Provider Listings

If you don't already have a Web provider, choosing one is likely to be your first decision made with this book. There are literally thousands of companies who will lease you space on the Internet for a minimal fee. For a complete list of affordable companies, visit **http://budgetweb. com/budgetweb/** (see Figure 2.14). This site is a clearinghouse for affordable hosting and other Web-related services.

FIG. 2.14

budgetweb.com is the premiere Internet site for finding cheap resources to work on and store Web pages.

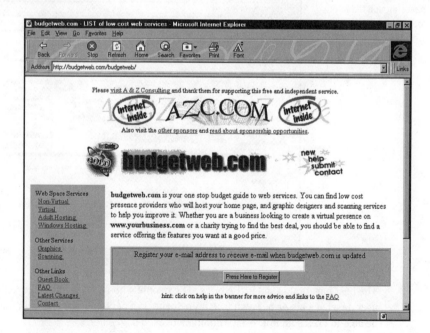

Read through the list because each Web provider is slightly different. Their prices are reasonable for the services they offer.

Another Web site you'll want to visit is the Free Page site (**http://www.thenet.pair.com/freepage/**) that lists over two dozen sites on the Internet where you can house your home page for free.

The following shows different Web providers that you may want to explore. There is a free site for beginners, an excellent (but slightly expensive) professional site that offers top-notch support and service, and some information on using the big online services—AOL and CompuServe—to host your Web pages.

Geocities

For a basic home page, Geocities (see Figure 2.15) is generally the best free site you're going to find. Everything here is free, from creating your home page to monthly (even daily) maintenance. Ample limitations on your home page file size, not much technical support, and few advanced home page features tend to limit this site to beginning users only. Stop by **http://www.geocities.com** for more information.

FIG. 2.15

Geocities hosts thousands of people's pages around the world for FREE!

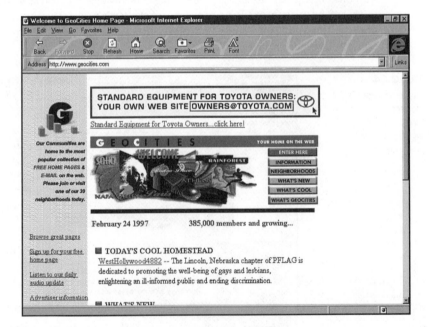

The best part of this site is the price. The people who run this site believe that every Internet user deserves his or her own free home page as a personal starting spot on the Internet. You'll be able to create an impressive complex of Web pages here.

A built-in home page editor enables you to create decent-looking home pages in just a few minutes, or you can upload your HTML files directly.

Personally, I like Geocities because its concept is to enable hundreds of thousands of users to have a spot they can call home. It isn't the best or the fastest site on the WWW, but it is free.

Forman Interactive

Most of the low cost and free Web providers are ideal for a personal Web page, but if you want to create one for a business, Forman Interactive is the place to start looking. It is a stable and well-entrenched Web site that runs an electronic mall—virtually guaranteeing that your Web site will get traffic. Visit **http://www.formaninteractive.com/index.htm** to get started (see Figure 2.16).

FIG. 2.16

Forman is a premier full-service Web provider.

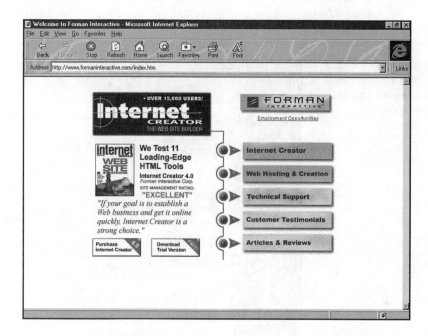

The best part is they offer a full Web Site Startup Kit free, which affords you amazing flexibility and customization for creating a cool site and adding image maps, shopping carts, forms, and many more advanced features immediately to your site. Stop by for a look. Be aware that they are not the cheapest company around and have some significant costs when developing a Web site. This company is geared towards helping businesses get online and sell information to visitors.

Online Services

Both major online services—CompuServe and America Online (AOL)—enable you to build your own Web page and give you your own corner of the WWW to work with. This space on the Web comes free with their standard accounts, which all begin at $9.95 a month. You get all the news, weather, sports, and family information that the online service has—and a Web page—for the same price of several of the other providers listed here in this appendix.

America Online   America Online is geared for casual computer users and has nearly three times as many members as CompuServe. Online, they have a great set of resources to assist you when building your own Web pages. Visit the Web Diner online (keyword: DINER). Another place to stop by online is the keyword **My Place**.

As far as online services go, AOL has the most hand-holding and user-friendly Web resources. AOL really goes out of its way to provide you with free graphics, multimedia clips, photo-scanning capabilities, and tools, without making you search for them.

You can use any standard AOL startup kit to get online for the Mac- and PC-compatible. Stop by **http://www.aol.com** (see Figure 2.17) or call 1-800-827-6364 and have them send you a startup kit for free.

FIG. 2.17

AOL is the best of the breed when it comes to online services.

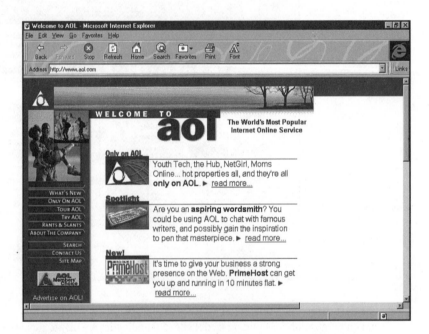

N O T E   If you are really serious about creating your Web pages on AOL, you might want to check out
Creating Your Own America Online Web Pages by Andy Shafran and Todd Stauffer, also
published by Que. This book is a complete guide to getting your Web page up and running on AOL. ■

CompuServe   CompuServe is a well-rounded and robust online service that has many things to offer besides Web pages. Over 2,500 services can be explored in the CompuServe world. Visit **http://ourworld.compuserve.com** (see Figure 2.18) to see CompuServe's collection of Web pages.

In addition, CompuServe has actual Web-page building software that you download and build your Web page with. This software automatically uploads it and helps you maintain it online. Called the Home Page Wizard, this software makes creating Web pages easy for the somewhat experienced user.

FIG. 2.18
CompuServe has millions of subscribers and includes Web hosting with its monthly fee.

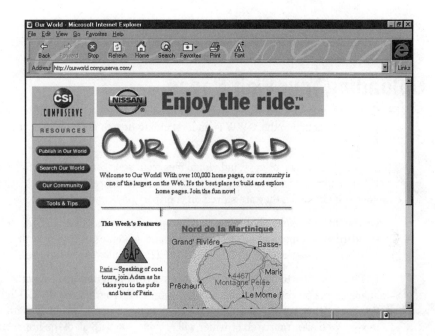

On CompuServe, you'll find virtually all of the same resources that AOL has, but sometimes they are more difficult to find. CompuServe has unparalleled forums of Internet discussions, where you can literally get any question—easy or complicated—answered. To obtain a free sign-up kit (with the first month free), call 1-800-848-8990.

One Alternative: Running Your Own Web Server

Another alternative to renting Internet space from a Web provider is setting up and creating your own WWW server on the Internet. With significant start-up and monthly maintenance charges, this option is for the truly Web-dedicated companies out there. Rough estimates start at an initial $2,000 investment for the computer and software and a $100 monthly fee for a full-time Internet connection (and that's a slow one—fast ones cost much more).

Running your own Web server offers unlimited flexibility when configuring and developing your own site. But, along with this flexibility comes more cost and complexity. Running a Web server is expensive because you have to buy the equipment described earlier, and invest the time and expertise into knowing how all the technology works.

Running your own Web server from scratch is out of the realm of this introduction to Web pages. But, there are several comprehensive and free resources available for you to learn more about how this process works. Visit **http://www.mcp.com/que/bookshelf/** for the complete text of several books that introduce and explain the whole Web server process. You can read several books there, including the *Running a Perfect Web Site* series that steps you through the complete process of getting a site up and running.

To learn more about WWW servers, visit **http://www.yahoo.com/ Computers_and_Internet/Software/Internet/World_Wide_Web/Servers/**.

Uploading Your Web Pages

Once you've selected a Web provider and you know how to create HTML files, the final step in your introduction to the WWW is understanding how to get files from your computer onto the Internet.

You need to upload, or copy, individual files from your computer to your Web provider's, each HTML and graphic, in order to make it available to the rest of the world. Creating HTML files does you no good if they are stored on your personal computer.

On the Internet, uploading is handled by a process titled FTP (File Transfer Protocol). FTP is a standard way computers talk to each other and send files back and forth. In Internet speak, FTP is used as a verb—as in "You need to FTP your files to the Internet."

On the CD

FTPing your files to the Internet requires a special program that is geared specifically towards enabling this process. You will find shareware FTP programs on the CD-ROM that comes with this book. Once you install an FTP program, you can use it to copy files from your computer to your Web site. Your Web provider will provide you with all of the important information required to send files to your Web site, including a username, password, and FTP address. FTP programs allow you to upload files, create subdirectories on your Web site, delete files, rename files, and much more. Figure 2.19 shows FTPing a file to a personal Web site.

FIG. 2.19

You'll need to understand how to FTP in order to make your Web pages available online.

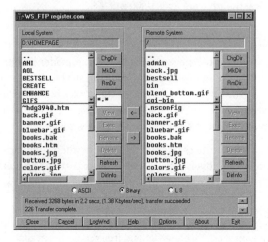

CHAPTER 3

Web Page Basics

HTML isn't a complicated language to learn, but there are some quirks. In fact, most HTML is intuitive and easy to read. When you go to England, the people there speak English but have their own vernacular colloquialisms (like realizing that a queue is when you stand in line—not a misspelled computer book publisher). Although it's not quite as easy as speaking British English, you won't have to learn an entirely new language (like Russian) to create a good home page.

Over the last couple of chapters, you were introduced to the WWW to help get you ready to create your home page. You saw several different types of home pages, learned the basics about the tools used in this book, and learned how to find a Web provider.

Now that you're finished with the planning stages of your Web page, it's time to get started! ■

How to use important tags
Learn about the handful of HTML tags that all Web pages need to have, no matter what.

Enlarge text to make headlines
Work with special tags that exist with the sole purpose of marking text to appear larger in headline form.

Make your text easy to read
Learn how to organize your Web page paragraph by paragraph so that all your text doesn't jumble together.

Understand the *<HR>* tag
Use horizontal lines to separate sections of a Web page logically.

Using the Standard Home Page Template

A sample home-page template has been included on the CD that comes with this book. This sample template contains tags preformatted for a simple, but elegant home page. All you need to do is add your own text! My home page uses the same general template.

Feel free to use, customize, and modify the home-page template to your heart's desire. It's meant to be flexible to your needs, not rigid. By the time you finish reading this book, you'll know how to use all of the tags found in the template and how to make your own personal modifications. Figure 3.1 shows a sample Web page using the home-page template on the CD-ROM. This sample template uses several important HTML features, including lists, tables, stylized text, and Web graphics.

FIG. 3.1

HTML tags that you can add to your home page are shown here.

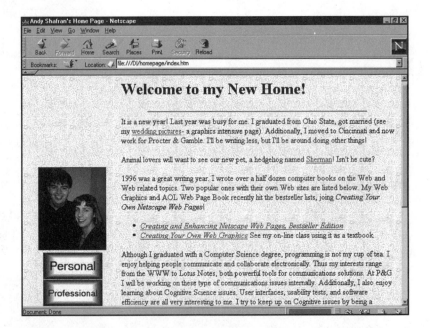

Although the template is included on the CD-ROM, you won't see much about it in the book. Instead, you learn how to build a Web page one tag at a time.

Important HTML Tags

No matter what your page looks like or what kind of information you want to display, there are four HTML tags that every page should have so they follow HTML and WWW standards.

■ <HTML>   Informs the browser that this document is written in HTML.

■ <HEAD>   Labels the introductory and heading part of the HTML document.

- ■ <BODY>   Marks where the body text and information appears.
- ■ <ADDRESS>   Contains an e-mail address to get further information about this Web page.

These tags are vital to telling your Web browser how to recognize different parts of the HTML document, but they don't directly affect how your Web page appears. They're necessary for future enhancements of HTML to be able to use your home page properly, and so your Web page looks the same in all WWW browsers. For example, your Web server might run a program that looks at every HTML document and tries to create a large listing of them all. It might only list the text that appears in the <HEAD> tag because that's where the title of the document should go. So, if your home page doesn't use the <HEAD> and </HEAD> tags, you wouldn't be included in the listing. In fact, that's how most of the popular WWW search engines work, they pick up information from the <HEAD> (and other) default HTML tags. In general, while they don't affect how your home page looks, using these tags is considered proper.

▶ **See** Chapter 12, "Publicizing Your Web Page," for more information on how WWW Search Engines index and publicize Web pages.

<HTML> and </HTML>

This tag is important because it tells browsers to interpret the text inside of these tags as HTML text. Since HTML documents are strictly text based, the <HTML> tag lets you know that a file is written in HyperText Markup Language.

Starting with a completely new HTML file, this is the first set of tags you want to add. To use these tags, put the tag **<HTML>** at the very top of your file. It should be the first typed text on your screen. Then type in its companion tag **</HTML>** at the very end of the file. All the text surrounded by these tags are now marked as written in HTML format. Did you notice the "/" in the second tag? The forward slash is used to indicate *ending* HTML tags. Most HTML tags come in pairs, surrounding the text they mark up. The closing tag of a pair will always start with a forward slash.

So far, your home page looks like this:

```
<HTML>

</HTML>
```

<HEAD> and </HEAD>

The next set of tags you want to include is the **<HEAD>** and **</HEAD>** tags. These tags identify and mark information in your HTML document that serves as the document's header, or title information.

Adding these tags to your home page is just as easy as the <HTML> tags. Type **<HEAD>** on the screen in between the <HTML> tags and then type in its companion tag **</HEAD>** on the following line.

<BODY> and </BODY>

Just like the <HEAD> tags, you use **<BODY>** and **</BODY>** to delineate a separate part of your HTML document. Text surrounded by the <BODY> tags represents the main meat of a document.

This is where most of your text and information will be typed because they are part of the document's body. Add **<BODY>** and **</BODY>** to your Web page and your document thus far looks like this (I added tabs to indent several spaces to make them easier to read):

```
<HTML>
     <HEAD>
     </HEAD>
     <BODY>
     </BODY>
</HTML>
```

<ADDRESS> and </ADDRESS>

You've added three sets of tags to your Web page, but no text. Now add the <ADDRESS> tags, another important HTML tag. The <ADDRESS> tags contain information about who to contact regarding this particular page. It is important to always put some kind of contact information on a Web page in case someone has a question or comment they want to ask you.

The <ADDRESS> tag is used to separate that important information from the regular text body. Follow these steps to add the <ADDRESS> tag to your home page.

1. In between the **<BODY>** and **</BODY>** tags, type your name and e-mail address like this:
   Andy Shafran—e-mail:andy@shafran.com
2. Now add the **<ADDRESS>** tag to your HTML file on the line above your name and e-mail address.
3. Finally, add the closing tag, **</ADDRESS>** to your HTML file after the name and e-mail address (this contact information can span multiple lines if necessary).

Now, save your HTML file and bring it up in your WWW Browser. You'll notice that you finally have some text on your Web page. Figure 3.2 shows the HTML on your home page with Netscape.

Your HTML so far looks like this:

```
<HTML>
     <HEAD>
     </HEAD>
     <BODY>
     <ADDRESS>Andy Shafran - e-mail:andy@shafran.com</ADDRESS>
     </BODY>
</HTML>
```

FIG. 3.2

Here's my simple home page so far.

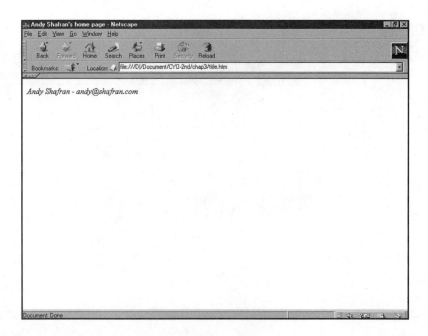

Part II

Ch 3

Titling Your Home Page

Now that your basic four HTML tags are created on your Web page, you can start adding some text to your page. Let's start by adding a title to your Web page with the **<TITLE>** and **</TITLE>** tags.

The Web page title is displayed in the browser's title bar when you visit that page. Additionally, it is the page's title that is saved when you bookmark that page for future reference as a place you'd like to visit.

Your title belongs within the **<HEAD>** and **</HEAD>** tags on your Web page. You can only have one title per HTML document. Type your Web page's title between the **<HEAD>** and **</HEAD>** tags. Now add the **<TITLE>** and **</TITLE>** tags around your newly typed text. Your HTML should look something like this:

```
<TITLE>Andy Shafran's home page</TITLE>
```

Now save your file and bring up your Web page in your browser. Figure 3.3 shows how this title appears on the screen.

FIG. 3.3
Your title is an important label for your home page.

Here's where the title appears in the WWW Browser

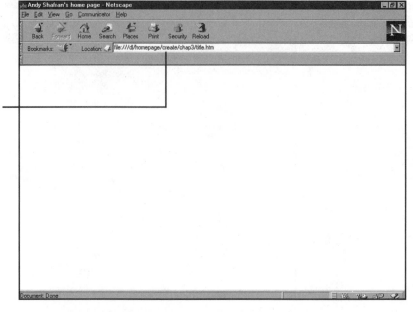

Make sure you use a short, to the point, and informative title.

 Bad home page titles are wordy, lengthy, and uninformative.

Titles should fit within the browser title bar, be easy to reference, and accurately describe the site they represent. Good home page titles include:

Andy Shafran's Home Page

Shafran's Web Page

Andy's Web Site

Visiting Andy's Page

Some bad home page title examples are:

My Page

This is the fantastic, wonderful place to visit on the Web where Andy Shafran's home page resides

Home Page, Sweet Home Page

Creating Headings

Once your title is in place, your next step is to add a heading that will appear on your Web page. Headings are similar to titles in that they should be succinct and useful. Headings come in six sizes (creatively numbered one through six, with one being the largest). Figure 3.4 shows how the different heading sizes appear. Heading tags are different than **<HEAD>** and **</HEAD>**. These tags mark how text appears on the screen, not a portion of your HTML document. You can think of headings as the headlines found on newspaper articles. They are much larger than the rest of the text and should be informative and inviting to the reader.

FIG. 3.4

Here's how the six heading sizes stack up against each other.

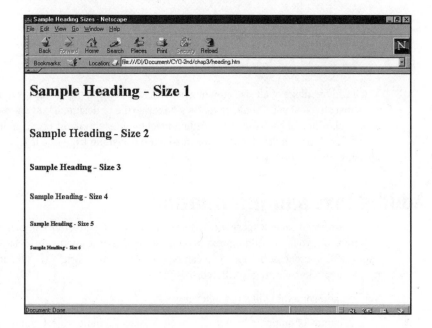

In WWW browsers, headings appear larger and bolder than standard text and are a great way to delineate different parts of your Web page.

To use a size one heading on your home page, you would use the **<H1>** and **</H1>** HTML tags around the text you want to mark. Try adding a heading to your current page. Make sure that your text falls within the **<BODY>** and **</BODY>** tags.

1. Type your heading text onto your Web page:

   Welcome to Andy's Home

2. Add the **<H1>** and **</H1>** tags around your text:

   `<H1>Welcome to Andy's Home</H1>`

3. Adding a secondary headline is just as easy. On the next line after your level one headline, type a secondary line of information, and add a size two heading with the **<H2>** and **</H2>** tags:

   `<H2>All visitors are welcome!</H2>`

4. Save and preview the Web page in your Web browser (see Figure 3.5).

You'll add headings of all sizes to your home page. You can use headings to organize the different subsections of your home page. As a general rule of design, if you use two headings right after each other, only change the heading level by one increment (go from level one to level two, or level three to level four). This makes the transition from one level of text to the next appear natural to the eye.

Adding Text and Information

With your home page properly titled and headlined, add some more information that tells your visitors about yourself. Adding text to your home page is arguably the easiest step in the home page creation process, because you can type directly into your HTML file, and it will appear as normal text when viewing it with a browser.

You can add something like the following:

Thanks for stopping by my Web page. It is an ongoing project and is continually updated. I try to add new information every two months or so. My personal interests include learning about computers, reading, and watching Broadway musicals. I live in Cincinnati with my wife and work full time in addition to occasionally writing computer books.

After typing the text, save your HTML file. Then preview what your page looks like by starting your Web browser (see Figure 3.6). You'll get a good idea of how your headings and text look on your Web page.

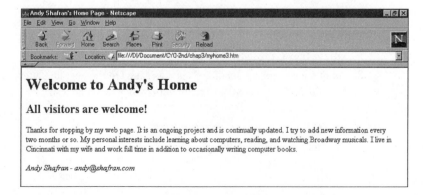

Breaking Text into Readable Chunks

Once you start adding text to your home page, you'll soon realize that your browser doesn't display your text exactly how you type it onto your home page. For example, the following text appears like this when typing it into an HTML file:

```
Here's a list of things I like to do in my spare time:
        Read books on Star Wars and historical fiction
        Travel abroad and domestically
        Surf the Internet
        Enjoy live theater
```

But it looks quite different when browsing it (see Figure 3.7).

Part

II

Ch

3

FIG. 3.7
All the text jumbles together.

Jumbled text ———

That's because Web browsers only format information according to your markup tags. HTML is a *formatting language* and tells browsers such as Netscape or Internet Explorer what to do with text. If you think the above example was jumbled, think of a large block of text that includes several different paragraphs. Since browsers ignore white space between paragraphs, you would only see one huge block of text! You need to have special tags in your HTML file that tell your Web browser when to start a new paragraph or indent text on the screen.

> **CAUTION**
> Web browsers ignore spaces, tabs, and line breaks between text unless you define them with the correct markup tags.

The following sections introduce you to some of the basic text placement markup tags. You'll learn how to break up your text into readable bits by using the paragraph and line break tags, as well as working with the *horizontal rule*—a line that is drawn across the screen to separate pieces of text.

Unlike most tags, these tags do not appear in pairs. Your browser recognizes the single tags and spaces your text accordingly.

Paragraph Tag

The paragraph tag (`<P>`) tells the browser to separate two paragraphs of information with a blank line between them. It's useful when you have many paragraphs of text in a row, such as an online book, or detailed personal information that needs to span more than one long paragraph.

Adding a paragraph tag is simple. Place your cursor in the spot where you want the tag and type `<P>`. Web browsers automatically understand what that tag means and will correctly display a paragraph break onscreen.

 TIP   The heading tags automatically include a carriage return and blank line after text surrounded with the `<Hn>` and `</Hn>` tags (where the n stands for the header level as described previously) without worrying about using the line break or paragraph tags.

Line Break Tag

The line break tag `<BR>` is similar to the paragraph tag, except that it does not add an extra line between the text it separates. After the tag, text continues directly at the beginning of the next line.

In your HTML file, move your cursor to where you need a line break to appear and type in `<BR>`.

You can use the line break tag when creating a short list of items:

```
<H3>My Favorite Musicals, in order:</H3>
Les Miserables <BR>
Jeckyll & Hyde <BR>
Cats <BR>
Pippin <P>
```

The `<P>` tag was used at the end of the list to separate the end of the list from the next paragraph (see Figure 3.8). The first list of information was fixed by using the `<P>` and `<BR>` tags.

N O T E   HTML also includes two derivations of the `<BR>` tag.

The word break tag, `<WBR>` marks where browsers should break up a specific word, should it need to wrap to a following line (particularly useful for long and extended medical terminology).

The opposites of `<BR>`, `<NOBR>` and `</NOBR>` surround text that should never be wrapped on subsequent lines automatically by the browser. The no-break tag disables automatic word wrapping and is useful when you need to ensure a group of text always appears on the same line. ■

FIG. 3.8
Some favorite musicals, browserized.

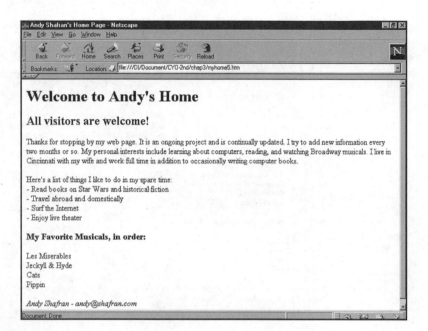

Horizontal Rules

The horizontal rule tag, <HR>, is one of the most useful and elegant tags available to help you separate and break up your Web page.

Adding this tag to your HTML document creates a line that goes across the screen. This line is useful for logically separating different parts of your home page from each other.

You can use the horizontal rule tag as an organizational and design tool. It helps people who view a Web page to understand which pieces are related to each other, and it also separates the page into different pieces. For example, the <HR> tag can be used right above an e-mail address on a Web page to split that information apart from the regular text on the home page.

You can use the <HR> tag anywhere within your HTML document's body. To add a horizontal rule tag, simply type <H> directly into your Web page. Like the <P> tag, Web browsers add a carriage return automatically after the horizontal line. Figure 3.9 shows a standard horizontal line on a Web page.

Keep in mind that too much of anything can be a bad thing. While horizontal lines are very useful and popular techniques for organizing Web pages, don't over use them by having dozens of different lines on a single page.

Part
II

Ch
3

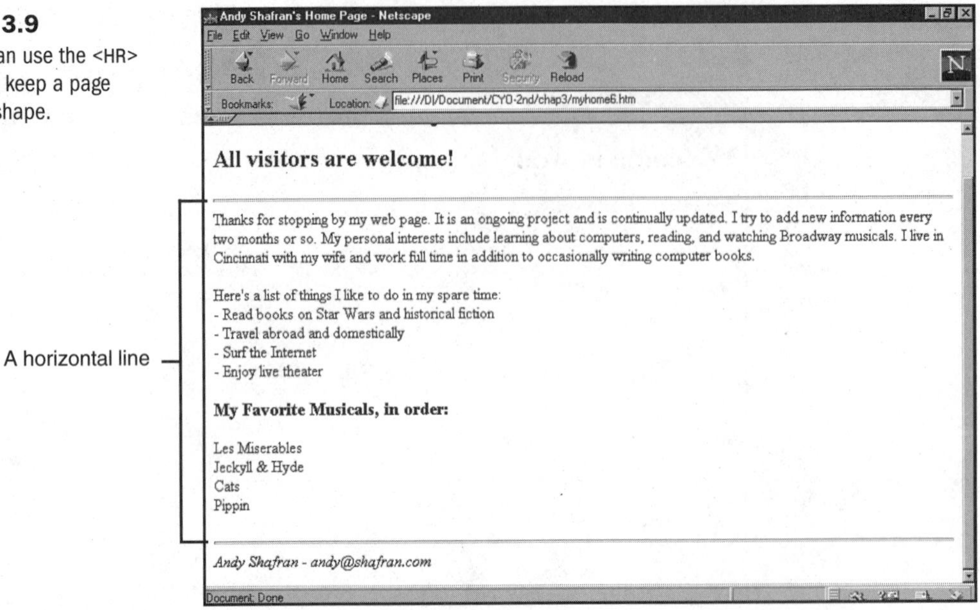

FIG. 3.9
You can use the <HR> tag to keep a page ship-shape.

A horizontal line —

Line Extensions

Although useful, Web page creators quickly became bored with adding simple lines to their Web pages. So, several years ago, the <HR> was expanded so that you could add special key-words that control the thickness, alignment, and length of a horizontal line on a Web page. A thin line across the page is useful in some cases, but occasionally you might want to have a different type of line. Using the <HR> extensions, you have significant control over your horizontal lines.

Horizontal line extensions are special keywords that are added to the <HR> tag. They tell your Web browser that you want a horizontal line to appear on the screen, but to give it some special traits. This section describes these extensions in details.

> **CAUTION**
> While useful techniques, horizontal-line extensions do not work with versions of Microsoft Internet Explorer before 3.0.

SHADE* or *NOSHADE   The first <HR> extension lets you decide if your horizontal line appears solid black or as a shaded line (the default setting when using a vanilla <HR> tag).

To change your horizontal line to use the NOSHADE options, simply add the keyword NOSHADE to your <HR> tag:

```
<HR NOSHADE>
```

Figure 3.10 shows an example page with horizontal lines using the shade and noshade option.

FIG. 3.10
Notice how the two lines look significantly different on a Web page.

Standard horizontal line

Noshade horizontal line

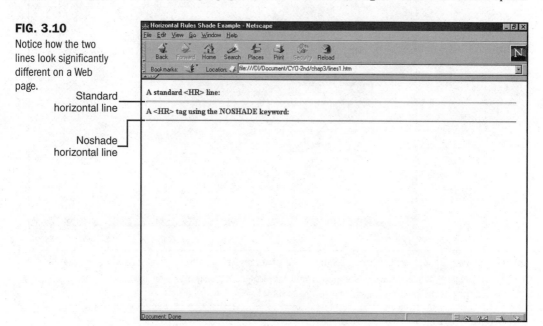

Line Width   The most popular horizontal-line extension allows you to control the width of the line across the page. With the standard <HR> tag, a line appears all the way across the screen. Often times, you may want to have the line only go halfway across the screen, or maybe even a quarter of the way across the screen, depending on how your page is designed.

You can control the horizontal line width by adding the WIDTH keyword to your <HR> tag and specifying a percentage value that tells the line how wide it should be. For example, if you wanted to create a simple line that goes halfway across the screen (50 percent), you'd use the following tag:

```
<HR WIDTH=50%>
```

Figure 3.11 shows several different lines of varying widths across the screen. By default, the horizontal lines appear centered on the screen, regardless of their width.

FIG. 3.11

You can make your horizontal line any width by changing the percentage value.

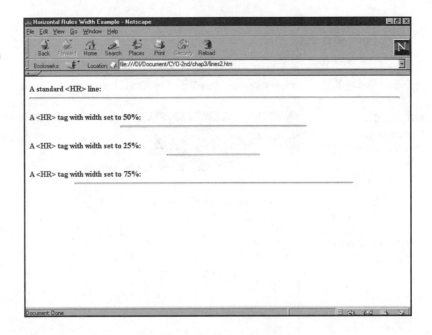

TIP Don't worry about the resolution or computer type of visitors who stop by your Web site. Since you are assigning a percentage value to the width, Web browsers automatically make the line appear that percentage wide, on any computer screen.

Alignment   Now that you can control the width of a horizontal line on the screen, occasionally you may want to control its alignment as well. Used in conjunction with the WIDTH keyword, you can set the line alignment with the ALIGN keyword. Line alignment has three settings: left, center (default), and right.

To make a horizontal line appear aligned with the left side of the page, you'd use the following <HR> tag (This line is only 50 percent wide):

```
<HR WIDTH=50% ALIGN=LEFT>
```

Figure 3.12 Shows an example page with horizontal lines using the SHADE and NOSHADE option.

FIG. 3.12
Alignment settings work
well when controlling
line width.

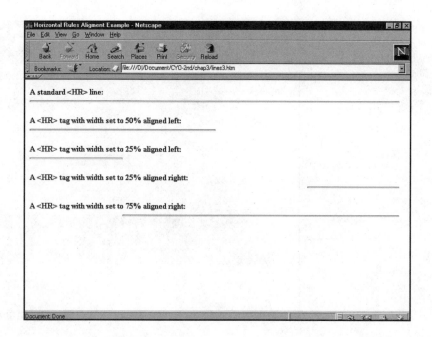

Line Thickness In addition to controlling line width on the screen, you can also manipulate line thickness as well. Line thickness allows you to create horizontal lines that can really section off and organize different sections of a Web page without adding graphics to the page or using any advanced HTML features like Tables. Line thickness is controlled with the SIZE keyword.

When using SIZE in the <HR> tag, you are assigning a pixel thickness to the horizontal line. The default pixel thickness of a line is two (SIZE=2). You can set the line thickness to be anywhere from one to 175 pixels thick with the SIZE keyword. Whenever you use SIZE to change your line thickness, you'll always want to use the NOSHADE keyword as well, so that your lines appear dark and filled in on the screen.

To add a horizontal line on the screen that is five pixels thick, use the following tag:

```
<HR NOSHADE SIZE=5>
```

Figure 3.13 Shows an example page with horizontal lines that have varying thickness.

Part

II

Ch

3

FIG. 3.13

The last line extension you can set is line thickness.

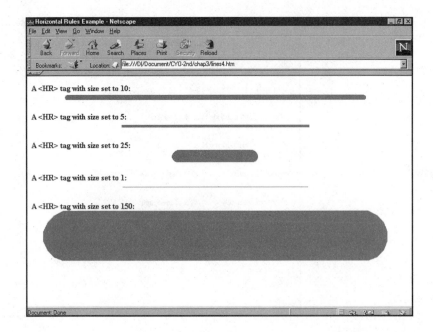

Preformatted Text

Sometimes, you don't want Web browsers to take care of the formatting automatically for you. You may want to type some information into your HTML file and have it look exactly the same in the WWW browser, without worrying about paragraph tags.

In that case, use the <PRE> and </PRE> tags for preformatted text. Any text that appears within the <PRE> tags will appear exactly the same in Netscape and Internet Explorer— spaces, tabs, line breaks, and all.

Add the preformatted tags into your Web page by typing <PRE> and </PRE> around the text you want to indicate.

▶ **See** "Table Alternatives," in Chapter 5, "Adding Lists and Tables," for more information (and an example) of using preformatted text on your home page.

CHAPTER 4

Adding Style to Your Text

In the last chapter, you learned how to add basic text and simple HTML tags to your Web page. You now have a fundamental understanding of how to organize paragraphs of text and use important tags.

There are many other ways that allow you control over how text appears on your Web page. Just like using a word processor, you can control whether text appears in bold, italic, or underlined, which font it appears in, and how large it looks on the screen. Additionally, HTML now gives you complete control over what colors text appears on the screen. You have literally millions of different colors and shades to choose from.

This chapter introduces you to these important text formatting techniques. You'll learn several new tags and how these styles can work together to make parts of your Web page really stand out. ■

Control text appearance on a Web page

You can make text onscreen appear in bold, italic, superscript, subscript, and many others with a few simple tags.

Color coordinate text

HTML offers a variety of different ways to control the color of text on the screen to add pizzazz and excitement to regular black text.

Work with the FONT tag to affect font appearance

When building Web pages, your text can be established in any font available, not just the standard *Times New Roman*.

Add special characters to pages

There are many characters you might want to use that aren't available on your keyboard. Learn how to build symbols like the copyright sign into a Web page.

Updating Text Appearance

Once you are familiar with the basics of building a Web page, the most requested technique to learn is how to have basic control over text appearance.

Sometimes, you might want to emphasize a specific word or italicize a phrase. Other times you may want to center a headline, or even make text stand out by having it blink intermittently. Several text-formatting features are available at your disposal and can be integrated into your Web page. These features can really add life to a home page.

Centering

Centering is probably my favorite text formatting feature. Using the center tags, <CENTER> and </CENTER>, you can make specific text and headlines stand out easily.

You can use the center tags for headings, so they span the area where text appears, instead of being trapped in the left margin. To center text, simply add the <CENTER> and </CENTER> tags around the text you want centered onscreen.

Try centering your main home page headline. After adding the tags, my HTML code now looks like this:

```
<CENTER><H1>Welcome to Andy's Home</H1></CENTER>
```

You can center headlines, horizontal lines, Web graphics, and paragraphs of text.

Bold Text

You can mark various words and phrases in your HTML document to be displayed in boldface by using the <B> and </B> tags. Text surrounded by these tags appears darker and thicker than standard text, and stands out nicely on your home page.

To mark text as bold, add the <B> and </B> tags around the selected text.

```
<B>This Text will appear in Bold</B>
```

NOTE You can also mark text to be darker by using the <STRONG> and </STRONG> tags. The strong tags are a more general term that tells browsers to make the marked text appear stronger onscreen. The strong tags are inherited from the parent language of HTML (SGML), but are not used as often now because each browser interpreted what strong text meant, creating some discrepancies. Everyone understands what bold means.

As mentioned in Chapter 1, "A Web Crawler's Beginning," logical versus physical formatting is often a common debate among HTML programmers. Nowhere can this debate be better witnessed than in deciding how to make specific pieces of text stand out in bold or italic. The physical answer to this question is to use the <B> and <I> container tags to mark text as bold or italic.

On the flip side, logical proponents suggest using the <STRONG> and <EM> (emphasis) tags to make text stand out. These two tags are used to describe how text should appear relative to normal text on-screen. Typically, the <STRONG> tag bolds surrounded text while the <EM> tag italicizes it, but this interpretation depends on each WWW browser's interpretation. For example, another browser might decide that <EM>phasized text should be bright red and in huge letters, while there's a much more standard approach to displaying <I>talic text—slightly slanted towards the right. With Logical Formatting tags, you're at the mercy of a WWW browser to interpret them however it likes.

Nowadays, most HTML programmers tend to use the physical tags (<B> and <I>) because of the underlying uncertainty of exactly how WWW browsers will display text marked with logical tags. In general, most popular Web browsers (including both Netscape and Internet Explorer) interpret the <B> and <STRONG> and <EM> and <I> tags identically. ■

Italic

Marking some text to be italicized is just as easy, only you use the <I> and </I> tags instead. Simply type <I> and </I> around your selected text in your HTML file.

```
<I>This Text will appear in Italic</I>
```

Blinking

Arguably one of the most annoying features of HTML, blinking text allows you to designate portions of your Web page to flash on and off intermittently.

Judicious use of the <BLINK> and </BLINK> tags is accepted, but be careful not to make your home page look like a bad used-car commercial.

To make text blink, surround it in your HTML file with <BLINK> and </BLINK>. See Figure 4.1 for a look at a Web page using several of these useful HTML formatting tags.

```
<BLINK>This Text will appear BLINKING</BLINK>
```

Part

II

Ch

4

FIG. 4.1
Here are several formatting tags in a Web page (of course, you can't see the blinking text).

Bold ⌐
Center ─

Italic ─

CAUTION

The <BLINK> tag does not work in Microsoft Internet Explorer. This is one of the slight differences in HTML that means you have to be particularly careful when using this tag because all of your visitors won't be able to see the page properly.

Strikethrough

When you want to make text stand out on your Web page, you'll likely enlist the <B> or <I> tags to make text appear in boldface or italic. There are also several other incorporated HTML tags to control text appearance, including the strikethrough tag.

Strikethrough text appears like regular text, but with a horizontal line crossing it out. Its uses are varied; in general, people use the strikethrough tag to indicate changes to a Web page or updates to a document. To mark text as strikethrough, use the <S> and </S> tags to surround the chosen text.

```
<S>This text has been struck through</S>
```

Underline

Another newly supported HTML tag is underlining. This tag wasn't supported by browsers until recently because it could easily be confused with text that links to other Web pages (See Chapter 7, "Linking Your Web Pages," for more information). To underline text on your Web page, surround the text with <U> and </U>. Remember that since hyperlinked text also appears underlined, visitors might get confused, so try to use the underline tag sparingly.

```
<U>This text appears underlined</U>
```

Figure 4.2 shows text with strikethrough and underlining.

Making Your Text Slightly Larger or Smaller

Sometimes, when you add text to your Web page, you want to slightly emphasize certain portions of text to make it stand out to the reader. HTML offers several alternatives. You can bold text (<B> and </B>), italicize it (<I> and </I>), or use any number of other tags that were described previously in this chapter.

There are also two other new tags that help you make text look slightly different onscreen—the <BIG> and <SMALL> tags. Neither one of these two tags drastically change the way words are displayed, but instead make slight, but noticeable, changes to the thickness and size of text marked with these attributes.

Surrounding text with the <BIG> and </BIG> tags makes it appear slightly larger and bolder onscreen. As you'd expect, the <SMALL> and </SMALL> tags have the exact opposite effect. Text surrounded with this set of tags is slightly smaller in font size.

FIG. 4.2
As you can see, a musical has been struck out.

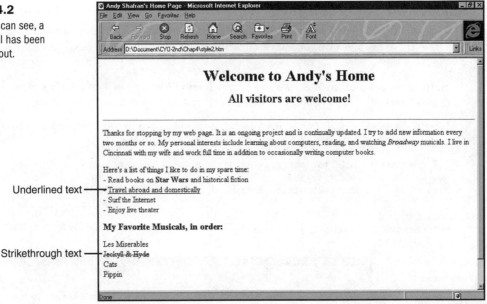

Underlined text ⟶

Strikethrough text ⟶

Here's the best way to think of the <SMALL> and <BIG> tags. Assume without any special tags, your regular text appears at 100 percent. Using the <SMALL> tag reduces the text size by about 10 percent onscreen while, conversely, the <BIG> tag increases the text size by about 10 percent.

The following is an example of the <BIG> and <SMALL> tags in action:

```
<BIG> Here's some BIG text</BIG> <BR>
Here's some REGULAR text <BR>
<SMALL>Here's some SMALL text</SMALL>
```

When used within large blocks of text, these tags can be significantly more subtle than using any of the other text attribute tags (see Figure 4.3).

FIG. 4.3
These <BIG> and <SMALL> tags allow for increased flexibility when displaying text on a Web page.

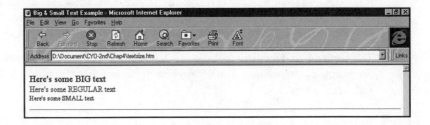

Subscript and Superscript

Two other new tags have been introduced with recent versions of HTML—subscript and superscript. These two tags give you increased flexibility for displaying specialized information in a Web browser.

You'll find yourself using these two tags sparingly, but they come in handy when you need to display information like chemical formulas (H_2O) or street addresses (1400 W 13th).

Use the _{and} tags to mark text that should appear in subscript, and the ^{and} tags for superscript information. The following are examples:

```
The chemical formula for water is H<SUB>2</SUB>O — Two parts
hydrogen and one part oxygen.
Stop by the holiday party this weekend. My address is 1400 W 13<SUP>th</SUP>.
```

Figure 4.4 shows how Netscape displays subscript and superscript marked text. These two font attributes can be added simply to an HTML file by typing the corresponding tag.

FIG. 4.4
Useful for specific pieces of information, the superscript and subscript tags aren't used very often.

Subscript ——
Superscript ——

Working with the *FONT* Tag

Web developers have long requested additional control over the way text appears on a Web page. They've been frustrated that they can only control simple text attributes for text, and have no control over how basic tags—such as <H1> appear in both style and color.

In answer to this complaint, newer versions of Web browsers support the <FONT> tag, which offers significant control over text style, color, size, and appearance, much more than the standard <B> and <I> tags. You can even have text appear onscreen in different fonts—besides the traditional Times New Roman that makes up most Web pages today.

This section introduces you to these new font control tags, as well as other important text and document appearance tags. You'll learn how to customize text appearance by using the <FONT> and </FONT> tags.

TIP The font attributes you have control over now are just the tip of the iceberg. Soon, you'll be able to build in default icons that can appear alongside your text, and create animation that makes your text move around onscreen. Keep an eye out for the latest HTML advances and innovative new ways to use the <FONT> tag and new forthcoming HTML tags by stopping by my Web page regularly (**http://www.shafran.com**).

Setting Actual Font Size

In Chapter 3, "Web Page Basics," you learned how to control the size of headings onscreen by using six different sets of tags, ranging from <H1> to <H6>. You could specify exactly how a heading should appear onscreen. The only drawback was you only used the <H1> tags for headlines. You didn't have that kind of sizing flexibility with regular text onscreen.

Now, with the <FONT> tag you have the same flexibility with regular text. Text can appear in seven different sizes onscreen ranging from 1 (the smallest) to 7 (the largest). Normally, without using the <FONT> tag, text appears in size 3. That means you have four new settings to make text larger (4–7) and two to make text smaller (1–2). All you have to do is surround the text whose font size you want to change, and add the SIZE= keyword like the following example:

```
<FONT SIZE=5> Here's text displayed in Size 5 </FONT>
```

The previous <FONT> tag sets the surrounded text to be size 5, two steps larger than text normally appears onscreen. Figure 4.5 shows you how all seven font sizes compare against one another.

FIG. 4.5
This figure compares the multiple text sizes.

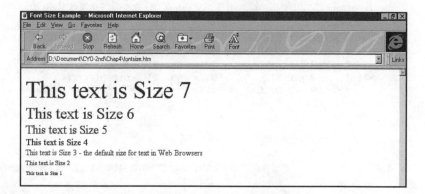

Part

II

Ch

4

TIP Just like using headings, make sure you change font sizes step by step. Jumping from size 1 to size 6 on subsequent lines makes a Web page look odd and out of place. Differentially sizing text should be used carefully and scrutinized closely.

Setting Relative Font Sizes

The <FONT> tag also has slightly more flexibility when setting the actual size of your text onscreen. Instead of setting your text size to be a specific number, you can instead give it a relative size, such as +3 or –1. The Web browser takes your relative size tag and adds to (or subtracts it from) the default font size being used (size 3). Take a look at the following examples:

```
<FONT SIZE=+3> A Relative Font Size Example </FONT>
```

```
<FONT SIZE=-2> Another Font Size Example </FONT>
```

Since the normal font size of text is size number 3, the first line in the previous code makes the surrounded text display onscreen in size 6 (3+3=6) while the second line displays text in size 1 (3–2=1). Figure 4.6 shows how the previous two lines of HTML are interpreted on a Web page.

FIG. 4.6

Relative font sizes let you increase or decrease the size of fonts on a step-by-step basis.

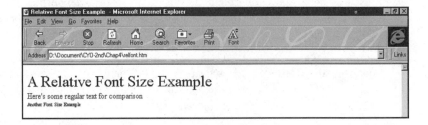

One very popular use of this dynamic sizing is the ability to make the first character in a phrase appear larger than the rest of the sentence. This method helps draw attention to this particular part of your Web page because it uses a larger than average first character.

Here's an example of where the first character appears larger than the rest of the sentence:

```
<CENTER>
<FONT COLOR=RED SIZE=6>E</FONT><FONT SIZE=5>xamples</FONT>
<FONT COLOR=RED SIZE=6>F</FONT><FONT SIZE=5>rom the</FONT>
<FONT COLOR=RED SIZE=6>B</FONT><FONT SIZE=5>ook</FONT><BR>
<FONT COLOR=RED SIZE=7>C</FONT><FONT SIZE=5>hapter</FONT>
<FONT COLOR=RED SIZE=6>4</FONT><FONT SIZE=5>: Adding Style to Your Text
➥</FONT><BR>
</CENTER>
```

Figure 4.7 shows how this example appears on screen.

FIG. 4.7

This is a popular stylistic technique for Web developers.

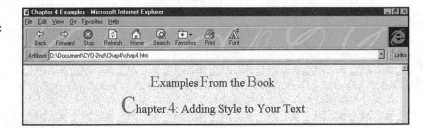

Embedding *<FONT>* Tags

You can also embed <FONT SIZE> tags within one another—but they don't work as you might assume. Let's say you wanted to make three words appear subsequently larger like this:

Big Bigger Biggest

Your first reaction might be to embed three <FONT> tags inside of each other, like the following:

```
<FONT SIZE=+1> Big <FONT SIZE=+1> Bigger <FONT SIZE=+1> Biggest </FONT> </FONT>
➥</FONT>
```

That way the first word, *Big*, would be enlarged by one size; then *Bigger* is enlarged another size; and *Biggest* is enlarged for a cumulative total of three sizes—but that's not how browsers work.

<FONT> tags are not cumulative in nature. Each of the <FONT SIZE=1> tags sets the surrounded text to be one size larger than regular—the result being that all three words are the same size.

To make cumulative changes in font size, you'd have to create your HTML like this:

```
<FONT SIZE=+1> Big <FONT SIZE=+2> Bigger <FONT SIZE=+3> Biggest </FONT> </FONT>
➥</FONT>
```

Figure 4.8 shows how these two examples appear.

FIG. 4.8
Remember that
<FONT> tags are not
cumulative in nature.

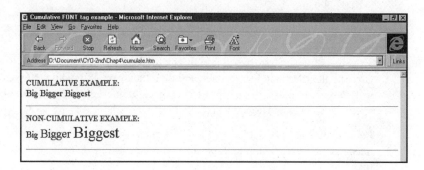

TIP If you change the relative size of text to be larger than +4 or smaller than –2, browsers just assume you want to display the information in the largest (or smallest) size available.

Font Faces

If you're like most people, you likely have many different fonts, or typesets available to you when you use your word processor. Windows 95 alone comes with dozens of different fonts that can each be used for different occasions.

Internet Explorer allows you to specify which fonts text appears in and when you use a new keyword that's part of the <FONT> tag. Here's how it works. Using the FACE= keyword, the browser attempts to display text in the alternative font you tell it to.

```
<FONT FACE="Arial">Here is some differently fonted text</FONT>
```

This snippet of code tells your browser to display the surrounded text in the **Arial** font—one of the standard fonts installed along with Windows 95. Figure 4.9 shows how Internet Explorer displays this text.

Here's how this new Font tag works. First, your browser looks at the Font you've specified—in this case Arial. It then checks the personal computer of the person visiting the Web page to see if the Arial font is installed. If so, it displays the text by using the new font. If for some reason, Arial can't be found, then it simply displays the text like standard regular text—as if the <FONT FACE="ARIAL"> tag wasn't even there.

FIG. 4.9

The Arial Font really stands out on a typical Web page.

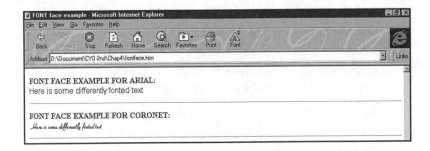

If you'd like, you can also specify a list of fonts that you want the browser to try to find before it uses the default.

```
<FONT FACE="Arial, Coronet, WingDings">Here is some differently fonted text
➡</FONT>
```

The preceding tag first tries to find Arial and display your text with that font. If that doesn't succeed, it'll then look for Coronet, and then finally try WingDings. If none of these three fonts work out, then Internet Explorer defaults back to the regular Times Roman font. You can specify as many fonts as you would like to try to find.

Remember that since you'll be adding this tag to your Web page that everyone who stops by needs to have a particular font installed on their machine in order to see the differently styled text.

The trick to using this new tag is properly naming the fonts you want to display text in. To get a list of fonts that are available on your personal computer, you need to see your system settings. Figure 4.10 shows just a smattering of all the fonts you can choose from and use on a Windows 95 personal computer.

 Try using your Word Processor—like Word or WordPro—and explore using the different fonts on your machine to find the one you want to use on your Web page.

To see a list of all the fonts available in Windows 95, click the Start button at the bottom of the screen and choose Settings, Control Panel, and double click the Fonts icon.

There are many different ways to use different fonts on a Web page. Figure 4.11 shows an example of a font that fits with the overall style of the Web page.

FIG. 4.10
Most computers have a plethora of fonts to choose from.

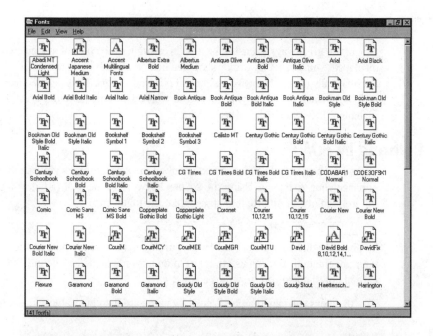

FIG. 4.11
This page just exudes a Vermont feeling.

Controlling Text Color

One of the great ways to customize text is changing the color of any piece of information being displayed. You can set a word or sentence in a paragraph, item in a list, or snippet of text, to automatically appear in any of millions of different colors. Netscape lets you choose from 16 different default colors, or you can create your own particular color creation by mixing and matching different shades of red, green, and blue.

Coloring by *FONT*

Changing the color of displayed text is one of the easiest things you can do to spice up and enhance your Web page. Using the COLOR= keyword in the <FONT> tag, you can specify several different colors for your text to appear, like the following:

```
<FONT COLOR=RED>Some Red Text</FONT>
```

You have 16 different default colors at your fingertips that are named and recognized within your imagination. You can use them as often as you would like on your Web page—just be careful not to make your text unreadable.

The 16 colors you can identify directly by name are listed in Table 4.1.

Table 4.1   The 16 Named Font Colors

Black	Maroon	Green	Olive
Navy	Purple	Teal	Gray
Silver	Red	Lime	Yellow
Blue	Fuchsia	Aqua	White

N O T E In case you're wondering where these 16 colors came from, they were the original 16 VGA named colors that Microsoft used in Windows. ■

Besides using the 16 named colors, you can also specify colors by mixing different shades of red, green, and blue. This literally gives you millions of different colors to choose from. See the section "Color by Hexadecimal" later in this chapter for more information.

Of course, the COLOR keyword can be used in conjunction with the SIZE keyword described earlier.

T I P Use the <FONT> tag to change text color for a small piece of your Web page. If you want to modify the text color for the entire page, see the following section, "Other Ways to Change Color."

Other Ways to Change Text Color

In this section, you'll learn how to change the default text color for the entire page by adding a new keyword to your <BODY> tag. This keyword uses the exact same color formula as described in Table 4.1—where you name the color you want to use from the 16 named colors.

You'll want to customize this option when you start using background images and colors on your Web page. By default, the text color is black, and the background is gray or white.

N O T E   This section shows you how to control the text color by using a keyword in your <BODY> tag. You also have several other color controls available.

Chapter 6, "Using Graphics to Excite Your Web Page," shows you how to change the background page color for your site and use images in the background as well.

Chapter 7, "Linking Your Web Pages," shows you three more keywords that work in the <BODY> tag. These new keywords let you control which color-linked text appears on the screen. ■

To change the default color of text on your screen, add the TEXT= keyword to your <BODY> tag, like the following:

```
<BODY TEXT=Lime>
```

The preceding tag sets all text on my Web page to lime green (how ugly). You can replace **Lime** with any of the other 16 named colors.

N O T E   Colors specified with the <FONT> tag, as described previously, override your default color setting from the <BODY> tag. ■

Color by Hexadecimal

Many times, you might want to use other colors not specified in the default-named 16 provided. Just like a painter, you want to mix and match different hues and shades to come up with your own color concoction.

Another way to set your COLOR= keyword inside of the <FONT> tag and the TEXT= keyword in the <BODY> tag is by using the six-character hexadecimal equivalent. Specific colors are indicated by a six-character hexadecimal combination that tells your computer how it should mix red, blue, and green together to get your specified color. Hexadecimal numbers range from 0–9 and A–F. If this sounds confusing to you, don't worry. I'll step you through the color process and show you how to figure out the six-character combination for many popular colors.

Here's how it works. On a computer monitor, all colors are a mix of red, green, and blue. Each of these three primary colors controls two of the six hexadecimal characters. By mixing and matching different shades of these colors, you have literally thousands of different possibilities to choose from. For example, let's say you wanted to use a pure shade of red on your Web page. For this, you'd use <FONT> in the following manner:

```
<FONT COLOR=#FF0000>Some Red Text</FONT>
```

Part

II

Ch

4

Notice the six-character color tag. Each primary color—red, green, and blue—is assigned to two characters correspondingly. So the previous tag, interpreted, says to mix 100 percent full vibrant red with zero percent of green, and zero percent of blue. Similarly, true green and blue are defined as:

```
<FONT COLOR=#00FF00>Some Green Text</FONT>
```

```
<FONT COLOR=#0000FF>Some Blue Text</FONT>
```

Unfortunately, this book doesn't appear in color. Otherwise, I could demonstrate how these colors work visually (I have several color examples linked to my home page, though). For a more complete listing of colors and examples, visit **http://www.imagitek.com/bcs.html** (see Figure 4.12). This Web site lets you pick any sample combination of hexadecimal colors to see what it looks like. Also, stop by **http://www.yahoo.com/Computers_and_Internet/ Internet/World_Wide_Web/Page_Design_and_Layout/Color_Information/** for a listing of other sites that help you choose corresponding colors to use.

FIG. 4.12

Here's a good site that lets you check out colors by hexadecimal.

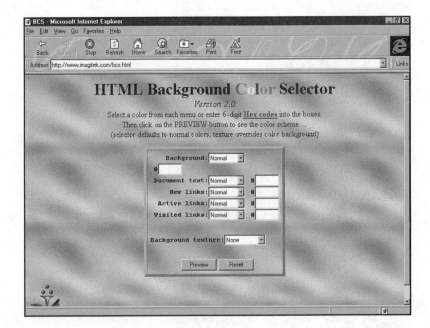

Next, I've listed a short table (see Table 4.2) of some of my personal favorite colors and the corresponding six-character codes. Feel free to experiment with your own creative mixes of colors. Since Hexadecimal counting uses 16 digits instead of the standard 10 we are all used to, each character can be a number 0 through 9 or a letter A through F.

Table 4.2   Several Hexadecimal Colors You Can Use with Text

Color	Six-Digit Code
Black	000000
White	FFFFFF
Yellow	FFFF00
Gray	C0C0C0
Maroon	8E046B
Hunter Green	215E21
Pink	BC8F8F
Navy Blue	04048E
Violet	4F2F4F

Adding Special Characters

Sometimes, you may have trouble making certain characters display within a Web page. Characters such as &, ", <, >, =, and more are integral to the definition of other tags. Other tags are not in the normal alphabet—such as , , --, or . Still other characters are present in foreign languages, but not English—for example, to correctly insert *français* in your Web page, you need to use a character called the *cedilla* instead of the c.

To include these individual special characters on your Web pages, you need to refer to them individually, each with a special HTML tag. Fortunately, there are HTML standards that agree on a default set of HTML tags that represent characters when found inside of an HTML file.

 T I P   If you find yourself using foreign language characters regularly, it might be worth your while to evaluate the Multilingual WWW Publisher and Browser produced by Accent Software (**http://www.accentsoft.com**).

Table 4.3 lists several popular characters that you may want to include on your Web page, and the appropriate HTML you must use—each beginning with & for them to appear.

Table 4.3   Some Special Characters to Use in Your HTML Page

Character	HTML tag
<	&lt
>	&gt
&	&amp

continues

Part

II

Ch

4

Table 4.3   Continued

Character	HTML tag
"	&quot
©	&copy
®	&reg
—	&emdash

TIP   For a more complete listing of all the special characters you can include on your Web page, visit the following site:

http://www.uni-passau.de/~ramsch/iso8859-1.html

CHAPTER 5

Adding Lists and Tables

Most people like watching the nightly news because a lot of information is packed into 30 minutes. The newscasters realize that they have to keep the viewers' interest or the viewers will switch channels. Your home page needs to follow this same practice. You have to organize your page and present your information in a concise and sensible way, or they'll leave your page faster than they click the remote control.

With a simple Web page under your belt, it's time to start exploring different HTML elements that can help you organize your page and present information more attractively.

This chapter teaches you how to add lists and tables to your home page. Lists and tables are HTML elements that make it easy to display groups of related information together in an easy-to-use format. You'll use lists to show itemized elements listed in order, while tables have a familiar row-and-column feel that allows you to display a lot of information in a concentrated area.

Although not difficult to use, lists and tables require a more thorough knowledge of HTML. ■

Determine when to use a list on your home page

Decide when and how lists can be useful in organizing Web pages.

Use three different kinds of lists

HTML provides you with several flavors of lists, and you'll learn how to use each of them.

Understand the differences between lists and tables

Evaluate the similarities and differences between using lists and tables in certain situations.

How to create a simple home-page table

Learn how to make a good-looking, simple table to organize and compare information.

Customize your table to make it look good

Take advantage of several advanced table tags and features that enhance your Web page.

What Are Lists and Tables?

Nowadays, lists are an integral part of virtually any Web page. With several different types available, lists allow you to separate pieces of text and information from the standard paragraph format. While paragraph text wraps around line after line in a traditional format, lists show text differently. Items in a list are indented, kept separate from other paragraphs of text, and are usually preceded by a bullet or number.

Proper use of a list makes a large amount of information readable, usable, and easy to spot on a Web page. Additionally, you can embed lists within each other to display data in outline format. You can, for instance, use lists on your home page to itemize your interests and to organize your page of hotlinks.

Tables, which are related to lists, use a row-and-column format to present information on your home page. Supported by nearly all Web browsers (including the new WebTV), tables have a very important role in controlling information layout and design on a Web page.

Tables are fantastic for displaying a lot of related information in a usable format that fits on-screen. Anything that you would organize in columns is fair game to present in a table. Companies commonly use tables to show products and pricing information. You can also, say, use a table on your home page to compare and contrast Broadway musicals.

Both tables and lists offer specialized formatting options to let you customize how they appear on your Web page.

What Lists Help You Accomplish

First, you're going to see what lists are and how you can use them in your Web page. Lists are extremely popular and can make a good Web page look great when used correctly.

Lists are especially good in three situations: when you have similar information that needs to be categorized in some fashion; when you have a lot of data that would be too wordy and un-readable in paragraph format; or when you have a step-by-step process that needs to be de-scribed in order.

Organize with Lists

Lists make it extremely easy to itemize information in a concise format. You don't have to bury important information inside a long paragraph—instead, use a list.

Take my home page (**http://www.shafran.com**) as an example. I originally had a paragraph that described my personal interests:

> Even though I work full-time, I still have quite a bit of time on my hands. Consequently, I have a varied group of interests. I work with a product called Lotus Notes, which is groupware software (which I am interested in, in general). Besides Lotus Notes, I love

browsing the WWW and seeing all the weird and useful pages. As one part of my career, I write computer books about a wide variety of products. In my spare time I like to read and listen to (and see) Broadway musicals and live theater.

Not only was the paragraph too wordy, but it presented a bunch of information repetitively and in an unorganized fashion. Below is a snippet of HTML which shows how I tidied it up by using HTML lists. Figure 5.1 below shows this list from a browser's point of view.

```
My Personal Interests:
<UL>
<LI> Groupware
<LI> Lotus Notes
<LI> Browsing the WWW
<LI> Writing Computer Books
<LI> Broadway Musicals and Live Theater
</UL>
```

FIG. 5.1
Here's how my list of
information appears in
a browser.

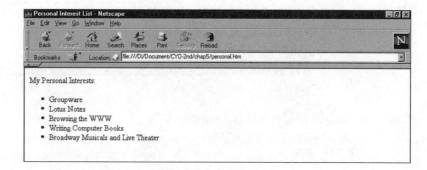

Lists help you organize information and make people more likely to read through your home page, because a quick scan through a list can find what they're looking for.

Simplify Large Amounts of Information

Whenever you have several items of related information, consider using a list to make it readable. For example, suppose that you're listing your favorite Broadway musicals. Rather than typing the names of the musicals in paragraph form, creating a list is perfect for this situation.

Each musical is indented and easy to read (see Figure 5.2).

N O T E The last chapter showed you how to use the <BR> tag to force Web browsers to display text on the next line—See "Line Break Tag" in Chapter 3, "Web Page Basics." Using the <BR> tag, you can emulate a simple list, although I usually wouldn't recommend it. Lists are indented, bulleted, and can even be numbered, making them much more powerful for displaying separate items than the <BR> tag. ■

Part

II

Ch

5

FIG. 5.2
Here are some popular musicals. Which is easier to read—the paragraph or the list?

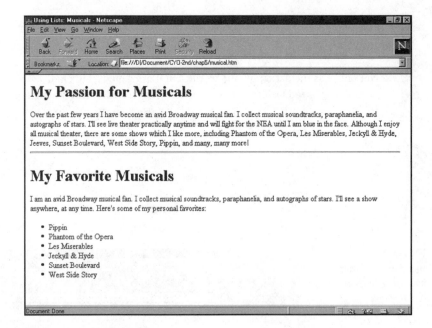

Describe a Step-By-Step Process

Another popular use of lists within Web pages is to describe a specific process one step at a time. HTML automatically numbers each step in ascending order, allowing you to ignore the actual numbering scheme for each step. This type of list is perfect to use throughout a training manual.

Whenever you need to outline a process or describe a complicated series of events, I recommend using a list on your Web page. Figure 5.3 contains a good example of when using a list makes sense for a step-by-step process.

FIG. 5.3
Here's a step-by-step process that needs to be explicit about the order of operations.

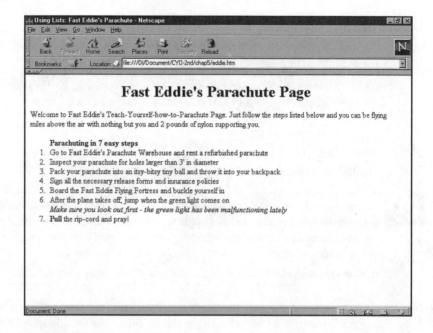

Add a List to Your Page

Now that you know when you can (and should) use lists, let's take a look at the different types of lists you can add to your home page.

Lists come in three basic flavors: unordered, ordered, and definition. Although there are others, these are the most commonly used—and most widely supported—types. Each is similar in that it lists each item on a subsequent line, and you can label selected text to make information stand out. The main difference between the three list types is how the listed items are numbered and structured.

Adding a list to your home page is relatively easy. First, add the list opening and closing tags (<UL> and </UL>, <OL> and </OL>, or <DL> and </DL>). Next, add a tag before the text identifying each item in the list—the <LI> tag. Finally, add the title of the list inside the header tags (</LH> and </LH>) and you're ready to go. Don't feel overwhelmed by all this HTML tagging; I'll step you through all the steps necessary to create a complete list.

T I P Notice the spaces after the <LI> tag and before the first letter in each element. Make sure that you follow the convention of either always including a space after the <LI> tag or never including a space. Mixing and matching spaces between text and the <LI> tag will make your list look jumbled, because browsers display any spaces you include. As long as you're consistent, all the items in the list will line up correctly.

Part
II

Ch
5

Unordered (Bulleted) List

The most common list you'll find on Web pages is the *unordered list*. Each item in an unordered list is identified by a miniature icon preceding it.

The HTML tags for the unordered list are `<UL>` and `</UL>`. Inside these tags, specify each list item with an `<LI>` tag. In your HTML page, type in the following snippet:

```
<UL>
<LI>
</UL>
```

On the line with the `<LI>` tag you can add your first list item.

TIP Although you can have as many list items as you want, be careful not to go overboard. A list with too many items is just as unattractive and unreadable as a large paragraph of text. As a general rule of thumb, limit yourself to no more than eight items per list. Generally, if you need more items than that, you can divide your list into smaller sublists that are easier to scan through.

If you feel you need more items, try using a table instead—you'll learn about these in a moment.

From here, you can choose the type of list you want to add, and can select your desired display options. Type your list's title in the List Heading box. The list title appears above your list and serves as a label describing it.

After the `<LI>` tag, type the information you want to appear for that list item. For subsequent list items, type in a new `<LI>` tag and then the item in the list. Finally, add a list header to your list with the `<LH>` and `</LH>` tags. Web browsers automatically make text marked as headers appear slightly different than standard text (and in this case I added the bold tags around this text as well). Ensure that all of your `<LI>` and `<LH>` tags are between the unordered list pair of tags—`<UL>` and `</UL>`.

Eventually, my sample list looks like this:

```
<UL>
<LH><B>Barney's Circus Animals</B></LH>
<LI>Elephants
<LI>Lions
<LI>Bears
<LI>Sharks
</UL>
```

Figure 5.4 shows how this simple list looks in a browser.

FIG. 5.4

Here's how the list looks when someone is viewing my HTML page.

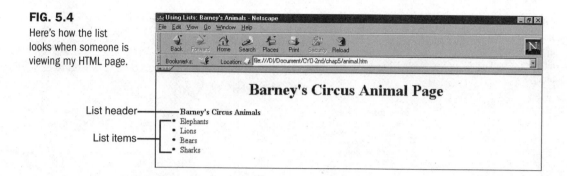

List header ——— Barney's Circus Animals

List items ——— • Elephants
• Lions
• Bears
• Sharks

Ordered (Numbered) List

The *ordered list* works in much the same way as an unordered list. The only difference between these two list types is that, instead of inserting graphical bullets in front of items of information, the ordered list automatically adds sequential numbers or letters in front of your list items. This saves you from manually typing a number for each item in the list. It's a real help when you insert an item somewhere near the top of the list and all the subsequent items are automatically renumbered.

An ordered list uses the <OL> and </OL> tags. As with an unordered list, you use the <LI> to identify each element. By default, ordered lists number each element beginning with 1.

You can use ordered lists to describe information that you want ranked in order (think of Top 10 lists from *The Late Show with David Letterman*), or to describe steps in a process that must be followed in order.

Adding an ordered list to your home page is as easy as adding an unordered list. Simply type the following snippet of HTML into your Web page:

```
<OL>
<LI>
</OL>
```

As with an unordered list, you can add as many <LI> elements as you want to your ordered list—just remember not to go overboard. The following is a listing for a simple HTML list that is shown in Figure 5.5.

```
<OL TYPE=1, 2, 3, ...>
    <LH><B>My Quick Europe Itinerary</B></LH>
    <LI>Fly into Paris
    <LI>Travel overnight to Berlin
    <LI>Catch a train to Vienna
    <LI>Charter a flight to Rome
    <LI>Stop by Nice
    <LI>Return to Paris and fly home
</OL>
```

Part

II

Ch

5

FIG. 5.5

This is the browser view of a European trip itinerary, showing the order of visits.

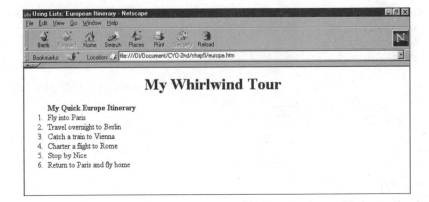

By default, HTML lists are automatically numbered with standard numerals—1, 2, 3, and so on. You can also specify lists to use alternative numbering, such as letters (upper and lower case) and Roman Numerals (I, II, III, IV, and so on). To change the default numbered list, add the TYPE keyword to your <OL> tag. The following list shows the five varying settings you can use with a numbered list:

- **TYPE=1**   Uses the standard numerical system for a numbered list—1, 2, 3, 4, 5.
- **TYPE=A**   Uses uppercase letters for ordered list items—A, B, C, D, E.
- **TYPE=a**   Uses lowercase letters for ordered list items—a, b, c, d, e.
- **TYPE=I**   Uses the Roman Numeral counting system for ordered list items—I, II, III, IV, V.
- **TYPE=i**   Uses the lowercase Roman Numeral counting system for ordered list items—i, ii, iii, iv, v.

Figure 5.6 shows the same list from Figure 5.5 using different numbering systems.

 Sometimes, you might not want your numbered list to start with a 1 (or letter A). In that case, you can add the SEQNUM keyword to your <OL> tag and set the list to begin with a different number. For example, to make an ordered list begin on the lucky number 13, use this tag:

```
<OL SEQNUM=13>

<LI>

</SEQNUM>
```

Make sure you set SEQNUM to a correct value that corresponds to your ordered list. For example, if you use uppercase letters, set SEQNUM to be equal to a letter, not a number or numerical value.

FIG. 5.6
Each numbering system
has its own place when
creating Web sites.

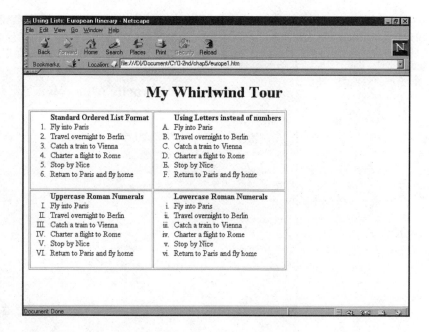

Definition List

While *definition lists* aren't as common as ordered and unordered lists, they can come in handy
in several situations. Using two lines instead of one for each list item, the definition list is useful
when you want to add additional information to your list elements.

Definition lists work slightly different than the other types of lists. Instead of having a single
`<LI>` tag for each element, the definition list requires two tags. The `<DT>` tag is used to identify
text listed as a separate element—that is, the term being defined. The `<DD>` tag places other
information indented below the `<DT>` text. This second line of information is referred to as the
definition. With one look at a definition list, you'll understand where it gets this name.

You add a definition list just as you add the other two lists, except that you now need to add two
tags for every list element:

```
<DL>
    <DT>
    <DD>
</DL>
```

A dictionary, of course, is the ideal use for a definition list. You can list each term and its definition easily in HTML. Soon, however, you'll think of many other uses for a definition list in your
home page.

Instead of using an unordered list to present popular Broadway musicals, you can use a definition list. This list displays the musical name, as the definition text, and a short explanation of
the show, as the text in the `<DD>` tag. Figure 5.7 shows this list in a browser.

Part
II

Ch
5

FIG. 5.7
This list of musicals has a little more style as a definition list than it did as an unordered list.

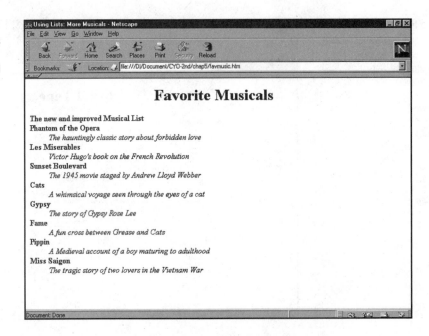

Listing 5.1 shows the HTML code of the definition list shown in Figure 5.7.

Listing 5.1   Musical Definition List

```
<DL>
<LH><B>The new and improved Musical List</B></LH>
     <DT><B>Phantom of the Opera</B>
          <DD><I>The hauntingly classic story about forbidden love</I>
     <DT><B>Les Miserables</B>
          <DD><I>Victor Hugo's book on the French Revolution</I>
     <DT><B>Sunset Boulevard</B>
          <DD><I>The 1945 movie staged by Andrew Lloyd Webber</I>
     <DT><B>Cats</B>
          <DD><I>A whimsical voyage seen through the eyes of a cat</I>
     <DT><B>Gypsy</B>
          <DD><I>The story of Gypsy Rose Lee</I>
     <DT><B>Fame</B>
          <DD><I>A fun cross between Grease and Cats</I>
     <DT><B>Pippin</B>
          <DD><I>A Medieval account of a boy maturing to adulthood</I>
     <DT><B>Miss Saigon</B>
          <DD><I>The tragic story of two lovers in the Vietnam War</I>
     </DL>
```

Lists Within Lists

One nice feature of lists is the ability to recursively place them inside each other. Creating lists within lists allows you to have several levels of organized material. You can embed several levels of lists on your Web page to increase order and decrease clutter.

Adding a list within a list is the same process as creating a single list. There are no special HTML tags—just the regular list tags. Make sure that you use the closing tag </UL> for each sublist, to avoid confusing the browser. You can even embed different types of lists within each other.

 When you embed lists within other lists, use tabs to line up each level of the list within your HTML file. Although the tabs won't show up in the browser, your home page will be much easier to maintain and read if the lists are organized well.

Figure 5.8 shows an example with several unordered lists embedded into a larger ordered list.

FIG. 5.8
The European itinerary
is shaping up.

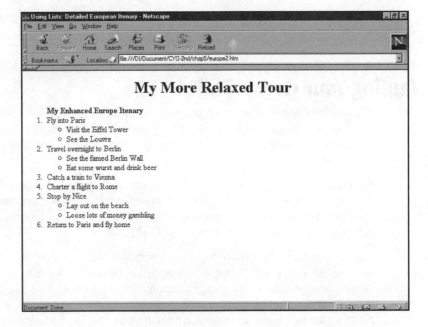

Part

II

Ch

5

Listing 5.2 shows the HTML for this example. Notice how each sublist is carefully indented. It is very easy to identify all of the sublists within the larger one.

Listing 5.2   Embedded List Code Listing

```
<OL TYPE=1>
    <LH><B>My Enhanced Europe Itinerary</B></LH>
    <LI>Fly into Paris
        <UL>
            <LI>Visit the Eiffel Tower
            <LI>See the Louvre
        </UL>
    <LI>Travel overnight to Berlin
    <UL>
            <LI>See the famed Berlin Wall
            <LI>Eat some wurst and drink beer
        </UL>
    <LI>Catch a train to Vienna
    <LI>Charter a flight to Rome
    <LI>Stop by Nice
        <UL>
            <LI>Lay out on the beach
            <LI>Loose lots of money gambling
        </UL>
    <LI>Return to Paris and fly home
</OL>
```

Tabling Your Home Page

The one drawback of using lists is that they're one-dimensional objects. This means that you can organize information only on subsequent lines. Tables, on the other hand, allow you to line up data in organized rows and columns. You get the flexibility of two dimensions to display information on your Web page.

It's important to understand which occasions are appropriate for using tables so they don't waste space on your Web page. Tables are good for comparing and contrasting similar pieces of information, because tables can have several different columns and rows. Each row and column can be labeled, allowing a spreadsheet-like appearance.

A good table can make your Web page look very neat and organized, while offering a lot of information to the viewer. A bad, or inappropriate, table splits up your page and introduces confusion to the point you're trying to convey. Figure 5.9 shows a sample table done well.

N O T E   Although the pitchers in the table aren't in any particular order, it's easy to see how listing them in a certain way makes using tables a powerful feature for Web pages. You could list them in order of ERA or Wins and Losses so that you know that the best (or worst) are listed at the top of the table. Organizing your table in a specific order provides even more information to visitors who see your page because it automatically provides a comparison and contrast for them to read. ■

FIG. 5.9
This table might come in handy for baseball fans.

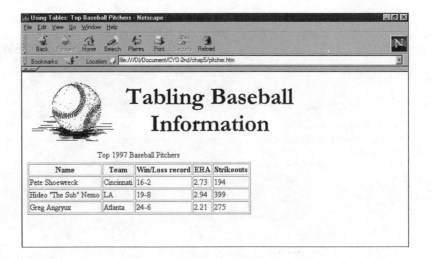

Add a Table

Adding tables to your home page can be complicated because several different tags are used. <TABLE> and </TABLE> surround the entire table, and several other tags define how information should appear. Table 5.1 offers complete descriptions of the table tags.

Table 5.1   HTML Tags Related to Tables

Tag	Description
<TABLE> and </TABLE>	These tags surround the entire table. <TABLE> tells browsers to expect the table tags listed below. Add the word BORDER (making the opening tag <TABLE BORDER>) if you want a grid to appear, separating each row and column with a thin line.
<CAPTION> and </CAPTION>	Text within these tags serves as the table's explanatory caption. You can also use <TC> and </TC> as well to depict information for a table caption.
<TH> and </TH>	Boldfaces and slightly enlarges text to serve as a row or column header.
<TR> and </TR>	Identifies each row in the table. The </TR> isn't critical, but makes your HTML code more complete and easier to maintain.
<TD> and </TD>	A pair of these tags surrounds the text for each cell of the table.

Part
II

Ch
5

If you're not careful, the need to use so many tags can make it confusing to create a multirow table. Remember the simple table for baseball fans shown in Figure 5.9? This requires many lines of HTML just to create a simple table. In Listing 5.3, you'll find the HTML used to create the table shown in Figure 5.9:

Listing 5.3   A Multirow Table

```
<TABLE BORDER>
<CAPTION ALIGN=top>Top 1997 Baseball Pitchers</CAPTION>
    <TR>
        <TH>Name</TH>
        <TH>Team</TH>
        <TH>Win/Loss record</TH>
        <TH>ERA</TH>
        <TH>Strikeouts</TH>
    </TR>
    <TR>
        <TD>Pete Shoewreck</TD>
        <TD>Cincinnati</TD>
        <TD>16-2</TD>
        <TD>2.73</TD>
        <TD>194</TD>
    </TR>
    <TR>
        <TD>Hideo "The Sub" Nemo</TD>
        <TD>LA</TD>
        <TD>19-8</TD>
        <TD>2.94</TD>
        <TD>399</TD>
    </TR>
    <TR>
        <TD>Greg Angryux</TD>
        <TD>Atlanta</TD>
        <TD>24-6</TD>
        <TD>2.21</TD>
        <TD>275</TD>
    </TR>
</TABLE>
```

Whew! All that for just a little table, and I spent extra time formatting the HTML into an easy-to-read format by adding tabs to line up each element.

Don't worry though; creating a table isn't very difficult if you are patient and carefully add tags to your Web page.

Your first step in working with a table is adding the generic <TABLE> tag:

```
<TABLE>
</TABLE>
```

To add a thin border around each cell in your table, add the BORDER=1 keyword to your <TABLE> tag. Otherwise, the cells will line up automatically but you won't see any lines separating the items of text.

Now you need to build each table cell, one at a time. First add a row to your table:

```
<TABLE BORDER=1>
    <TR>
    </TR>
</TABLE>
```

Now within your first row, add a cell that is marked as a table header. Browsers display table header cells slightly darker so they stand out.

```
<TABLE BORDER=1>
    <TR>
        <TH>Year</TH>
        <TH>Model</TH>
        <TH>Make</TH>
    </TR>
</TABLE>
```

Now, you've got a single row of information in your table, with each cell in that row marked as a table header. It's time to add several other rows of information to your table. Make sure that each row has the same amount of columns—in this case, three.

```
<TABLE BORDER=1>
    <TR>
        <TH>Year</TH>
        <TH>Model</TH>
        <TH>Make</TH>
    </TR>
    <TR>
        <TD>1986</TD>
        <TD>Toyota</TD>
        <TD>Corolla</TD>
    </TR>
<TR>
        <TD>1986</TD>
        <TD>Chevrolet</TD>
        <TD>Nova</TD>
    </TR>
<TR>
        <TD>1996</TD>
        <TD>Plymouth</TD>
        <TD>Neon</TD>
    </TR>
</TABLE>
```

Figure 5.10 shows this simple table—notice how it has three columns and four rows. You can easily match up how each row (`<TR>` and `</TR>`) in the HTML listing corresponds to the table in the figure.

You can use tables of multiple columns and rows on your Web pages.

 T I P It's a good idea to take some time and format your table tags and text to be read easily, in case you want to make changes later. I spaced my table out to make it readable by using tabs and carriage returns.

Part

II

Ch

5

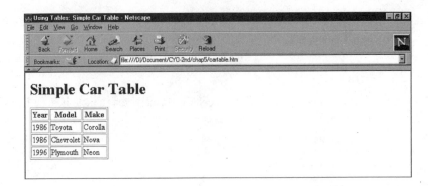

FIG. 5.10
Although simple,
making this table
introduces the basic
table-making
techniques.

Using Advanced Table Features

Now that you can create a good-looking, simple table, let's try adding a little flavor to it.
Current browsers offer several impressive ways to customize your tables.

Each of these techniques requires that you carefully calculate the number of rows and columns
used in your table so the information is appropriately organized. For this section, you'll see a
modified version of the simple baseball table you saw in Figure 5.9.

Lines Spanning Multiple Rows

When you start using tables more often, you'll occasionally find situations where you want your
information to span multiple rows. That's where the ROWSPAN keyword is useful.

ROWSPAN is a special keyword that you add to the <TD> tag for a specific cell. To have a cell span
two columns instead of the default of one, replace something like <TD>Your Cells Text
Here</TD> with the following:

```
<TD ROWSPAN=2>Your extended Text HERE</TD>
```

When your table displays, the cell you added ROWSPAN to will now take up two rows. Here's how
ROWSPAN was used to change the baseball table:

```
<TR>
<TD>Pete Shoewreck </TD>
<TD ROWSPAN=2>Cincinnati</TD>
<TD>16-2</TD>
<TD>2.73</TD>
<TD>194</TD>
</TR>
<TR>
<TD>Jose Rio</TD>
<TD>28-2</TD>
<TD>1.92</TD>
<TD>199</TD>
</TR>
```

Figure 5.11 shows the changed table.

FIG. 5.11
Here's how ROWSPAN
can shape up a table.

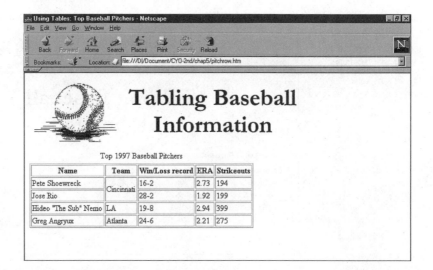

Spanning Multiple Columns

Just as ROWSPAN enables specific cells to span multiple rows, COLSPAN enables specific cells to span multiple columns. Using the COLSPAN keyword, you can instruct your table to span across as many cells as you want. Consider the following example:

```
<TR>
<TH COLSPAN=2>Personal Information</TH>
<TH COLSPAN=3>Statistics</TH>
</TR>
<TR>
<TH>Name</TH>
<TH>Team</TH>
<TH>Win/Loss record</TH>
<TH>ERA</TH>
<TH>Strikeouts</TH>
</TR>
```

Figure 5.12 shows the results of this use of COLSPAN.

Part
II

Ch
5

FIG. 5.12
You can use ROWSPAN
and COLSPAN in the
<TH> and <TD> tags.

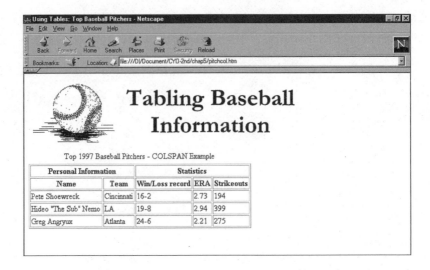

Embedding Lists into Tables

Tables can be combined with other HTML elements, and can contain any of the list types described earlier in this chapter. All three list types perform the same when embedded within a table. Make sure that you carefully add all necessary closing tags whenever you add a list to your table—they're easy to lose track of.

In Figure 5.13, a simple unordered list has been added to the baseball table.

FIG. 5.13
Lists inside of tables
look really slick—don't
you agree?

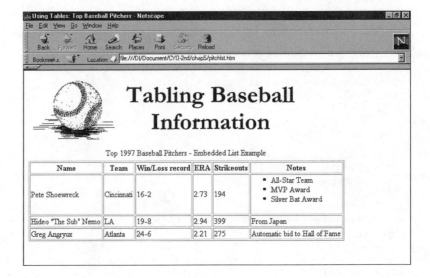

N O T E   If you're looking for a challenge, try embedding a table within a table. The effects are neat, but keeping track of your HTML can be a bear! You've got to make sure that you use all the </TABLE> closing tags properly, and lining up each element is difficult. Embedded tables often don't need any headers or borders. ■

Setting Your Text Alignment

Tables let you customize the alignment of each cell both vertically and horizontally. Set by special keywords, ALIGN and VALIGN, these alignment settings offer you increased flexibility for how your table looks. You can set table alignment within the entire table (in the <TABLE> tag), in a specific row (in the <TR> tag), or in a single cell (in the <TD> tag).

The ALIGN and VALIGN keywords each have three possible settings and are used in the same spot as the spanning keywords above—within the <TD> tag. Table 5.2 details the use of these two keywords.

Table 5.2   Keyword Setting Descriptions

Keyword Setting	Description
ALIGN=LEFT	Left-justifies text in the cell (the default setting).
ALIGN=CENTER	Centers text horizontally within the cell.
ALIGN=RIGHT	Right-justifies text in the cell.
VALIGN=TOP	Starts text at the top of the cell (particularly useful when information in the row has multiple lines of information).
VALIGN=MIDDLE	The default setting, centers text vertically within the cell.
VALIGN=BOTTOM	Positions text at the bottom of the cell.

Continuing to work with the baseball example, add VALIGN=TOP to the entire row that has the list in it, so that text doesn't appear to float in the middle of that cell. Change the <TABLE> tag to the following:

```
<TR VALIGN=TOP>
```

Figure 5.14 shows how this setting affects the baseball table.

T I P   Some Web pages use ALIGN and VALIGN to organize graphics within a table. By removing the table's border, you can perfectly line up sets of graphics in an organized fashion.

Part
II

Ch
5

FIG. 5.14
One of my pitchers' information has been moved to the top of the cell.

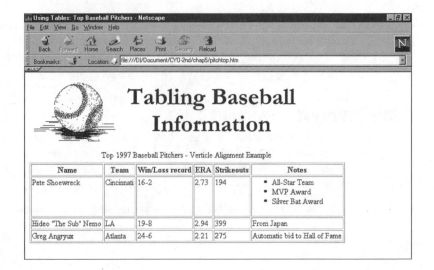

Table Colors

Until recently, you haven't been able to control the colors of the tables on your Web page. Table borders had to be black, and the background color of each and every cell had to be whatever was used for the rest of the Web page. This sometimes made it difficult to add spot color to a particular cell that had important information, or to use a variety of colors when developing your Web pages.

With several new HTML tags, you can now control the color of your table's background and borders. Most importantly, you can add the BGCOLOR keyword to your standard <TABLE> tag, as follows:

```
<TABLE BORDER BGCOLOR=YELLOW>
</TABLE>
```

Now the background color of the entire table is set to yellow. You can set your background color to any of these 16 default colors by specifying the color name (see Table 5.3).

Table 5.3 Available Named Background Colors			
Black	Maroon	Green	Olive
Navy	Purple	Teal	Gray
Silver	Red	Lime	Yellow
Blue	Fuchsia	Aqua	White

Besides the BGCOLOR keyword, there are several other new color enhancements you can choose from, as follows:

BORDERCOLOR	Sets the lines of the table border to the color you specify.
BORDERCOLORDARK/BORDERCOLORLIGHT	Used to change the colors of your table border to give a three-dimensional effect. By setting both attributes, it creates the appearance that your table is in 3-D. Try experimenting with it and use a thick table border (BORDER=6).

All together, the following is a simple example of the new table keywords in action:

```
<TABLE BORDER BGCOLOR=YELLOW BORDERCOLOR=RED BORDERCOLORDARK=BLUE
BORDERCOLORLIGHT=GREY>
</TABLE>
```

As you can see, these new keywords add a lot of flexibility to the appearance of your tables. But wait—there's more! You can also add these keywords to each individual cell or row of data to control the color of that particular element. The HTML code below customizes each cell color individually (see Figure 5.15).

```
<TABLE BORDER=2 WIDTH=300>
<TR>
    <TD BGCOLOR=YELLOW> Don't you think</TD>
    <TD BGCOLOR=BLACK><FONT COLOR=YELLOW>That this Table</FONT></TD>
</TR>
<TR>
    <TD BGCOLOR=BLACK><FONT COLOR=YELLOW>Looks similar to</FONT></TD>
    <TD BGCOLOR=YELLOW>A BUMBLEBEE!!!</TD>
</TR>
</TABLE>
```

FIG. 5.15

Color can be assigned to each cell and row.

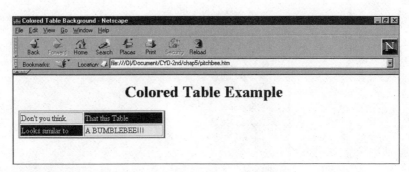

You can also add these new keywords to the <TR> tag to control an entire row's color coordination. Notice how the color of the text was changed by using the <FONT> tag. This is to ensure the background and text colors contrast so the text is readable.

▶ **See** Chapter 4, "Adding Style to Your Text," for more information on using the <FONT> tag.

Part

II

Ch

5

Table Alternatives

If you are concerned that some visitors won't be able to see your tables because they are using a nontable supporting browser (like Lynx, or an older version of Mosaic or Netscape), find tables too bulky to use, or prefer not to use them at all, you'll be pleased to know that there are a few popular alternatives to using tables.

The two most popular options are using extra lists, or using the <PRE> and </PRE> HTML tags. These two workarounds offer table-like functionality but are limited in nature.

Lists Can Replace Tables

Even though lists are one-dimensional displays of information, you can replace virtually any table with a couple of lists if you use them properly.

Returning to the baseball player table, you can replace that table with a few lists (see Figure 5.16). Of course, these lists aren't as easy to read as a table, and they make the user scroll through the screen because of the way the information is presented. In general, lists tend to be more spread out than tables and make it more difficult to compare information between the items.

FIG. 5.16

Although they present the same amount of information, lists aren't as flexible as tables.

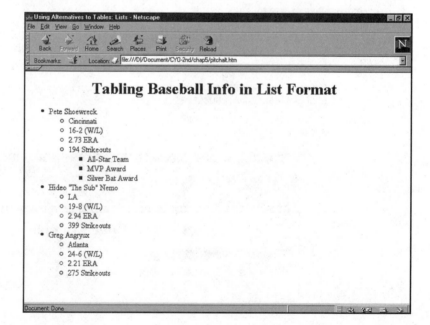

Preformatted Text

Chapter 3, "Web Page Basics," discussed the <PRE> and </PRE> tags that cause browsers to display information on your home page exactly as you type it, without any interpretation of how the information should be presented.

You can use these tags to emulate a table. The result is not as flashy as a table, and you cannot have graphical borders, but most people won't notice the difference. Using carriage returns, spaces, and tabs, preformatted text has been used to present the same baseball information (see Figure 5.17).

```
<PRE>
<B>Name      Team        (W/L)     ERA      Strikeouts</B>
Jon Happy      Cincinnati    16-2    2.73      194
Hideo "The Sub" Nemo    Los Angeles    19-8     2.94          399
Greg Angryux     Atlanta     24-6    2.21      275
</PRE>
```

FIG. 5.17
The <PRE> tag lets you present this simple "table" with no problems.

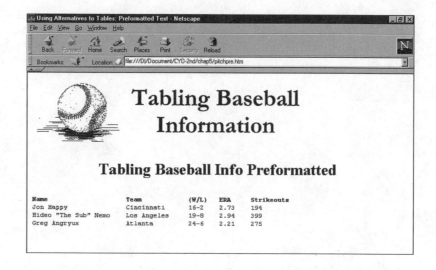

 TIP Notice that you can use text-formatting tags within your preformatted text to add bold or italic to parts of the table.

Part
II

Ch
5

CHAPTER 6

Using Graphics to Excite Your Page

You're already in Chapter 6 of this book, and you've got a decent-looking Web page to prove it. So far, you've seen how to plan and produce a good-looking Web page that isn't too complicated to update and maintain.

Now that you're familiar with lists, tables, and text-formatting features, you can organize your page however you like. But text formatting isn't the real reason that the WWW is so popular—its popularity results from the ability to add cool graphics and pictures to your page alongside your text.

As you've probably already noticed, almost every page on the WWW uses graphics or pictures to enhance its site and make it more enjoyable to visit. This chapter teaches you how to spice up your home page with vivid graphics, colorful backgrounds, and useful icons. You probably won't even recognize your own Web page when you're finished with this chapter! ■

Use the images included on the Web page CD

I've spent countless hours putting together thousands of images for you to use. You'll learn how to use them directly from the CD-ROM included with this book.

Add images to your home page

Images are the spice of life on the Web. Learn how to captivate visitors with all sorts of colorful and fun images.

Advanced graphics tags

HTML has many keywords associated with placing images on Web pages. Learn how to use several of these for better performance when graphicalizing your Web page.

Customize your home page with icons

Get familiar with using small navigation icons to convey a message graphically for browsing your Web site.

Change your page's background

Use colorful background colors and patterns to change the whole style of your Web page easily.

Pros and Cons of Web Page Graphics

You've probably spent a lot of time browsing through many different sites on the Web. You've seen personal pages, commercial pages, and lots of other unique Web sites, and I'll bet that almost every one of them used images in some fashion. Everything from business logos and snazzy icons to pictures of pets and famous paintings can be found on the WWW. Remember the Warner Brothers example from Chapter 2 "Weaving Your Own Web"?

Images and graphics are vital to the Web's existence. The WWW is the only Internet tool that lets you look at images and text on the same screen at the same time. Imagine picking up an issue of *Newsweek* that had no pictures in it. It might be pretty boring, no matter *how* they formatted their text. Looking at a Web page without any graphics is like reading a coffee table book that has no pictures—it just doesn't make sense.

You'll learn in this chapter how to easily add images and pictures to your home page to make it more attractive and fun to browse. Figure 6.1 shows a prime example of a Web site that utilizes graphics.

FIG. 6.1

It's practically impossible to imagine the Louvre Web site (**http://www.emf.net/wm/paint/auth/michelangelo/**) without pictures.

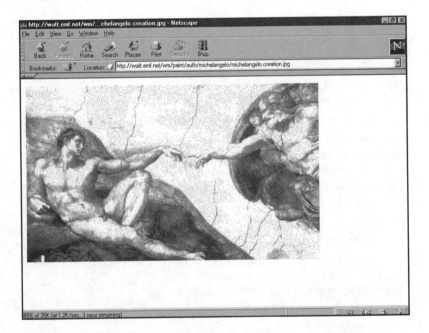

Of course, there are times when you should avoid using images on your Web page, but they're few and far between. Generally, if you aren't taking advantage of the WWW's ability to display images, your pages are probably pretty boring.

On the flip side, you've got to be careful not to overdo your home page by adding too many images. Before you read this chapter and decide to add 100 plus images to your one Web page, remember that it's easy to go overboard. With too many icons and images cluttering your home page, your text will get lost in the shuffle, visitors won't understand what they're looking at, it takes forever to download, and all your efforts at a great-looking Web page might be for naught.

The best solution is to balance your use of graphics in your Web page. If you're not sure whether your Web page is too plain or too busy, ask some friends for their opinions, but remember that your Web page ultimately should reflect you and your personality.

Where You Can Find Graphics, Images, and Pictures

Now that you're convinced you need to add an image or two to your home page, where do you find them? Acquiring images can be the most difficult task in the entire process. Whether you want a simple icon or a panoramic view of the Grand Canyon, it's hard to find that perfect image to stick in your home page.

However, you'll find a lot of help on this book's CD-ROM, where there are hundreds of different images, icons, and backgrounds. You have a vast array of pictures and images available at your fingertips. If these don't fit your needs, you'll also find included some tips on how you can use your own images in your home page.

On the Enclosed CD-ROM

When the CD-ROM was put together, the following question was asked: What kind of stuff would people find useful on a CD-ROM in this book? The obvious answer was graphics—images, icons, pictures, drawings, sketches, and lots more! This CD is your main resource when creating your own home page, and you'll find included all the appropriate material. Feel free to use as many of them as you like.

Besides the standard icons and images, you'll find a sample collection of 3-D icons, banners, buttons, and graphics from several companies and professional software/clip art packages.

The images on the CD-ROM are organized into three main categories:

- Pictures—You can find shots of animals and other images that should look familiar. This is a generic set of pictures that you might want to use in your home page.

- Icons—Icons are used to represent information in a familiar and graphical way. On the CD, you can find construction icons, home icons, navigation icons, and even spiffy lines that can replace the <HR> tag!

- Backgrounds—Web browsers allow you to place an image behind your text so that it appears as a background (covered later in this chapter). This gives your home page some flair and makes it much more colorful. Several hundred sample backgrounds are on the CD, so you have plenty of choices.

There are several ways for you to get graphics from the CD-ROM onto your Web page. The easiest method is to use Windows 95 Explorer (or Windows 3.1 File Manager) and copy the appropriate graphics from the CD-ROM to the subdirectory on your PC that contains your HTML files. Alternatively, check out the following section, "Borrow from Other Pages," to

Part
III

Ch
6

learn how to use your browser to browse the CD-ROM and save images directly to your computer.

More details on the images and pictures that are available on the CD-ROM are contained in Appendix D, "What's on the CD-ROM."

Borrow from Other Pages

Another common way to obtain images for your Web page is to borrow them from other pages that you visit. Built into both Internet Explorer and Netscape is a feature that allows you to save any image you see with just a few mouse clicks.

CAUTION

Be aware that images you see when browsing the WWW might be protected under copyright laws. Even though you can save images with a browser, you must have permission to use borrowed images on your own home page.

While many individuals on the Web don't mind if you borrow icons and images from their Web pages, businesses and corporations often have a different point of view. Their images usually are custom-developed, and they—and the court system—view saving a copy of their images as stealing. Be careful when taking images from sites around the Web. Many images and graphics are copyrighted, and the owners can—and sometimes do—take legal action against people who infringe upon their copyrights.

One good example, which makes it easy for everyone to see, is browsing cartoons on the Web. Dilbert, one of the world's most popular cartoon strips can be found at **http://www.unitedmedia.com/comics/dilbert/**. Every day a new cartoon is online, displayed as an image. This cartoon, however, has a copyright, and you are not allowed to save or use it on your Web site in any fashion, no matter how fitting it is or how funny it may be.

If you ever are unsure whether an image has a copyright or not, send e-mail to the person in charge of the Web page and ask. You have permission to use all the images found on the CD-ROM included with this book.

For more information on copyright and other legal issues surrounding the WWW, see Appendix C, "Legal Issues with Web Pages," where you'll find a discussion of these very important issues.

Borrow with Netscape   Here's how to save an image you're looking at in Netscape for Windows.

1. View any page on the WWW, and move your pointer onto the image you want to save separately on your computer. Go to **http://www.shafran.com**.

2. Right-click the picture of the two people at the top of the screen to bring up a Netscape shortcut menu with several options (see Figure 6.2).

3. Choose Save Image As to bring up the Save As dialog box shown in Figure 6.3.

4. Netscape fills in the default file name automatically. Select where on your hard drive you want to save the image, then choose Save.

FIG. 6.2
Netscape doesn't support copyright laws very well, does it?

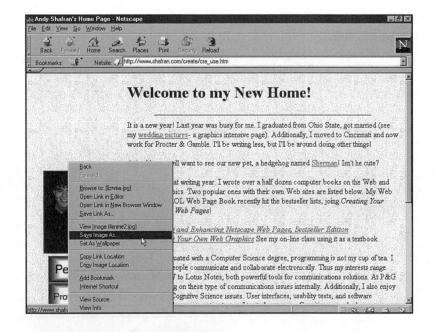

FIG. 6.3
Once you click Save, the image is yours forever.

Borrow with Internet Explorer   Of course, you can also borrow images if you use Microsoft Internet Explorer. Here's how:

1. Again, go to **http://www.shafran.com**.

2. Right-click the image at the top of the screen to bring up an IE shortcut menu with several options (see Figure 6.4).

3. Choose Save Picture As to bring up the Save As dialog box (just like Figure 6.2).

4. Like Netscape, Internet Explorer fills in the default file name automatically. Select where on your hard drive you want to save the image, then choose Save.

Linking to Images   A different way to borrow images from other Web sites is to link your page to an image on another site. Currently, you can only do this easily with Netscape. To do this, right-click the image you want to link to, and choose **Copy Image Location** from the pop-up menu (see Figure 6.5).

Part
III

Ch
6

FIG. 6.4

Internet Explorer allows the same picture poaching technique.

FIG. 6.5

Linking to images on other sites is not the same as "borrowing" (that is, stealing) them.

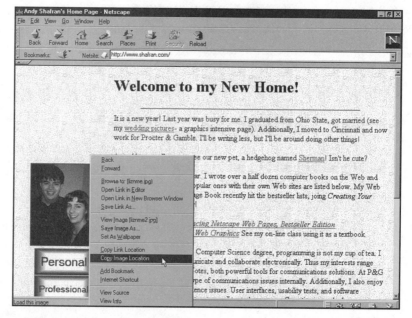

This copies the URL of the image you selected to your computer's Clipboard. From there, you can go to your HTML editor and choose Edit, Paste (or press Ctrl+V). The URL of the image you want to display appears wherever you perform the paste operation. Make sure that you build the <IMG> tag properly. For example, if you want to include a link to an image on your Web page, you first copy the URL to your Clipboard, then paste it as part of the following <IMG> tag:

```
<IMG SRC="http://www.shafran.com/liznme.jpg">
```

Whenever someone visits your Web page, the browser retrieves the image you linked to, and displays your Web page the way you want.

You can also discover the URL of the image you are loading with Microsoft Internet Explorer. In IE, simply view the Web page's source code (View, Source). Then you can find the URL of the image and type it into your HTML editor.

> **CAUTION**
>
> This practice of linking your Web page to images elsewhere on the Internet falls into a gray area of the legal world. By linking to an image, you are giving credit to the original owner, but might very well be using the image in a manner not originally intended by the author/creator. Be aware that some individuals and companies request that you do not link to images and pictures on their Web page.
>
> Also, when you link to another person's site, you have no control over when an image gets updated or deleted, often causing broken links.
>
> Read Appendix C, "Legal Issues with Web Pages," for an in-depth discussion of these issues.

Other Existing Images

Although the attempt has been made to put a reasonable collection of images, tools, and multi-media clips on the CD-ROM accompanying this book, it's hard to accommodate everyone.

You might want to look at the book *Internet Graphics Gallery* by Paul DeGroot and Dick Oliver. This book lists hundreds of sites on the Internet and WWW where you can find images of all kinds. You'll be impressed with the encyclopedic approach this book takes towards finding creative and unique images on the Internet.

Another possibility is using stock images and clip art for your Web pages. *Stock images* are sold in bulk quantity—usually on CD-ROM—and can be used in any manner once purchased. You can find stock CD-ROMs (for the Mac and PC) at your local computer store, specializing in all types of images. A great one comes from Expert Software. For $19.99, you can purchase a CD-ROM that comes with 3,000 full-color, professional photographs. They produce similar CDs full of clip art. Many of the examples and images used in this book come from those CD-ROMs. If you're interested, you can contact Expert Software directly at 1-800-759-2562 (1-305-567-9996 for overseas callers).

Create Your Own

While you'll probably find lots of useful images on the CD-ROM, you're likely to want a few of your own pictures on your home page. You might want to show yourself, your family, or a pet.

Part
III
Ch
6

I have pictures of myself and my family interspersed throughout my home page as well as icons and buttons created myself.

For more information on creating Web graphics from scratch, and advanced details on building animation, performance friendly graphics, and more, pick up *Creating Your Own Web Graphics* by Andy Shafran and published by Que.

Using Paint Shop Pro

There are many useful software tools and graphics programs that let you create, change, and manipulate images for your Web pages.

A great one is Paint Shop Pro. You can create new images from scratch, modify existing ones, or combine text and images. In addition, Paint Shop Pro also lets you convert your images into virtually every graphical file type you'll ever need (GIF, JPEG, and PNG included). Figure 6.6 shows me in action working with another image for my Web page.

FIG. 6.6
Paint Shop Pro is the best of the tools out there for creating and manipulating images.

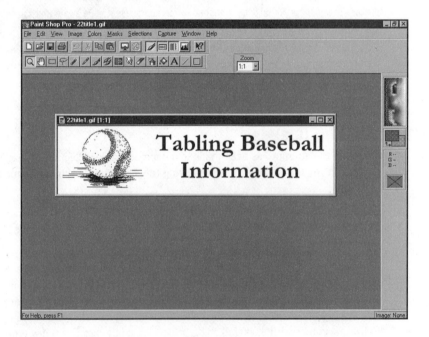

 For the latest edition of Paint Shop Pro, you can always stop by **http://www.jasc.com** to download the newest shareware version.

Current Scanner Quality and Detail

When you want to include personal pictures and drawings on your Web page, sometimes the only way is to use a digital scanner. Scanners come in all different price ranges and quality. You can find an affordable black-and-white scanner for $79, but high-end color scanners can run $999 or more, depending on the quality you are looking for.

Scanners are rated according to *resolution*. Resolution is the number of itsy-bitsy dots that a scanner observes when digitizing your photographs and drawings. Resolution is important because the better resolution your scanner uses, the more detailed your digitized images appear.

When looking for a scanner, you should get at least a 300×300 dpi resolution. This means that for every inch scanned, 90,000 dots are picked up by the scanner. That may sound like a lot, but a standard fax machine uses 200×200 dpi resolution—and you're probably familiar with how blurry faxes can sometimes be. Often, a scanner comes with software that enhances the resolution of scanned images significantly.

High-resolution scanners often cost a premium, and can be overkill if you are simply scanning pictures in for your Web page. Often times, 300×300 or 600×600 dpi is enough resolution for casual users.

To put personal images on your home page, you need to scan them directly into your computer. Figure 6.7 shows one of the pictures that's been scanned.

FIG. 6.7
The resolution of the image looks fine.

N O T E I use a Logitech PageScan Color scanner. For about $400, it has a 400×600 dpi resolution and comes with all the necessary software to scan color and black-and-white images, and can even make photocopies and send faxes. All of the photographs on my Web page were scanned at this level, so you can visit my page to get a good idea of the type of resolution you might want when buying a scanner. ∎

 Initially, for my home page, I couldn't afford a scanner, so I went down to my local Kinko's (or other copy store). They usually have scanning equipment available to rent for just a few dollars. I was able to scan in several pictures for around $20—this is much cheaper than buying your own scanner. Along the same lines, many local public libraries also have multimedia equipment as well—and those are free!

Adding an Image to Your Home Page

Now that you know where to get images from, it's time to start adding them to your Web page. This section describes adding graphics to your Web page and teaches you how to use various HTML options when adding images.

First, you'll see what you need to understand about images and their file types. Next, there's a description of how to add a simple image to your home page. There are also some image tips and tricks that will make your home page easier to use and more enjoyable for visitors who stop by.

Using the Proper Image File Types

Images can be saved in several different formats. Each format has its own advantages and disadvantages. On the WWW, two main image formats, GIF and JPEG, are supported.

The *Graphical Interchange Format* (GIF) file type was pioneered by CompuServe (an online information service) to provide information in a standard graphical format. GIF set the image standard years ago and was the first file type supported by the WWW.

More recently, the *Joint Photographic Experts Group* (JPEG) format was developed and has proven to be significantly more efficient than GIF in several circumstances, especially with larger images. JPEG files tend to be smaller—and consequently download quicker—when browsing the WWW. JPEG uses a special image compression technique that makes it better for pictures and snapshots. JPEG also handles colors and detail better than GIF.

N O T E Recently, a new type of image has gained in popularity. Billed as the replacement for GIFs, Portable Network Graphics (PNG, pronounced *ping*) images soon will be supported by the leading browsers.

PNG graphics are very similar to GIFs but are more efficient and can better handle a vast array of colors. Soon, you'll probably see a phasing out of GIF images to use PNG instead. Although Netscape and Internet Explorer don't support PNG images yet, other popular browsers such as Mosaic 95 already do.

PNG graphics can be displayed as transparent images, and you can choose to save them in interlaced or noninterlaced format.

For more information on the PNG graphics type, visit a great PNG information center at **http:// quest.jpl.nasa.gov/PNG/**. It's good to know that Paint Shop Pro can also convert images into PNG format if that's what you want.

Rather than bore you with all the details, here's a quick summary of why PNG exists. Several years ago, CompuServe (an online services company) created GIF as their international image standard, and many people adopted it as their standard as well.

A few years ago, Unisys realized that CompuServe had used some of their patented computer code when developing the GIF format, and decided to enforce their patent. Not wanting to be dependent on another company's patent, CompuServe (along with other developers on the Internet) introduced PNG to be the community-wide graphics format standard. PNG has started to develop significant popularity because of its advantages over the GIF file format—such as not having to tussle with Unisys over who owns the PNG format. ■

Both IE and Netscape support GIF and JPEG files. I use JPEG for most of my images because of the significant file size difference, but in this book I'll talk about using both types of images.

TIP IE and Netscape allows you to use other image formats (such as PCX, TIF, and BMP), but you need a different image viewer to see pictures in these formats. Check the CD-ROM for additional image viewers.

Alternatively, feel free to use newer plug-in technology that allows you to build these other image types into your Web page in many situations. See **http://home.netscape.com/comprod/products/navigator/version_2.0/plugins/index.html** for more information on available plug-ins.

Adding the Image

This example should look familiar to you. I'm using Barney's Circus home page to show you how adding graphics can make quite a difference. We'll build a special page for the human-eating tigers (they are gender indiscriminatory)! Figure 6.8 shows a plain, text-only page.

FIG. 6.8
Here's the initial, boring tiger page.

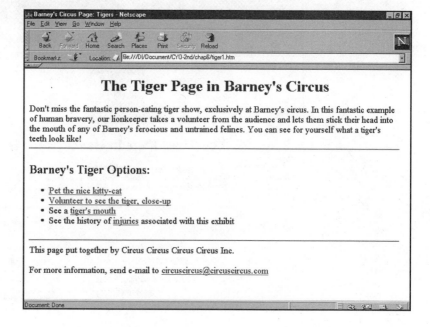

Part

III

Ch

6

Adding images to a Web page is pretty easy. All you need to know is how to use the `<IMG>` tag. IMG is short for Image (as you probably guessed). Using the `<IMG>` tag, add the `SRC=` keyword to tell the Web page which graphic should be loaded, and that's it. Images can be added anywhere on a Web page, in titles, tables, lists, or as part of the flow of text, just make sure they appear between the `<BODY>` and `</BODY>` tags. For my tiger page, I'm going to add the image to the top of the page, right above the `<H1></H1>` header.

To insert a GIF file named TIGERS.GIF to your home page, here's the single line of HTML to add:

```
<IMG SRC=TIGERS.GIF>
```

This tag tells browsers to display an image whose source file name is TIGERS.GIF. When you view your Web page, the image appears, integrated with your text. By adding this tag, you are assuming that the file TIGERS.GIF is saved in the *same* subdirectory as your HTML file. If not, the browser won't be able to find the image you're referring to.

Of course, you can point to any GIF file to add to your Web page. Let's say you had a file named BEARS.GIF; you would add virtually the same tag:

```
<IMG SRC="BEARS.GIF">
```

Figure 6.9 shows the page from Figure 6.8 after the TIGERS.GIF image has been added to it.

FIG. 6.9
Just one image makes
a page instantly more
attractive!

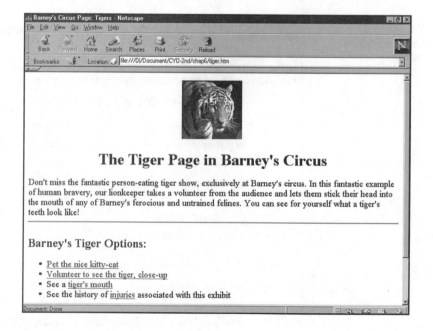

N O T E Linking correctly to your images requires that you understand how to point to files that are in a different file directory, or even on a different drive.

For example, if your image (TIGERS.GIF) is located in exactly the same directory as the HTML file, you don't have to point to other drives or directories. Your HTML tag is simply this:

```
<IMG SRC=TIGERS.GIF>
```

Sometimes, however, your home page images and HTML files aren't located in the same directory. If your images are located in a subdirectory named Images, for example, your tag is this:

```
<IMG SRC=IMAGES/TIGERS.GIF>
```

If your images are located in a directory one level above the directory that contains your HTML files in your hard drive structure, then you use this tag:

```
<IMG SRC=../TIGERS.GIF>
```

If your images are located on a separate drive—like drive D—then you use this tag to tell your browser to look for the correct file:

```
<IMG SRC=FILE:///D:\TIGERS.GIF>
```

Any combination of these tags can be used to tell browsers where to look for images when trying to display your Web pages. ▪

Based on the information in the previous note, it's easy to tell if you've pointed to the wrong location for a GIF (or JPEG) file. When you preview the page, the browser displays a simple broken icon image instead of the picture you're expecting. Figure 6.10 shows the bad-image pointer icon. This icon means one of three things:

- The image file name you specified is incorrect and doesn't point to a valid file (maybe you typed in TIGRESS.GIF by accident).

- The image pathname you specified points to an incorrect location. Try copying the image file into the same subdirectory as your HTML file and then pointing to it.

- The image file is at the location you specified, but it has incorrect file permissions set. Because Web pages have to be uploaded to the Internet, your files sometimes are modified to make sure that nobody can look at your HTML files or GIF images. In this situation, once you're *sure* that the full pathname is correct, contact your Internet service provider for information about setting your file permissions correctly. In general, this involves using the UNIX chmod command. If my file name is TIGERS.GIF, for example, I might issue the following at my UNIX prompt:

```
chmod 755 TIGERS.GIF
```

You won't have this problem on your personal machine—only when uploading the Web pages. The numbers in the preceding command basically mean that you are setting security provisions so that visitors who come to your Web site can look at your image, but not delete it or replace it with something else.

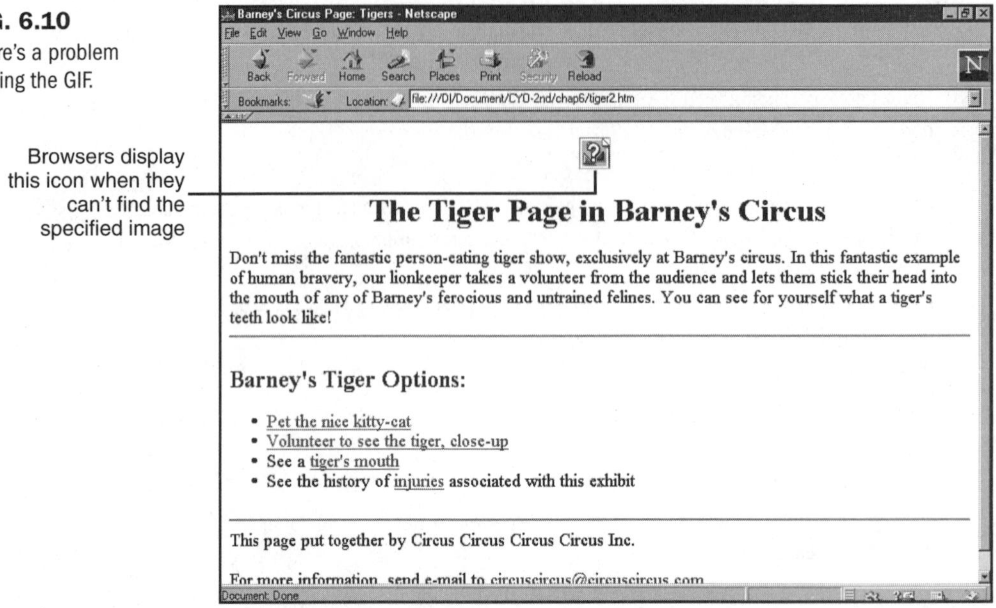

FIG. 6.10
There's a problem
finding the GIF.

Browsers display
this icon when they
can't find the
specified image

Image File Size Guidelines

One of the most important things you should think about when it comes to using images in your Web page is file size. Usually, whenever someone visits your Web page, they must download all the text and images to their personal computer. Although text doesn't take very long to download, images can take a while, so you must be aware of how large your Web page is and how long it takes to download. You want to make your home page downloadable in a reasonable time.

Think of when you call a company for technical support, and you have to push different buttons on your phone to be sent to the correct extension. After that, you often have to wait until a support representative becomes available. You're on the phone just waiting, when you could be doing other things you would enjoy more (just about anything). If you hang up and call back later, you still have to go through the same rigmarole. This is similar to what happens when people stop by your Web page. Your Web page immediately starts appearing, but they have to wait until all the text and images are loaded before they can continue. They have to watch their computer download each image, one at a time. Of course, the longer they wait, the more impatient they become.

Since waiting around is nearly universally annoying, the following sections offer pointers for making sure that visitors don't have to get a cup of coffee every time they access your Web page. (If they do, then after one or two visits they might never come back again.)

Maximum File Size   As a general rule of thumb, I try to limit any image on my Web page to 20K. With a 20K limit, the images can be of sufficient detail, yet not make visitors chew off their fingernails waiting for the page to download. Actually, I use 20K as a very rough guideline. In the next section, when I talk about icons, you'll see that most of them are extremely small (2K–6K) and download quickly. Occasionally, you might find a fantastic image that's larger than 20K. Don't worry too much about using it; just be aware that if you incorporate too many larger images, your visitors' waiting time increases greatly.

 It's a good idea to keep track of your entire Web page's file size. Add the size of your HTML file and the file size of each image you use. Your total should rest below 150K, preferably between 30K and 70K. With a 14.4 baud modem, visitors who stop by must spend 1–2 minutes downloading before they can enjoy the full glory of a 150K page. That's a long time to wait.

Resizing and Thumbnailing Your Images   If all the images you like are larger, you have several other options for including them on your home page without making each visitor download them. You can resize most of your images, making them smaller on screen, and decreasing their file size as well.

 Several professional packages, such as Adobe Photoshop, allow you to manipulate image sizes. Included on the Web Pages CD you'll find several shareware tools that let you resize your images. Although not nearly as robust as Photoshop, they're much cheaper (free) and can accomplish most of what you need for your home page. I use Paint Shop Pro or WinJPG to resize and create thumbnails of all my graphics. For simple tasks, they're nearly as good as commercial graphics packages.

Resizing makes your image smaller, and therefore possibly harder to see. Some images look fine when shrunk, but others become barely visible. I've had great success resizing my images. One image I use was originally the size of the entire screen and took up 190K (what a long download for a single image). After resizing it to about one-fourth of the screen size, the picture is down to about 43K, a reasonable size for my Web page (although still large).

Another option related to resizing your images is creating *thumbnail images*. Thumbnail images are miniature duplicates of larger images. You can create a small thumbnail of a large image on your Web page, and include a link to the full-size image that visitors can see if they want to. (Read "Linking Your Images" in Chapter 7, "Linking Your Web Pages," for more information on how to do this.)

Thumbnails are extremely popular because they let visitors pick and choose which full-size images they want from a cornucopia of miniature ones. Figure 6.11 offers an example of how I use thumbnail images in my home page.

 If your images are all in GIF format, try converting them to JPEG format. You might notice as much as a four-to-one file size difference from GIF to JPEG for certain images!

FIG. 6.11
The thumbnail image is at the top of my home page. Clicking it brings up the same image at its full size.

Thumbnail image ——

Full-size image ——

Manipulating Your Home Page Images

With images added, you'll notice a big difference in the attractiveness and appearance of your Web page. However, there are several other HTML options that can help you manipulate and organize images. One of the most important of these lets you provide alternative text for visitors to read if they can't view your images for any reason.

You can set image alignment, text flow around images, and size images manually on your Web page. I'll show you how to set these options and explain them individually.

Providing Alternative Text

Some browsers don't support both GIF and JPEG, and others don't support any images at all. Although most common ones support both of these image types, you want your Web page accessible to everyone in the world. Additionally, sometimes it takes a while to load an image on the screen and you don't want visitors to see just a bunch of white space where your images will be.

Often times, people will browse the WWW and tell their browser to stop loading the images from Web sites. Since downloading images takes the lions share of time browsing, they find it quicker and easier to not see them by default. Providing alternative text is useful to these users because they can read a brief description of what the image represents and then view it if they desire. You can control whether images are automatically loaded by choosing Edit, Preferences from your browser menu bar.

To compensate for these issues, you want to use the ALT keyword in the <IMG> tag. ALT adds a piece of text on the screen where the images should (or will) be on your Web site.

It's considered common courtesy to always provide *alternative text* descriptions of the images you include on your home page. Alternative text is part of the <IMG> tag. You add the ALT keyword to your tag and type text inside quotation marks. When I add alternative text to the TIGERS.GIF example from earlier in the chapter, the new tag looks like this:

```
<IMG SRC=TIGERS.GIF ALT="Barney's Tigers">
```

When I am downloading the graphic, the alternative text appears on screen. Figure 6.12 shows how alternative text appears on WWW pages.

FIG. 6.12
ALT text is useful when downloading large images.

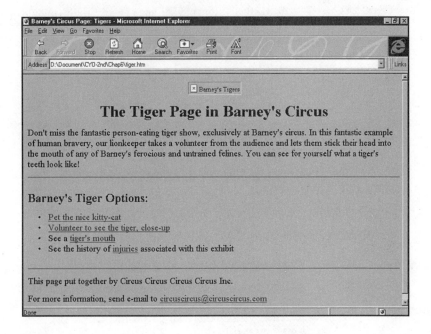

Aligning Your Image

When you place images on your home page, you have several options for how they're aligned on screen with respect to text on your page. Browsers recognize the ALIGN keyword as part of the <IMG> tag.

With ALIGN, you have control over where the image is placed on screen and how text appears around it. Table 6.1 lists the eight ALIGN options.

Part
III
Ch
6

Table 6.1 Image Alignment Possibilities

Option	Action
LEFT	Lines up the image on the left side of the page with multiple lines of text wrapped around the side of the image on the right.
RIGHT	Works like LEFT, but the image appears on the right side of the page.
TOP	Aligns the image to the tallest item on the line.
TEXTTOP	Aligns the image to the tallest text item on the line (usually appears the same as TOP).
MIDDLE	Aligns the bottom of your line of text with the middle of the image.
ABSMIDDLE	Aligns the middle of your line of text with the middle of the image (very similar to MIDDLE, but used for small images).
BOTTOM	Aligns the bottom of your line of text to the bottom of the image.
BASELINE	Identical to BOTTOM.

Since they're very similar to other keywords, I recommend avoiding TEXTTOP, ABSMIDDLE, and BASELINE in your Web page; they'll just confuse you in the long run.

To set the tiger image's alignment to LEFT, for example, I added ALIGN=LEFT to the <IMG> tag, resulting in the following:

```
<IMG SRC=TIGERS.GIF ALT=Barneys Tigers ALIGN=LEFT>
```

Now, my text appears to the right of the tiger image (see Figure 6.13).

FIG. 6.13

ALIGN lets you control where your image is placed.

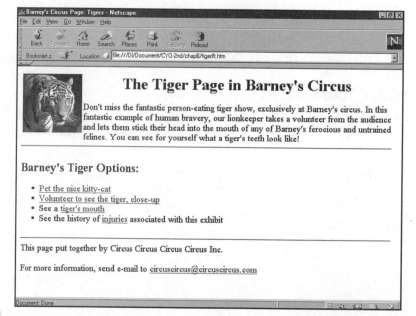

N O T E When using the LEFT and RIGHT keywords, you also might want to add the enhanced <BR> tag to your HTML document. You can add <BR CLEAR=LEFT> and <BR CLEAR=RIGHT> to make sure the text appearing after the image ends up below the image instead of next to it. Since I only want the headline (The tiger page in Barney's Circus) to appear beside the text, I use the <BR CLEAR=LEFT> tag. Figure 6.14 shows how the tiger page aligns and flows when I've included this modified <BR> tag. ■

FIG. 6.14

When using alignment, be aware of the <BR> tag modifications.

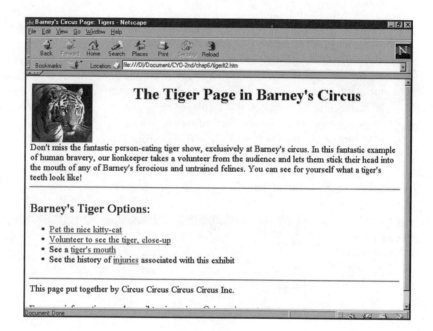

Sizing Your Image

Besides aligning your image, you can manually control the height and width at which images appear on your page. Normally, the image is displayed at its regular size, but with the HEIGHT and WIDTH keywords you can shrink or enlarge an image's appearance without altering the actual image. Additionally, the HEIGHT and WIDTH keywords allow your browser to mark room for the image on the screen and flow the text around it. That way the rest of the page can be seen while images are being downloaded. Many people use the HEIGHT and WIDTH tags for this reason, even if they don't change the sizing of an image on their site.

You must define HEIGHT and WIDTH in pixels, thus specifying the size of the picture on screen.

N O T E A *pixel* (picture element) is a unit of measurement that's used to calculate monitor resolution. To get an idea of how large a pixel is, consider that a standard VGA screen is 640×480 pixels (that is, 640 pixels wide by 480 pixels high). Super VGA is 800×600 pixels. Thus, an image 320×240 pixels in dimension takes up approximately half of a VGA screen. ■

Part
III

Ch
6

Add the HEIGHT and WIDTH keywords to your <IMG> tag the same way you add alignment and alternative text keywords. When I add HEIGHT and WIDTH keywords to my tiger picture, the HTML code looks like this:

```
<IMG SRC=TIGERS.GIF ALT="Barneys Tigers" ALIGN=LEFT WIDTH=240 HEIGHT=260>
```

TIGERS.GIF is now set to appear at the predefined size of 240 pixels across and 260 pixels down.

Actually, setting HEIGHT and WIDTH is another useful way to control the appearance size of an image on your home page. You can add an image to your home page and use smaller HEIGHT and WIDTH dimensions to make it appear thumbnail size. Figure 6.15 shows how you can change the appearance of the same image to several different sizes. Remember though that using the HEIGHT and WIDTH dimensions don't change the amount of time required to download an image, it just affects how it is displayed on your screen. Using the keywords does help performance somewhat though. The browser automatically allocates the required HEIGHT and WIDTH space on the Web page and can fit text around it correspondingly before the image is downloaded. Normally, it must download the image first and then place the text, because the Web browser doesn't know how big it will be. The keywords help define this information to your browser ahead of time.

FIG. 6.15
Each image here is proportionally twice as large as the next.

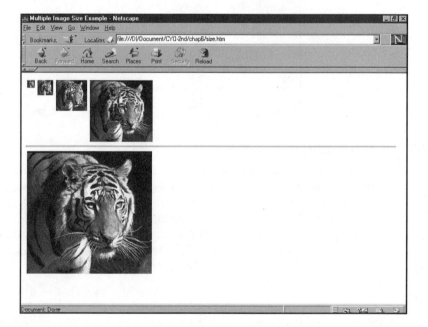

Adding Icons to Your Home Page

Besides adding full-color images and pictures to your home page, you can place all sorts of icons on the page as well. While icons technically fall under the term "images" (they're usually

GIF and JPEG files), they're typically extremely small (2K–6K) and are used for design, aesthetic, and navigational purposes on home pages.

Icons come in many shapes and sizes. Ranging from miniature construction icons to colorful lines and buttons, you can find a wide variety of them on pages across the WWW. You sometimes don't even realize that you're looking at icons when you browse a home page, because they're so well integrated with the design.

On the CD

I've included a vast array of icons on the CD. I can practically guarantee that you'll find several icons that will look great on your Web page. Let's take a brief tour of some of these icons, and I'll show you some uses for them on your Web page.

Lines and Bars

Chapter 3, "Web Page Basics," explains how to use the <HR> tag to separate pieces of your Web page. It's also common practice to use *line graphics* (simple graphics of lines and bars) to replace the <HR> tag.

Line graphics exist in all shapes, colors, and designs, and are significantly different from using the <HR> tag. On the Circus home page, I've added a red bar named BAR.GIF (found on the CD-ROM that accompanies this book) to the Web page, replacing the <HR> tag.

The page is more attractive, colorful, and fits better with the circus theme. I've added the following HTML code:

```
<CENTER><IMG SRC="bar.gif"></CENTER>
```

N O T E Actually, I've added this HTML twice, to make the same bar appear in two different spots. ■

Bullets

Bullets are commonly used to replace the dots that appear when you add an unordered list to your home page. You'll find bullets of many colors and sizes on the CD-ROM that accompanies this book.

When I use bullets, I usually don't use an unordered list in my home page. Instead, I add each list item with the <BR> tag after it. The overall effect is a simulated list with neat icons serving as the bullets instead of the circles and squares that go with an unordered list.

Here's a sample of the HTML code I've used to add graphical bullets to the Circus home page:

```
<BR><IMG SRC="redbull.GIF" ALIGN=CENTER>
```

Notice that I haven't used any alternative text—there's no point to doing so in this situation.

T I P Make sure that you use the ALIGN keyword when placing bullets on your home page, to ensure that your text lines up with the image correctly.

Part III

Ch 6

New Icons

Many sites use *New icons* to label new additions to their home page. This helps visitors quickly locate recent changes and information that has been added since their last visit. Several New icons are included on the CD-ROM that accompanies this book. Figure 6.16 shows how the Circus home page uses the New icon, colorful bullets, and a bar instead of a horizontal line.

FIG. 6.16

Here's the spiffed up Circus page, bullets and all.

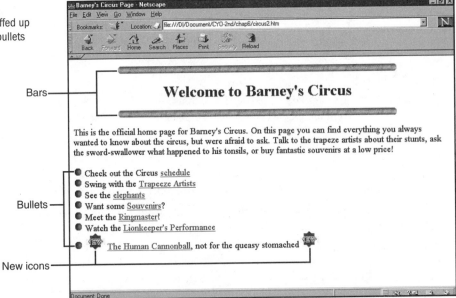

TIP Make sure that you don't leave a New icon on your page for months and months. It's common practice to label a new item on your home page for the first month or so that the item's on there. After that, drop the New icon for that item.

Construction Icons

Construction icons became popular a while ago, when everybody's home page was new, and constantly being modified. These cute icons labeled the Web page as frequently changing, or not yet finished.

These days, they're not quite as common, but you still see them regularly on brand-new pages. They let visitors know that you are currently modifying or making your Web page. Like the New icon, don't have a construction icon on the page for all eternity.

Navigation Icons

Navigation icons are probably the most useful icons to professional HTML developers, and least useful to people creating a basic home page. They come in handy when you have a large

Web site with many pages linked together. Since your home page is likely to be simple, you might not find navigation icons very useful.

These icons usually come in the form of arrows pointing one way or another. These arrows allow you to symbolize which way to go to bring up the next Web page. For example, if you're reading a book at a WWW site, you'll probably see three icons on each page: a left arrow, a right arrow, and a Home icon. The left arrow returns you to the preceding page, the right arrow brings up the next page, and the Home icon takes you to the very beginning of the book. This saves you the trouble of picking your way through with the Back and Forward buttons on the browser toolbar.

Navigation icons are only useful if you're trying to tie together multiple pages at a site, because they graphically link Web pages to one another.

Give Your Home Page Some Background

One of the neatest features of HTML is the ability to control what the background of your document looks like. Instead of creating pages that have the standard gray color behind text, you can change the background to any color you want. If you still aren't happy with the plain color, you can place images behind your text to add plenty of color, texture, and fun to your home page.

Adding Background Colors

A long time ago, people weren't too choosy about the kind of car they drove. Everyone drove a Ford Model T, which came only in black. That car suited several generations of people, until it dawned on buyers that cars could come in any color and shape they imagined. Today, when you're driving down the road, you can see cars ranging from neon purple to iguana green— variety enough for everyone's taste.

Colorizing home pages evolved in the same fashion. Originally, all home pages had a white or gray background because that's how viewers like Mosaic and Netscape displayed them. After a while, some people became bored with the *status quo*, and the BGCOLOR keyword was born. BGCOLOR lets you change the background color of Web pages on the WWW. With the BGCOLOR tag, you have 16,777,216 background colors to choose from. That's all the colors of the rainbow, and then some. Fortunately, it's easy to change background color because you have 16 default colors to choose from by name.

Part
III

Ch
6

You can identify the following 16 colors directly by name:

Black	Maroon	Green	Olive
Navy	Purple	Teal	Gray
Silver	Red	Lime	Yellow
Blue	Fuchsia	Aqua	White

The BGCOLOR keyword is added to the standard HTML <BODY> tag that surrounds most of your home page text. If you add BGCOLOR=RED, your background color is red—it's that simple. Follow similar steps for all 16 colors previously listed.

Here's how my HTML looks:

```
<BODY BGCOLOR=RED>
```

TIP Besides using the 16 named colors, browsers allow you to specify colors by mixing different shades of red, green, and blue. This gives you millions of colors to choose from. See the section "Color by Hexadecimal" in Chapter 4, "Adding Style to your Text," for more information.

For a fantastic list of useful background colors, stop by **http://www.infi.net/wwwimages/ colorindex.html** and see over 100 excellent red, blue, and green combinations.

Using Background Images

Besides standard colors, you can add customized background images to your home page. These patterned graphics give a cool effect to your home page when used properly. Background patterns consist of itsy-bitsy GIF images that are tiled next to each other so that they cover your entire background (it's like wallpapering your background with a colorful GIF). Your text and images are placed on top of the background image.

Background patterns are added in the same way that you change the background color, except that they use the BACKGROUND keyword. Simply add BACKGROUND="*FILENAME*" to your <BODY> tag, and the browser loads the background image automatically. You'll find hundreds of sample background images on the CD with this book.

I use a background image named BD.JPG in the circus page (see Figure 6.17). Here's the HTML that does so:

```
<BODY BACKGROUND="BD.JPG">
```

FIG. 6.17
Background patterns add texture to home pages.

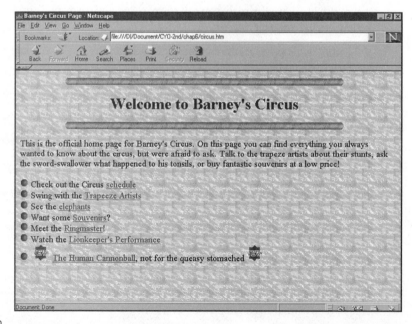

To access the same image in a subdirectory named IMAGES, I'd use the following HTML:

```
<BODY BACKGROUND="IMAGES/BD.JPG">
```

If your background image doesn't appear, the most likely problem is that you aren't pointing to the proper file, and the browser can't find the file you wanted to use. See the troubleshooting procedures listed in the "Adding the Image" section earlier in this chapter for more information on pointing to the proper directory structure.

Background Problems

Before you go hog wild with background colors and patterns, it's important to keep some issues in mind.

Many careless uses of colors and patterns cause the original page to become absolutely unreadable. Some Web creators choose a dark color, or an extremely busy background pattern, and it's virtually impossible to read text on those pages. As a good rule of thumb, use only light colors, and calm, easy-to-read backgrounds for your home page. Above all, make sure that you check out each page to make sure it's readable.

NOTE You can also change the color of the text that appears on your Web page. Chapter 4, "Adding Style to Your Text," covers this in detail. ∎

Moreover, adding background images to a Web page can considerably increase the amount of time it takes for visitors to experience your page. All the background images on the CD are sizes that are reasonable to use. If you borrow another background pattern, or create your own, make sure that you limit it to a maximum of 10K.

Creating Transparent GIFs

Throughout this chapter, I've talked about GIF and JPEG images interchangeably. I mentioned some of the differences between the two formats, but for the most part they both allow you to put graphics on a Web page. This section talks about one specific feature of GIF images which allows them advanced integration on Web pages—transparency.

GIF images allow you to specify one color within the file that WWW browsers ignore, and treat as transparent, or see through. The end result is that your WWW browser displays the normal GIF image, but ignores one of the colors in the picture and shows the Web page's background color or pattern instead. Much like an overhead machine displays transparencies with its projector, Netscape and Internet Explorer use transparent GIFs to make images appear more natural on a Web page.

Transparent GIFs are a powerful tool in a Web developer's toolbox. Creating effective images for the World Wide Web requires understanding and using transparent GIFs to enhance your entire Web page experience.

Understanding what transparent GIFs are and how they work is easy. Just think of how an overhead projector works. An overhead projector takes pieces of clear plastic with writing on it

Part

III

Ch

6

and displays only the writing onto a screen. Since the plastic is clear and transparent, it isn't projected onto the screen. Transparent GIFs work in a similar fashion. The GIF file format allows you to specify one of the 256 colors as transparent, or clear when shown within a WWW browser.

Any color can be specified as transparent. In this section, I'll use Paint Shop Pro a popular graphics-editing tool to work with transparent GIFs.

Often, transparent GIFs are used in images which normally use the color white in the background of the image. By setting white to be transparent, Netscape ignores the background, and the image appears to be "floating," or fit in with the actual Web page better.

Figure 6.18 shows an example of this phenomenon. This is Barney's Web page with transparent and nontransparent icons on it.

FIG. 6.18
The transparent icons don't have the white background.

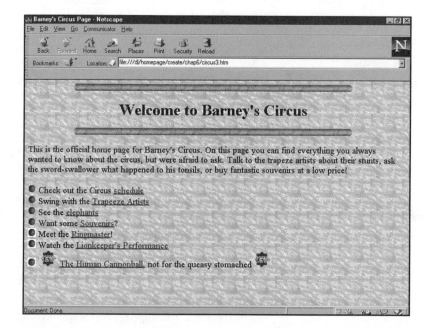

I have two different Red Bullet icons in this image. One is transparent, the other is not. Notice how the nontransparent GIF shows the white background, which is unattractive on this page because I use a background image. Transparency functionality is why most icons and bullets are saved in the GIF format instead of JPEG.

How Web Browsers Treat Transparent GIFs

When you set a color to be transparent, that information is saved into the actual GIF file. Since it is part of the file downloaded and displayed on Web pages, WWW Browsers can easily recognize and ignore that particular color.

When designing GIFs, you have literally millions of colors to use when colorizing your image—16.7 million shades and hues of reds, greens, and blues can be used. Although you have millions of options, only 256 different colors can be present at any one time in a GIF file. Each color is represented by a number ranging from 1 to 256. That's how graphics programs such as Paint Shop Pro and Web browsers recognizes each color. It doesn't recognize "blue," instead it might know color 175.

When your WWW browser displays an image, it divides the image up into quadrants that each get displayed in a different color. It's just like when you painted by number as a kid. The image was broken into many different sections, with a corresponding number telling you what color to paint each part. Although WWW browsers have 256 colors to choose from (for GIFs), the concept is still the same. Each part of the Web image is painted according to the number of the color specified.

Here's where the transparency issue comes into play. With transparent images, you can tell your WWW browser **NOT** to paint one particular color of an image—leaving it blank instead. Since nothing gets painted in that particular part of the image, it is transparent, and you can see right through it. Web browsers allow you to place colors and images in the background of your page, behind all the images and text. With a transparent color, you see the background designs, if any, instead of the particular color assigned to that section of the Web image.

As you can see, Web browsers aren't very complicated pieces of software when it comes to displaying images and graphics. Understanding how they display transparent GIFs shows insights on how Web graphics can be designed to take advantage of their simplicity and flexibility.

Making Transparent GIFs

Now that you are familiar with what transparent GIFs are and how WWW browsers such as Netscape or Internet Explorer display them, it's time to learn how to create your own.

Creating a Transparent GIF from Scratch

Making transparent GIFs doesn't have to be tricky, but there are some steps in the process which can be misleading if you aren't positively sure of how to proceed. I'll use Paint Shop Pro (which can be downloaded at **http://www.jasc.com**).

1. Start Paint Shop Pro and open up the GIF you want to work with. Figure 6.19 shows Paint Shop Pro editing the Red bullet.

2. You need to tell Paint Shop Pro which color should be deemed as transparent. Paint Shop Pro assigns whatever color is currently in the background of the paint brush to be the default transparent color. To do this, click the Dropper icon from the rows of icons at the top of the screen.

Part

III

Ch

6

FIG. 6.19

The Dropper icon selects colors in Paint Shop Pro.

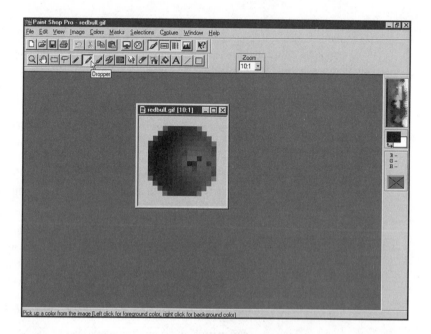

3. Now move your mouse to anywhere in the background of your image and click the *right* mouse button. The eye dropper lets you select colors by pointing and clicking them. The left mouse button controls the foreground and the right mouse button controls the background.

   In the Color Palette on the right side of the screen, the background color switches and becomes whichever color you are pointing at. For this example, my background color is gray, but it would work the same if my color were blue, red, or green—any color.

4. Finally, you are ready to save your newly minted transparent GIF. Choose File, Save As from the Paint Shop Pro menu bar to bring up the Save As dialog box (see Figure 6.20).

5. Click on the button labeled Options to bring up the File Preferences dialog box (see Figure 6.21). From here you can indicate exactly how you want Paint Shop Pro to save the color you indicated as transparent.

6. Select the radio button labeled **Set the transparency value to the background color**. This tells Paint Shop Pro to make a special note that the current background color (as defined in the Color Palette) is now the one that should appear transparent on a Web page.

7. Give your image a file name and save it. Now it is ready to be used on a Web page with the correct color marked as transparent.

FIG. 6.20
Your image is about to be saved.

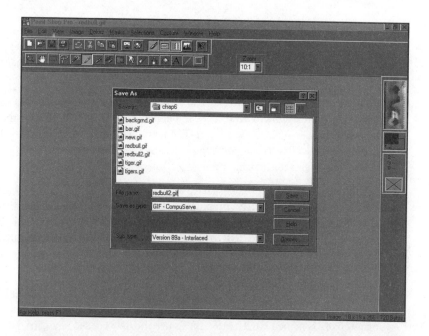

FIG. 6.21
Four GIF transparency options can be selected.

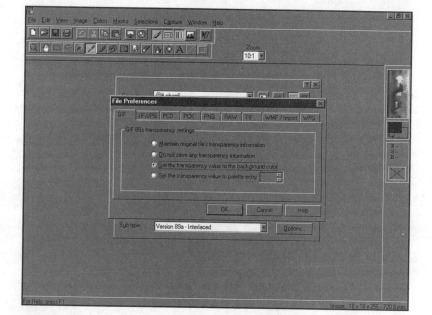

Part
III

Ch
6

Overlaying Images

As you can see, working with images can increase the time it takes to load a Web page significantly. Unfortunately, many Web developers still prefer using bright and colorful images on their Web pages, and use very LARGE images. Visitors tend to enjoy colorful images more, and will come back to visit more often when they remember and like a particular Web site. Web developers are often in the juxtaposition of choosing between brilliant colors and great file performance for a Web site.

To solve this dilemma, a new HTML keyword was added to the `<IMG>` tag which allows Web developers and visitors to experience the benefits of both worlds. Called the Low Resolution keyword (`LOWSRC=`), this new bit of HTML lets you tell your WWW browser to first load and display a smaller, low resolution image file, and then when the whole page is finished loading to begin displaying a normal, high resolution image.

In practice, often Web developers have a large, color image that is simply too big to use on a Web page. Instead, they use a graphics package like Paint Shop Pro to create a reduced file size (black and white or a smaller, resized image) to make a smaller version of the same Web Graphic. The Web browser first loads the image specified with the `LOWSRC` tag onto the page. Then, once it is finished loading the rest of the page, it loads the regular image specified in the standard `SRC=` tag.

For example, let's say I have two images, one called LOWCAR.GIF, which is a 16-color, less detailed black-and-white picture of two automobiles. My colorful, high-resolution image using many colors is named HIGHCAR.GIF. To use the new `LOWSRC` keyword, I'd add the following line of HTML:

```
<IMG SRC="HIGHCAR.GIF" LOWSRC="LOWCAR.GIF">
```

That's it! Figure 6.22 shows this process in action. First, the browser loaded LOWCAR.GIF, and this figure depicts the middle of HIGHCAR.GIF being displayed on top of the black-and-white image.

FIG. 6.22
Although difficult to tell, half of this image is in color and half is in black and white.

CHAPTER 7

Linking Your Web Pages

A Web page without links to other WWW spots is an isolated island. Once people visit, there's no way for them to get to other spots. Since you don't want to strand people on your Web page, it's a good idea to include links to several other pages on the WWW. That way, you can help to build the spider-like Web yourself.

Chapter 6, "Using Graphics to Excite Your Page," showed you how to combine graphical images with your home page. Now that you're familiar with using images, icons, and background graphics on your Web page, it's time to take the next step and learn to link different pages on the WWW.

Linking Web pages together is the most basic feature of the WWW. Any document can contain a link to another WWW document with a special HTML tag. This chapter is about using these hypertext link tags to connect Web pages to one another. You'll learn the proper way to link your home page to other HTML documents anywhere on the Internet. ■

Understand and dissect an HTML link

Learn how to recognize and use all of the different parts of a hypertext link when addressing a WWW document.

Link your home page to another WWW page

Work with your Web page to link it to another site on the Internet.

Make your images serve as links

Graphics may be pretty, but they can also serve as hypertext links once clicked upon—if you set them up properly.

Organize and keep track of your links

Lots of Web pages use links indiscriminately and end up with a confusing jumble of tags and text. Learn how to use links effectively, so they make sense to visitors who stop by.

Avoid common linking pitfalls

Avoid mistakes that most people make when linking their WWW site to another, so your visitors don't see confusing error messages.

Understanding Hypertext Links

As a Web surfer, you've probably already experienced *hypertext links* on the Web pages you've seen. While scanning through a page, you notice some text that is underlined and appears in blue. Text displayed this way is called *hot text* because clicking it links you automatically to another Web page.

Every URL requires three parts: a protocol, an Internet site, and a file name (including the full path, if necessary). A *protocol* is the way two computers speak to each other; this chapter talks mostly about *http*, the default WWW protocol. You must supply the Internet site and file name.

For example, the WWW address online that is dedicated to this book is:

http://www.shafran.com/create

Translated into English, this means that the browser should use the special WWW communication method (http) to connect to the Internet through computers to the specific location shafran.com (my own Internet site). Then, the browser should find the Web page in the create subdirectory.

Hypertext links are often used because they can transparently join two documents on opposite sides of the world. Documents and files on the Internet are each referred to by a unique address, called the *uniform resource locator (URL)*. To link two documents, home-page designers insert an URL into one of them. Using an URL is like addressing e-mail. The Internet computers understand how to translate the URL and find the exact spot to connect to.

If the Web page is in Manhattan, for example, it doesn't matter if the linked document is in the Bronx or New Zealand—the WWW treats it the same way. Browsers use each URL to find documents on the Internet and bring them up automatically for you. As a Web surfer, you don't have to worry about using URLs, connecting to Internet sites around the world, or locating the correct document. Your computer takes care of all that hassle for you.

With the WWW, you can link to HTML documents (Web pages), files (via FTP), Internet newsgroups (like UseNet), and even popular information sources such as Gopher and WAIS directly from your Web page.

N O T E This chapter explains how to link HTML documents to each other. For more information on how to access other Internet features from your home page, see "Linking to Other Internet Information" in Chapter 9, "Customizing Your Web Page." ▪

On your Web page, links must be created one at a time. You get to decide what text to make hot, and more importantly, what link each bit of hot text represents. You can add as many (or few) links to your Web page as you like, and can organize them in any fashion.

Anatomy of a Link

Linking Web pages to each other isn't very difficult, but you have to understand how to add links to your home page, including the necessary HTML syntax.

Just like every other HTML element, links have their own HTML tag pair. The opening tag (called the *anchor tag*) is <A>. You then specify what file you're linking to, and what text should be hot when your Web page is viewed through a browser. You conclude with the closing tag, </A>.

Here's an example of what a link on my home page looks like in HTML:

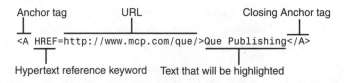

Figure 7.1 shows how this link appears in my home page.

FIG. 7.1
Since Que Publishing is hot text, it appears underlined.

This is my hot text

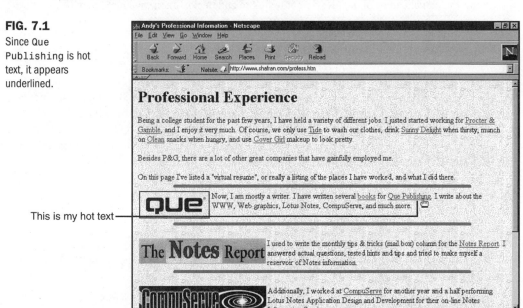

Creating a Link

Now that you've read about using links and have seen them in action, let's add one to your Web page. We'll add two different (but similar) kinds of links to your home page.

First, let's see how to link *local documents* to your home page. A local document is one stored at the same Internet location as your home page. Local documents are easier to link to because you don't have to know the complete URL—you need only its path and file name relative to your home page.

Then, using an almost identical process, you'll learn to link documents when they are located at different spots on the WWW. For this type of link, however, you need to add an entire URL to your Web page.

Linking to Local Web Pages

You often might have multiple HTML documents in one spot. There might be too much information to put in one document, so you split it into several different HTML files. In your main Web page, you want to link to each of the separate documents easily and quickly; perhaps your Web page is even set up like a table of contents to link to several different pages.

For my circus home page, for example, I want to add links to other related pages, such as the tiger and elephant pages I created earlier in the book. This process is relatively painless. Also, I want to identify what phrase of text will link to this particular HTML file. The first step is to know the actual names of the files I want to link to and decide upon my linked text.

Linked Text	File Name
Tiger Page	TIGER.HTM
Elephant Page	ELEPHANT.HTM

Next you add the `<A HREF=>` tag to your Web page. The `<A>` tag is called an anchor tag. Anchor tags are used to link text on a Web page to other pages. The HREF keyword in the anchor tag tells your browser where you want this text to be linked as a hypertext reference. Also, don't forget the closing `</A>` tag! To create a link to TIGER.HTM I'd add the following snippet to my HTML page:

```
<A HREF="TIGER.HTM">Tiger Page</A>
```

That's it. Tiger Exhibit will appear on the screen as linked text. When visitors click that text they are whisked away to the file TIGER.HTM.

Make sure that you include a subdirectory path to linked files, if necessary. For example, if my TIGER.HTM file were saved in a subdirectory named Exhibits, I'd type Exhibits/TIGER.HTM with the HREF keyword instead.

```
<A HREF="Exhibits/TIGER.HTM">Tiger Page</A>
```

So far, only the text Tiger Exhibit appears on this fictional circus home page. I'll add another link, this time to the elephant exhibit, by following the same steps.

```
<A HREF="ELEPHANT.HTM">Elephant Page</A>
```

Figure 7.2 shows how the circus home page looks once I've added the links to the animal pages.

You can test your link by clicking it and ensuring that you go to the correct Web page. Before you click a link, Web browsers display the full URL you are going to visit in the status bar at the bottom of the screen.

FIG. 7.2
Here's my circus home
page with the new links
added.

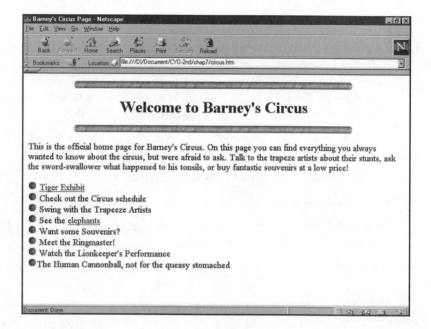

Linking Elsewhere on the WWW

You also should learn how to link your Web page to other HTML documents that reside on WWW sites besides your own. Linking to these sites requires you to know the full URL to the document, not just the path and file name as in the previous examples.

The link, however, looks the same. You still use <A HREF=> and </A> tags to surround the file name and hot text. When you're linking to other HTML documents on the Web, your URL always starts with the following:

HTTP://

That's so browsers know to go looking on the WWW for a document, not search for a file saved at your own Web site. The rest of the URL consists of the Internet path of the site, plus the full name of the document you're linking to—it's much like addressing an envelope in that you need to specify all parts of the address correctly for the address to be found.

Part
III

Ch

7

T I P   If you don't specify a file name, the browser automatically loads the file INDEX.HTML or INDEX.HTM when you link to a site. Since this is a WWW standard, nearly every site has an INDEX.HTML file. At my site, my home page is named index.htm.

To show you how to build a link elsewhere on the Internet, I'll add a link to the Yahoo! list of WWW circuses (there aren't too many) to Barney's Circus Page.

The first step is to identify the full URL you need to access that document. Next identify what text should link to that document in the browser window.

I want the following URL for the Yahoo! circus list:

http://www.yahoo.com/Arts/Performing_Arts/Circuses/

For my link text, I'm going to choose something more concise than that long URL. For my example, I'll type **Yahoo Circus List**.

Now add the `<A HREF=>` and `</A>` tags to your document and—Voila!—your new link looks like this:

```
<A HREF=" http://www.yahoo.com/Arts/Performing_Arts/Circuses/ ">Yahoo Circus
List</A>
```

Now that the link has been added, you can easily jump from one page to another as shown in Figures 7.3 and 7.4. Notice that in the status bar at the bottom of the screen, the browser displays the full URL of the spot you're going to link to when your mouse hovers over the hypertext link.

 T I P   One tip Web developers may find handy is to copy and paste Web URLs from the Browser Address Bar into your HTML file. In the Address bar at the top of the screen, highlight the full URL with your mouse and hit Ctrl+C to copy the address to your computer's clipboard. Next switch to your HTML file and you can paste the URL automatically by hitting Ctrl+V, saving you time and errors from retyping the entire address.

N O T E   When typing in the full URL and file name of the spot you want to link to, keep in mind that some Web Servers require the name to be case sensitive. So linking to TIGER.HTM might be different than tiger.htm, and so on. As a general rule, always try to match the case sensitivity of the file and subdirectories you want to link into. Fortunately, most Web Servers are moving away from case sensitivity. ■

FIG. 7.3
Clicking a link in the circus home page brings up the linked document.

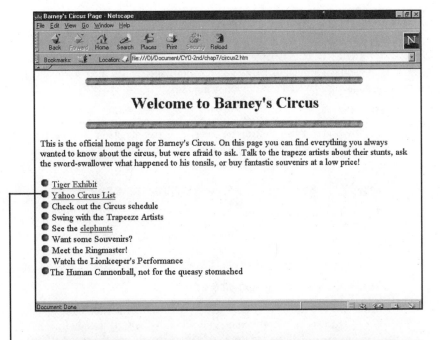

FIG. 7.4
This is the linked document.

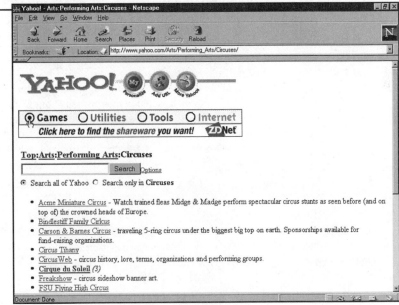

Link Color

You can also change the color of "hot" text that links your Web page to another spot on the World Wide Web. In Chapter 4, "Adding Style to Your Text," you learned how to use the <BODY> tag to add color defaults to the text on your page. To set the color of all of your standard text on the page to red, you'd use the following tag:

```
<BODY TEXT=RED>
```

Similarly, you can also control the colors of text that appear as hypertext links. There are three new keywords which control the color of linked text on a Web page, listed in Table 7.1.

Table 7.1   Keywords that Control Linked Text Colors

Keyword	Description
LINK	The LINK= keyword is used just as you used the TEXT= tag previously. By setting LINK=BLUE (or any other color), all links on the page that have never been activated (clicked upon) appear in blue. `<BODY TEXT=RED LINK=BLUE>`
VLINK	You may have noticed that sometimes linked text appears in a slightly different color, indicating that you've already traveled that particular thread of the WWW. You can change the color of Visited Link text on your Web page with the VLINK= keyword. The color of links on this Web page tones down silver when you've visited it already: `<BODY TEXT=LIME LINK=AQUA VLINK=SILVER>`
ALINK	The final color customization you can make is what color text appears as it is being clicked upon. This text is signified as Active Link text and uses the ALINK= keyword. When someone visits your Web page, the color of linked text is set with LINK=. But when it is clicked on, for a brief moment it changes to the color you specify with ALINK=. To go along with the other atrocious colors I've selected for this example, Active Linked text is now set to bright yellow. `<BODY TEXT=LIME LINK=AQUA VLINK=SILVER ALINK=YELLOW>`

N O T E These color settings can be overridden manually in Netscape by choosing Options, General Preferences, and setting them individually on the Colors tab. By setting these traits in Netscape, visitors ignore the background and color settings on your Web pages. ■

Using Images as Links

Not only can you use text to link to other WWW pages, but you can use images as well. Chapter 6, "Using Graphics to Excite Your Page," explained how to add images to your Web page.

Now you'll learn how to make them *clickable*—this means that when you click your mouse on an image, a separate WWW document is linked to and appears.

You can link an image on your Web page to another HTML document the same way you linked text. The only difference is that, instead of designating text to be hot, you assign an image. By default, in Web browsers, a blue box appears around the *hot image* and links visitors to a different page when they click anywhere on the image. You can use any kind of image, picture, or icon—except background images—to link WWW documents.

Another popular way to use images as links is as a clickable image map. A clickable image map lets you take any Web graphic and link to different files depending on where in the image you click. You can learn more about building clickable image maps in Chapter 8, "Image Map Education."

 Using images to link pages is very common. Make sure that you use recognizable images, however, so that visitors know where the links go. For example, if you're going to link your home page to a list of your favorite songs, use an icon that's music related. It's also extremely important to use the ALT keyword when linking images. This ensures that visitors who can't see images will be able to use your links from page to page.

Additionally, some people browse the WWW and turn off the image loading option when browsing. This allows them to browse quickly through lots of pages since images aren't downloaded. The ALT text is important for them as well, so they know what they would be seeing!

I link several graphics in my home page to Web sites. For example, I have the Que logo displayed prominently in the list of my past and present employers. I have the logo linked to the publisher's home page so that if you click it, you're immediately brought to the Que site on the WWW.

This link is the same one I used at the beginning of the chapter, with one key change. Instead of typing Que Publishing between the link tags, I use HTML code to display an image. Here is the HTML code:

```
<A HREF="http://www.mcp.com/que/">
<IMG SRC="gifs/quelogo.gif"ALIGN=LEFT>
</A>
```

Notice how it is the same anchor tag as before, linking to the same site, but instead of typing in linked text, I added an <IMG> tag. It's that easy to link graphics on your Web pages.

Figure 7.5 shows how the newly linked image appears. Notice that the mouse pointer turns into a small hand when hovering over a hot image.

N O T E With some advanced HTML programming, you can create clickable *image maps* that take you to different pages depending on where in the image you click. Image maps are slightly more complicated to create and maintain than simple linked images. For more information on using image maps, see Chapter 8, "Image Map Education." ▪

Part
III

Ch
7

FIG. 7.5
The Que logo now is
wired from my home
page.

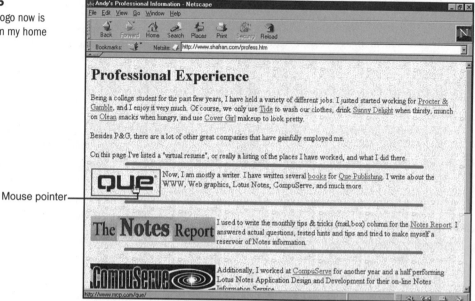

Mouse pointer—

Using Anchors on Your Home Page

Now that you're an accomplished HTML linker, you can connect your home page to any other file on the Internet. However, there are a few other uses for the <A> and </A> anchor tags, most notably using them as internal document references and pointers.

Suppose that you've picked up a large book because you want to read the contents of Chapter 26. You don't want to have to flip through the first 25 chapters just to locate Chapter 26. Instead, you go to the table of contents, find out what page Chapter 26 begins on, and go there immediately.

Anchor tags work similarly. When you have a large HTML document, you can add anchors to various points in the document. In this example, if the large book was a single, extremely large HTML file, you'd probably have an anchor at the beginning of each chapter. At the beginning of the HTML file, you'd have a table of contents that linked to each separate anchor in your file (one for each chapter). When visitors clicked the one labeled "Chapter 26," their browser would take them automatically to the Chapter 26 anchor in the same file; they wouldn't have to scroll through countless pages of information. Remember that anchors are used only for maintaining one large HTML file. Use regular hypertext links to organize multiple files.

Figure 7.6 shows an example of a Web site that uses anchor tags in this fashion. Visit **http:// www.mcp.com/que/developer_expert/htmlqr/toc.htm** to see the book *HTML Quick Reference* online. This site is the complete text of the book and is broken into several different HTML files. But within each HTML file there are several named targets so that you can look at the Table of Contents and click directly on the area that interests you. You are immediately brought to the section of the HTML page which corresponds with your named target.

In Figure 7.6, notice how the mouse is hovering over a hypertext link—the URL is shown in the status bar at the bottom of the screen. Look at that URL carefully:

```
http://www.mcp.com/que/developer_expert/htmlqr/reference.htm#newsgroups
```

Notice how it points to a particular Web site (**www.mcp.com**), and then to a file called reference.htm in a subdirectory on the site. After the file name there is #newsgroups. That information tells your browser to open up the reference.htm file and find the anchor in that page named newsgroups. Figure 7.7 shows what happens after clicking that link. You are brought into the reference.htm file—not to the top of the page, but to the section labeled newsgroups.

FIG. 7.6
This Web site uses anchors extensively.

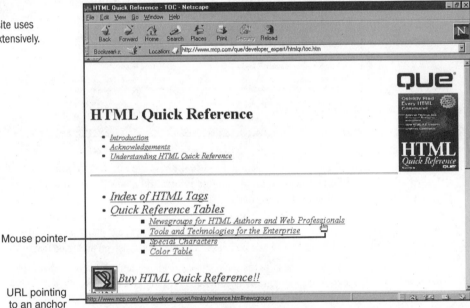

Mouse pointer

URL pointing to an anchor

Pretty nifty, huh? Anchors work the same way as linking to other documents on the WWW, except that you're linking to internal spots of a single document. Just like regular links, you can have as many anchors and tags as you want, but you shouldn't go overboard.

These anchor tags are also called *targets* by different HTML editors and Web developers when used this way as references. I can use such targets on my home page to lump everything about me together in one file. Instead of having four or five different files to work with, all the information is united into one file. This big file can become unwieldy, however, so for the benefit of visitors stopping by, I add anchor tags at the top of the page to provide links to several different areas in which I've organized my interests. Clicking the hot text for any of these links takes you to a different part of my home page. Of course, you can get there by simply scrolling down the

Part
III

Ch
7

page, but the table of contents at the top lets you jump instantly to the area of my home page you're looking for.

FIG. 7.7

The linked anchor helps point to the right section of this HTML file.

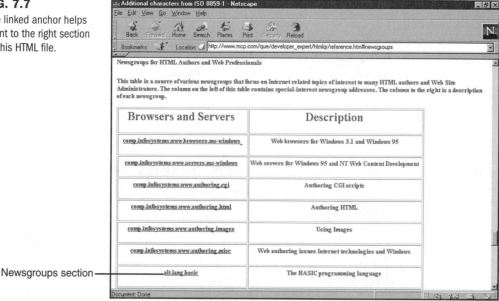

Newsgroups section

In this situation, my anchor tags are labeled to break the page into four distinct parts: Personal Information, Professional Information, Academic Information, and Publications. Let me show you how to add these anchor tags to manage the intradocument links.

N O T E Instead of using name anchors, many people split their home page into separate pages. See Chapter 9, "Customizing Your Web Page," for more information on how to do that.

Originally, I used anchors in my home page (as shown throughout this example), but eventually I split my home page into separate pages. If you visit now, you won't see any anchors there. ■

Creating and Naming an Anchor

When working with Intradocument anchors, there are two important parts. First, you must identify each section within an HTML document that can be linked into, and second, you then build the <A HREF=> tag that points to the named section.

On your Web pages, you can add named anchor tags wherever you like. Each tag you add allows you to jump directly to that spot with a link. For this example, I include four anchor tags and links in my home page.

Here's the necessary HTML format:

```
<A NAME="Named Anchor"> Anchor text displayed </A>
```

This adds an anchor tag around `Anchor text displayed`. To jump to this tag, a visitor must link to the target labeled `Named Anchor`.

You can add anchors to your page easily. The first step is to identify the part of your HTML document that acts as an anchor. For this example, I picked out a part of my home page that talks about my professional information:

```
<H1>Andy's Professional Information</H1>
```

Then I added the `<A NAME=>` tag around my original text. When using the NAME keyword, you must give each anchor in your file a unique name. I named this anchor `Professional` on my home page. Here's the snippet of HTML code:

```
<A NAME="Professional">
<H1>Andy's Professional Information</H1>
</A>
```

There's now an anchor on my home page at the beginning of the section that lists my professional information.

N O T E You don't have to place your target around text if you don't want to. Often, they appear right above the section of the HTML document that is to be anchored. ▪

 T I P Make sure that you put the anchor tag at the very top of the place you want to jump, because Web browsers place the line with the anchor at the top of its screen. If your anchor is below your headline, visitors won't see the headline when they jump to that spot (unless they scroll up to see it).

Repeat these steps until you have created specific anchors for all the desired areas on your Web page.

Linking to an Anchor

Once you have created all the anchors on your Web page, it's time to create your own table of contents, a set of links to each specific target.

By now, you've created several different anchors on the Web page. Creating a link to that anchor is simple, you just use the `<A HREF=>` tag, just like you do for standard WWW links. The only difference is that you must have the # to tell the Web browser that this is an internal document reference. So to build a link to my Professional Information section, I'd use the following HTML:

```
<A HREF="#Professional">
See my professional info
</A>
```

The symbol # used with the HREF keyword tells the browser to look for a target instead of a separate HTML document. Visitors see this hot text just as it would display the hot text for any other link. Instead of looking for a different file or going to a separate WWW site when the hot text is clicked, however, you are linked to the anchor within the current HTML file.

Of course, the name you point to in the <A HREF=> tag must be identical to the one specified with <A NAME=> when you set the anchor.

N O T E You can link directly to anchors in any HTML document on the WWW. If you want to create a link on your home page to the Professional Information section of my home page, for example, just use the following piece of HTML on your home page:

```
<A HREF="http://www.shafran.com/index.htm#Professional Information">
Link to Andy's Professional info
</A>
```

To link to a specific target on another page, view the HTML source code of that document (choose View, Document Source from the menu bar) and find the target you want to link to.

In general, however, this is a bad idea unless you maintain that Web page yourself. Linking to an anchor at my Web site, for instance, is generally futile because I change my anchors and targets so often, sometimes adding new ones and sometimes removing a few. ■

Organize Your Links with Lists

Now that you've started using links in your Web page, it's important to keep them orderly so that they're understandable and simple to use. It's easy to let your links become disorganized and fall into disarray. Every time you add new HTML to your Web page, you need to make sure that the page remains organized and easy to read.

One popular method for keeping links organized is using a list. As explained in Chapter 5, "Adding Lists and Tables," lists can present many different pieces of information in a crisp, bulleted format. Lists work perfectly when you want to include a bunch of links on your home page. For example, almost everyone has their own compilation of neat WWW pages. On my list are many popular places that I like to visit when I'm browsing the Web. If they weren't in list format, these links would be an unusable, jumbled mess.

To create an unordered list of links, simply use the standard <UL> and </UL> tags. Give each link a separate <LI> tag so that you have only one link per line. Figure 7.8 shows how I use a list to organize my hot links. I actually have multiple lists inside of lists—that's how many links I want to keep track of! I guarantee that even a simple list does more for organizing a bunch of links than practically any other trick you can use for organizing your page.

FIG. 7.8
I use lists within lists
to keep my links
ship-shape.

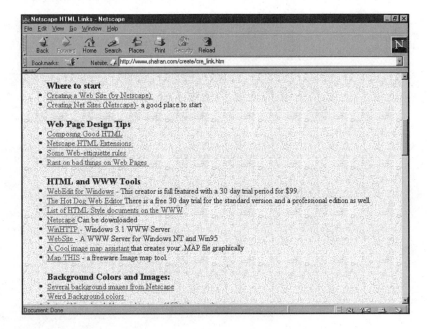

Useful Linking Tips

Knowing how to add WWW links to your Web page adds a powerful skill to your HTML authoring repertoire. Along with increased power and flexibility, however, comes the opportunity to make your Web page much more confusing and difficult to use for people who stop by for a visit.

Here's a list of some important issues to remember when adding links to your home page. Some are common sense, but others might seem more obscure. By following this short set of tips, you won't have to worry about making your Web page more confusing when you add links.

Don't Over Link

Nothing is more confusing than stopping by a Web page with 200 words of text, where 180 of them are linked to different spots on the WWW. Figure 7.9 shows a page containing too many links. Since linked text appears underlined and in blue, having too many links in a paragraph (or page) makes it completely unreadable, and makes it difficult for visitors to enjoy stopping by.

Visiting various Web pages is a lot like window shopping. If you see a store that has a hideous, cluttered front window, you're probably less inclined to go in and shop. Keep this in mind when adding links to your Web pages. If you do want to include many different links, consider adding a simple (but organized) list at the bottom of your page.

Part
III

Ch
7

FIG. 7.9
I get a headache just looking at this page.

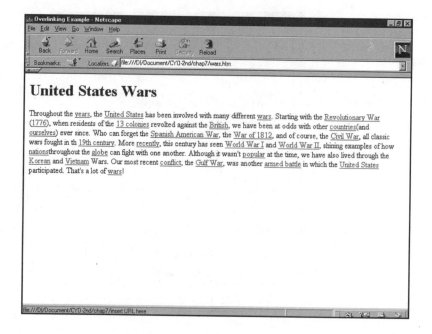

Link Specific/Descriptive Words

Although the WWW relies on links that connect pieces of information with each other, try to make your links transparent. Here's an example of what I mean (the links are in bold). The following paragraph includes a link that is *not* transparent:

> Barney's Circus is a barrel full of fun. Individuals and families of all ages and backgrounds can come to the circus and enjoy themselves. **Click on Barney's Circus** to see a picture of what the big-top tent looks like. The tent is world famous as the tallest tent being used today.

Here's similar text with a transparent link:

> Barney's Circus is a barrel full of fun. Individuals and families of all ages and backgrounds can come to the circus and enjoy themselves. You won't want to miss the **big-top tent** to see the world's tallest tent still in use today.

Your links shouldn't interrupt the flow of text as the link in the first example did by saying the words "Click on…". You can assume that readers know that clicking underlined text brings them to a related area.

CAUTION

One of my largest criticisms of Web page creators is that they often highlight useless pieces of text as links to other places. Of course, the most notorious culprit is the word **here**. You should *never* have the word **here** highlighted as the text that links your visitors to another page.

Even if you don't use here as hot text on your page, you still need to be careful when choosing the hot text for links to other pages. One way that I determine if I've accurately labeled each link is to imagine that my Web page is displayed only as linked text. I then decide if I can get a decent idea of what information will appear for each link, based on the link name without the context of the rest of the sentence.

Describe Large Links

Whenever you link your Web page to large graphics, files, audio bites, or video clips (even extremely large text files), you should let visitors know the file size before they click the link. They deserve fair warning because large files can take a while to download. Chapter 10, "Making Your Web Page Multimedia," discusses this in more detail.

Keep Your Links Current

As you become more experienced and continue to build your home page, you're likely to compile a collection of links to various parts of the Web. Occasionally, these links might become obsolete. A Web page you reference might be deleted or move to another site. Whatever the reason, it's likely that some of your links will be lost every few months.

Visitors who stop by and see a neat link in your Web page will try to use that link, and will be disappointed if they find that the page no longer exists. If you're going to have links on your Web page, you should periodically check to make sure that they all work. Otherwise, you shouldn't include them on your Web page. ●

CHAPTER 8

Image Map Education

In Chapter 6, "Using Graphics to Excite Your Page," you learned how graphics work as the glue behind the World Wide Web and make pages exciting and interesting to explore. In this chapter, I'll show you how to take your images one step further and put them to work for you.

These enhanced Web graphics, called *image maps*, are easy to use and quickly becoming a popular tool among Web creators all over the world. Using image maps, you can link different areas of a single image to different HTML files, or URLs. This lets visitors to your Web page navigate from page to page by using their mouse to select different areas of an image. Image maps are inherently easier to use than regular text links because there's no need to explain what the link does. A person doesn't have to read where a link might take him; he just sees it.

Though this may sound like image maps should be used everywhere, that's not true. There are some things to consider before using image maps. You also have to make sure it makes sense to put in image maps where you want them.

This chapter discusses the ins and outs of adding image maps to your Web pages, taking advantage of technology that makes creating image maps easier than ever. Anyone can add an image map, called a *client-side image map*, to his or her Web page in a matter of minutes. ■

Understand how image maps work

Clickable image maps are easy to use and add to Web pages, as long as you understand exactly how they work when visitors stop by.

Distinguish between client-side and server-side image maps

Image maps come in two flavors. Learn which format is better and how to recognize each of them.

Build a simple image map for your Web page

Nothing shows how easy image maps are to create except for making one on your own—with the right tools.

Decipher new HTML tags that support client-side image maps

Understand the new HTML tags that control your image map.

Link sections of an image to HTML files on the Web

Learn how the mechanics of the HTML tags actually link different sections of a picture to separate HTML files.

How Do Image Maps Work?

You are already familiar with adding inline graphics to Web pages. By embedding the <IMG> tag inside of a hypertext reference, you can create links from images, just as you would from text. Look at the following HTML example:

```
<A HREF="ROME.HTML"> <IMG SRC="ROME.GIF"> </A>
```

Shown in Figure 8.1, this example adds an image of the Coliseum in Rome to my Web page. When visitors click the image, the browser automatically loads the file ROME.HTML.

FIG. 8.1

Linking an image to an HTML page is easy to do.

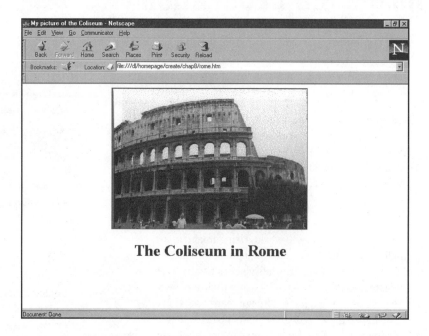

No matter where on the picture you click, you always link to ROME.HTML. This is where an image map could come into play. Using an image map, you can link different areas of an image to different HTML files, based on what section of the image is clicked.

This is an extremely useful technique because it lets visitors who see this Web page get accustomed to a single image, and lets them navigate from page to page by clicking different sections of that image.

Look at the Magnavox home page (**http://www.magnavox.com**) for an excellent example of an image map (see Figure 8.2). Here, the developers have included a picture of a remote control with several buttons drawn on it. Each section of the image brings you to a different spot on the Magnavox Web site. For example, clicking Company Info in the image brings up information about Magnavox, while you can easily imagine what kind of stuff appears when you click Fun & Games.

FIG. 8.2

Magnavox's image map is smart...very smart.

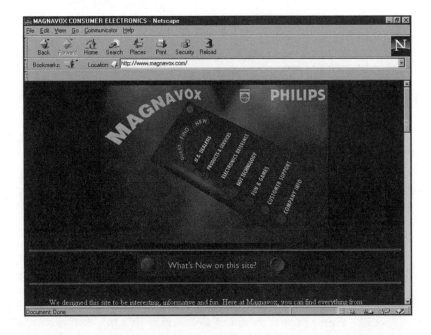

There are many good uses for image maps. For example, Italy might place a virtual map online. Using your mouse, you would click whichever region or city of Italy you wanted to learn more about. Clicking Rome might bring up the Coliseum, and Pisa could link to the famous leaning tower. Or Boeing might place a picture of its new 777 plane on the WWW. Visitors could click different parts of the cockpit to learn how the plane operates.

Virtually any image can become an image map—and they're easy to create. With the right tools, image maps can easily be designed and incorporated into a Web site within minutes.

Image Maps Are Not New Technology

Clickable image maps have been around for a long time. You have always been able to add one to your Web page if you knew the right steps to follow. With the release of Netscape 2.0, though, adding image maps to your Web page has become significantly simpler and less complicated.

Previously, to add a clickable image map to your Web page, you were dependent on your Web server software. Your server software controls all access to Web pages at a particular Internet site. To add an image map to your page, you had to find the right image, decide how each part of the image would link to a different HTML file, and then set up and customize your server properly. This was quite a hassle, even for those people who could understand every step—and some Web servers didn't permit image maps to run on them. Therefore, using image maps on Web pages was effectively limited to professional Web developers and larger companies; few individuals used image maps on personal Web pages.

Today, though, creating image maps is much easier. A new development called *client-side im-age maps* makes it easier for individual Web page developers—like you—to add a clickable image map to a Web page. More image maps are being created every day because of their relative ease of use.

Differences Between Server-Side and Client-Side Image Maps

As previously mentioned, *server-side image maps* have been around for a couple of years, but they were awkward to use and carried several disadvantages when working with them. In this section, you'll learn exactly how server-side image maps run, and why they've been pushed aside for newer technology.

Here's how a server-side image map works. When visiting a Web page, you might see a large image that has several different sections on it that are clearly delineated. Each section, when clicked, looks like it will take you to a different Web page. After looking at the image for a while, you click one area (like one of the buttons on the Magnavox remote control in an earlier example in this chapter), presumably to take you to a corresponding page of HTML. Web browsers store the coordinates that you clicked as an X,Y pair (the measurement is in pixels) and then send that information to the Web server. The server takes those coordinates and runs a separate CGI (Common Gateway Interface) program that translates those coordinates into an URL—the file name of the linked area clicked. Then the Web server sends that file name back to the browser, which loads the correct file.

As you probably can gather, server-side image maps aren't extremely efficient and can be difficult to use for several reasons:

- Server-side image maps cannot be used when running your site locally off a hard drive because they require direct interaction with a Web server.

- Not everyone can use server-side image maps. To create this type of image map, you need access to execute a CGI program on your Web server. Many WWW sites do not permit CGI access, and thus, you cannot include a server-side image map at your site.

- They can bog down Web servers. If you have a Web server that is extremely popular, it can spend all its time running the special program that translates pixel coordinates into an HTML file. This puts a heavier load on the Web server, and slows access for everyone reading pages at that particular Web site.

Fortunately, a new type of image map has taken the WWW by storm. Client-side image maps (called CSIM for short) are significantly simpler, easier to use, and are more efficient when interacting with Web servers. As far as users can tell, the same image appears onscreen, but what happens when they click the image is different. Instead of exchanging information with the Web server, Web browsers automatically know which HTML file to link to—and take you there automatically. This process is significantly quicker to process (you don't have to wait for the Web server) and easier for the browser to interpret. Each region in the image has its pixel coordinates defined within the same HTML file as the rest of the Web page, so you can link to another page of HTML just as if it were using a normal <A HREF> tag.

Client-side image maps are more efficient, easier to create, and better for users who visit your Web pages. Eventually, client-side image maps will entirely replace image maps that are dependent on the Web server.

N O T E   You always can tell whether you are using a server-side image map or a client-side one. Take a look at the status bar at the bottom of the screen while you move your mouse over an image map. If you see scrolling numbers, then you know it's a server-side image map (those pixel coordinates are sent to the server when you click). If you see a file name instead of coordinates, then you're using a client-side image map. ▪

Creating an Image Map

Since client-side image maps are much easier to create, maintain, and use, server-side image maps are rarely created nowadays. Although many exist on the WWW today, server-side image maps are older technology and will eventually be out of use completely. Now that you understand the difference between the two types of image map technologies, it is time to see how to build an image map on a Web page. You'll see a step-by-step process for building and adding an image map. This chapter focuses almost entirely on creating client-side image maps for your Web pages.

This section creates an actual image map from start to finish. You'll learn how to select the right kinds of images, link the different areas to separate HTML files, and add the correct tags to your Web page.

Finding a Good Image

When creating image maps, the first step is selecting a good image to use. You want to make sure that visitors who see the image understand that there are several different areas on the picture that they can select to link to different items. You need to select definitive images that have different regions easily delineated onscreen, and that make sense to visitors.

Figure 8.3 shows a sample image that will make for an excellent client-side image map for the ACME Block Company.

Image maps can be created from virtually any graphic that you can add to your Web page. Icons, buttons, bars, pictures, and images of all types can be sectioned out and presented as an image map for visitors. Not all images, however, make sense for use as image maps. In general, pictures become difficult image maps because they often lack clearly defined areas for the user to click. Recall the picture of the Coliseum earlier in the chapter (refer to Figure 8.1)—that image wouldn't be a good image map because there aren't any well-defined areas other than the large image of the Coliseum.

People and animals aren't always bad candidates for image maps, but you need to make sure that users will understand they can access different Web pages by clicking different parts of the image (for instance, body parts). Visit **http://www.cs.brown.edu/people/oa/Bin/ skeleton.html** for a prime example of how a picture of a person (in this case, a skeleton) can be used as an image map (see Figure 8.4).

FIG. 8.3

The big blocks make it easy for users to identify the different regions of the image map.

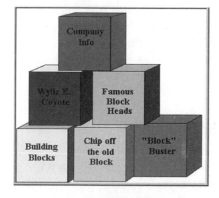

FIG. 8.4

Now, where's that funny bone?

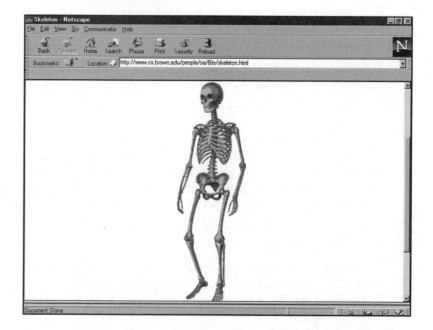

Figure 8.5 shows my block image loaded into PaintShop Pro, a graphics-editing application that allows you to customize and modify Web graphics. You can download it from the JASC Web site **On the CD** at **http://www.jasc.com**.

FIG. 8.5
The big blocks make it easy for users to identify the different regions of the image map.

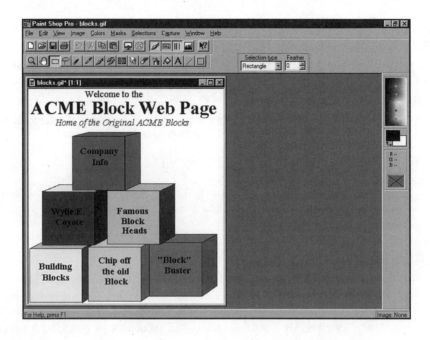

Planning the Map

Once you've selected an image, the next step is to logically divide it into different regions, and define how you want the image map to work.

For this sample block graphic, each individual block should be linked to a separate Web page (see Figure 8.6).

FIG. 8.6
Planning each link from your image map is an important step.

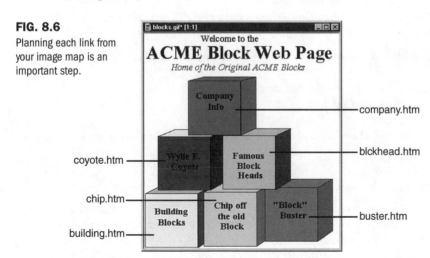

Once you have a good idea of how to divide your image map, you're ready to move to the next step, adding the necessary HTML tags to your Web page.

When you create an image map, it is important to realize that you are now working with multiple Web pages. You are now creating a path that visitors can use to explore the different aspects of your site.

▶ **See** "Expanding Your Web Page into a Web Site," in Chapter 9, "Customizing Your Web Page," for more information in splitting your Web page into a Web site.

> **CAUTION**
>
> Make sure that each HTML file your image links to exists. It's easy to forget to create one or more of the HTML files if you create your image map when they don't all exist.

Adding the Image to Your Web Page

With the correct image selected, it's time to start learning the new HTML tags that support client-side image maps. Adding image maps is similar to adding regular images except that you need a new keyword and a couple of new tags. Fortunately, you won't have to learn all the complicated HTML if you don't want—this section focuses on using a useful tool that avoids all that work.

If you're going to add the proper HTML yourself, first embed the image into your Web page by using the <IMG> tag with the USEMAP keyword:

```
<IMG SRC="BLOCKS.GIF" USEMAP="#ACME Block Image Map">
```

This tag tells browsers to display BLOCKS.GIF on the Web page. USEMAP tells your browser that the image is a client-side clickable image map, and to look for a named section named ACME Block Image Map in this HTML file. This named section of HTML describes how to interpret clicks on different coordinates of the image.

The # is very important because that's how browsers recognize named references within a file.

N O T E   You must name each set of image-map coordinates so that you can have multiple client-side image maps within a single page. ■

The next section describes how to tell your browser which portions of an image link to which HTML files.

Mapping Your Image

With the image embedded in your Web page, the next step is to define each region on the image graphically. Think of each image as a large piece of graph paper, where you have to identify the exact X and Y coordinates for each section that links to an HTML file. For images, coordinates are measured in pixels (the dot resolution of your computer monitor). You have to specify the pixel dimensions of each section for it to properly link to an HTML file.

Fortunately, several easy-to-use tools exist that make it easy for you to specify each distinct section for the image map. One of the best, MapThis!, is included on the CD-ROM accompanying this book. With MapThis!, you use your mouse to draw each section on the image, and thereby create a link to an HTML file. Alternatively, you can download MapThis! at **http://galadriel.ecaetc.ohio-state.edu/tc/mt/**. It is free software.

On the CD

This section uses MapThis! to create a complete image map from start to finish.

1. Start MapThis!. You can run the program directly from the CD-ROM or copy it to your personal computer. A blank screen appears.

2. Choose File, New to create a new image map from scratch. The Make New Image Map dialog box appears (see Figure 8.7).

FIG. 8.7

First you need to tell MapThis! which image you're mapping.

3. Click Let's Go Find One! to reach the Open Existing Image File dialog box (see Figure 8.8) where you can specify the image you want to map.

4. Select the image you want to edit (MapThis! currently supports only GIF and JPEG image formats—not PNG) and then click Open to bring up the mapping window shown in Figure 8.9.

FIG. 8.8

Select your mapped image in the Open Existing Image dialog box.

5. Once the image is opened, you can draw three types of shapes to indicate sections on your image: rectangles, circles, and polygons. Click the shape you want to draw and then use your mouse to make your shape on the screen.

6. Draw as many different shapes and sections on your image as you need. For this sample image, there are six different sections, one for each of the blocks. Figure 8.10 shows the image with each section marked.

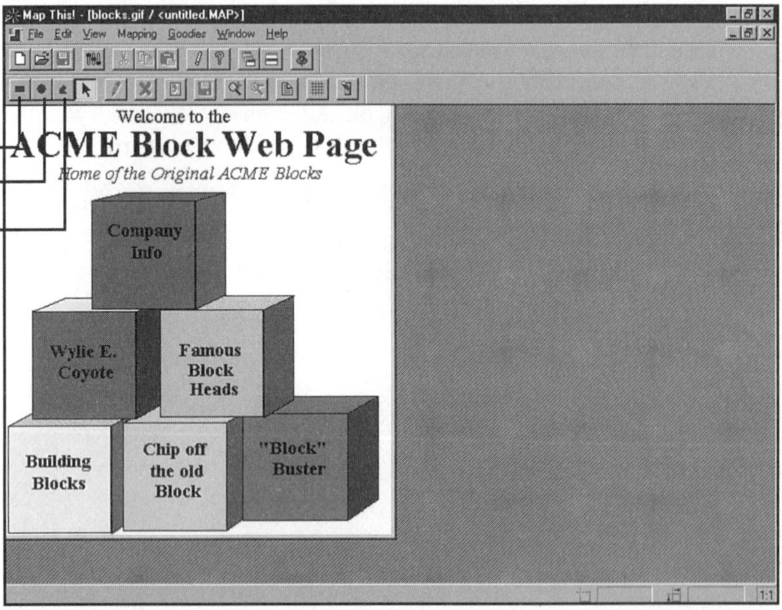

FIG. 8.9

From here, you can map the image with your mouse.

Rectangles

Circles

Polygons

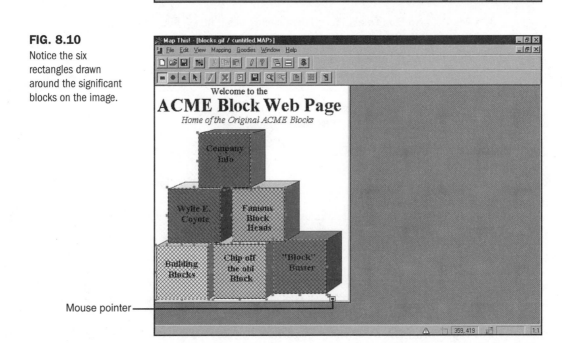

FIG. 8.10

Notice the six rectangles drawn around the significant blocks on the image.

Mouse pointer

7. Now, click the Show/Hide Area List icon on the toolbar to bring up the Area List dialog box (see Figure 8.11).

FIG. 8.11
From the Area List dialog box, you can link regions on the image to specific HTML files.

Show/Hide Area List icon

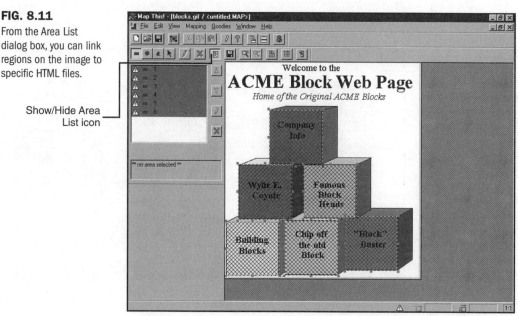

8. Select a listed area, and then click Edit to bring up the Settings dialog box (see Figure 8.12). Here, type the URL of the file you want linked to this region. Click OK after you've typed the URL.

FIG. 8.12
For each area, tell MapThis! what you're mapping.

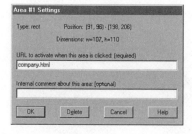

TIP When entering the URL of the file you want to link to, remember that you have the option of typing in a full URL like the following:

`http://www.shafran.com/~shafran/ACME/block1.html`

or a relative URL and file name like:

`ACME/block1.html`

Make sure that you correctly type the full path for the HTML file you want linked to this region.

9. Repeat Step 8 for every region defined on your image. After you finish, your Area List dialog box lists each region along with the corresponding linked file.

10. Choose File, Save from the menu bar to bring up the Info about this Mapfile dialog box (see Figure 8.13).

FIG. 8.13

Set your image map options here, and you're nearly finished.

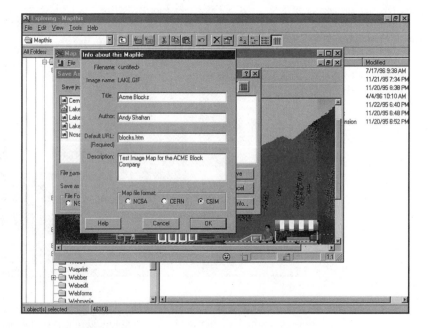

11. Enter the map's title, and make sure that the CSIM radio button is selected as the map file format. (Remember that CSIM stands for client-side image map.) You also can type in a default URL to link this image to if users click a part of the image outside of the regions you've defined.

CAUTION

For your image map to work properly, make sure that the title you type in the Info about this Mapfile dialog box corresponds exactly to what you entered following the USEMAP keyword earlier.

12. When you finish setting your image map options, click OK; MapThis! prompts you to save the client-side image map to an HTML file.

Here's a copy of the finished file for the example being discussed:

```
<BODY>
<MAP NAME="ACME Block Image Map">
<!-- #$-:Image Map file created by MapThis! -->
<!-- #$-:MapThis! free image map editor by Todd C. Wilson -->
<!-- #$-:Please do not edit lines starting with "#$" -->
<!-- #$VERSION:1.20 -->
```

```
<!-- #$DESCRIPTION:The client-side Image Map for ACME Block Company. -->
<!-- #$AUTHOR:Andy Shafran -->
<!-- #$DATE:Mon Mar 29 21:38:26 1996 -->
<!-- #$PATH:C:\ -->
<!-- #$GIF:blocks.gif -->
<AREA SHAPE=RECT COORDS="91,96,198,204" HREF=company.html>
<AREA SHAPE=RECT COORDS="29,206,136,314" HREF=coyote.html>
<AREA SHAPE=RECT COORDS="2,322,110,428" HREF=blckhead.html>
<AREA SHAPE=RECT COORDS="124,319,230,426" HREF=building.html>
<AREA SHAPE=RECT COORDS="161,205,269,311" HREF=chip.html>
<AREA SHAPE=RECT COORDS="247,310,355,416" HREF=buster.html>
</MAP>
```

13. Now that you've successfully created your image-map definition, all you have to do is add it to your HTML document (preferably just below the <IMG> tag), and you're all done. You've just created your own personalized client-side image map.

Figure 8.14 shows what the example image map looks like in Netscape Communicator. Notice how the status bar at the bottom of the screen indicates which HTML file will be linked to as the mouse hovers over a particular block.

FIG. 8.14
Here's the finished product—the ACME Block image map.

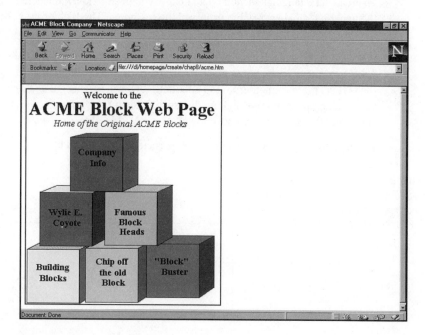

Understanding the Image Map Shapes

Although you'll probably only create an image map with MapThis! or a similar program, this section describes the different aspects of creating an image-map definition from scratch, so you can understand all the tags used in the file in the last section.

Once you've added the image tag to my Web page, the next step is to add the `<MAP>` and `</MAP>` tags:

```
<MAP NAME="ACME Block Image Map">
</MAP>
```

These are new HTML tags used to tell browsers where each region of the image is linked. Make sure that the value following NAME corresponds *exactly* to the value used with USEMAP earlier. Otherwise, your Web browser cannot interpret the image map links correctly.

The `<MAP>` tag indicates that this section of your HTML file describes how each region of the image map should work.

Within the `<MAP>` tag pair, you need to add an individual `<AREA>` tag for each section of the image you want mapped to another HTML file. You can have three different shapes: rectangles, circles, and polygons.

Rectangles

To create a rectangular section on an image, you need to know the actual pixel coordinates of the upper-left and lower-right corners of the rectangle. The Web browser then assumes that the area between these two points is associated together as a shape on your Web graphic.

Pixel coordinates come in pairs, with the upper-left corner of an image always identified as `0,0`. The first number is the horizontal measurement from left to right and the second number is the vertical measurement from top to bottom. You will be specifying a rectangular section on your Web graphic and then linking that section to an HTML file. So, you need to know the two corners of the rectangle you want to link.

For example, let's say you want to create a rectangular section like that shown in Figure 8.15.

FIG. 8.15
Let's use these coordinates to create this exact rectangle.

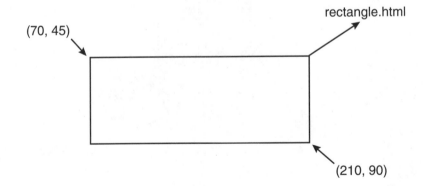

I labeled the pixel coordinates on this image. To add this section to your HTML file, therefore, your `<AREA>` tag would look like this:

```
<AREA SHAPE=RECT COORDS="70,45,210,90" HREF=rectangle.html>
```

The SHAPE keyword defines a rectangular shape. The COORDS keyword requires four values: X and Y coordinates for the upper-left and lower-right corners of the rectangle. Finally, the HREF keyword indicates which HTML file you want loaded when the user clicks this particular area.

 TIP In case you have forgotten, squares are rectangles with four equilateral sides. To add a square shape to your image map, therefore, you still use AREA=RECT.

Circles

Mapping circular shapes is almost as easy as rectangles, but there are a few differences. To map the shape of a circle, you only need three coordinates (as opposed to four for a rectangle). You need the X and Y coordinates of the circle's center, and the length of the circle's radius (see Figure 8.16).

FIG. 8.16
Use these coordinates and the length of the radius to create this circle.

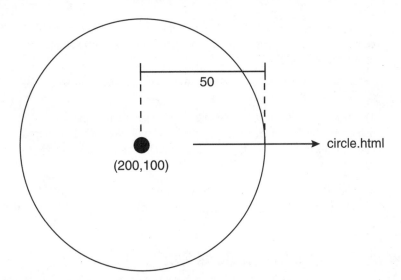

As you can see, the center of the circle is located at 200,100 and the circle has a radius of 50 pixels. The corresponding <AREA> tag looks like this:

```
<AREA SHAPE=CIRCLE COORDS="200,100,50" HREF="circle.html">
```

Polygons

The final shape you can define on an image map is a polygon. By specifying a polygon, you can identify a shape of any size with any number of sides. Simply indicate the coordinates of every corner of the shape. Take a look at the five-cornered polygon shown in Figure 8.17.

FIG. 8.17
You can figure out the
coordinates to draw this
polygon.

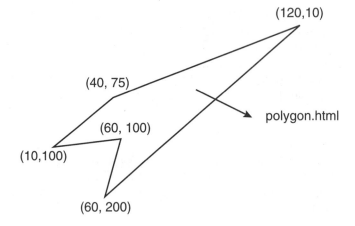

Adding the appropriate <AREA> tag is simple; the only difference is that you need to list a pair of coordinates for each corner of the polygon. Thus, for this example we have six pairs of X,Y coordinates:

```
<AREA SHAPE=POLY COORDS="40,75,10,100,60,100,60,200,120,10,40,75"
➥HREF="polygon.html">
```

The key to creating polygon regions on an image map is that the first and last pair of coordinates must be the same, so that the region can be closed. While there are six sets of coordinates in this example, notice that the first and last sets are identical.

> **CAUTION**
> MapThis! only supports up to 64 sets of corners for a polygon when you draw the shape with your mouse.

How Do Overlapping Regions Work?

When creating image maps, you may have two or more different areas that overlap (see Figure 8.18).

In this example, there is a small *overlapping region* for the two rectangles. How do browsers interpret a click in the overlapping region? The answer is simple—it links to the first region listed in the <MAP> tag. The example is coded this way:

```
<MAP NAME="Overlap Example">
<AREA SHAPE=RECT COORDS="70,45,210,90" HREF=rectangle1.html>
<AREA SHAPE=RECT COORDS="150,60,290,120" HREF=rectangle2.html>
</MAP>
```

Therefore, you link to `rectangle1.html` if the overlapping region is clicked.

FIG. 8.18
Notice the overlapping region in this drawing.

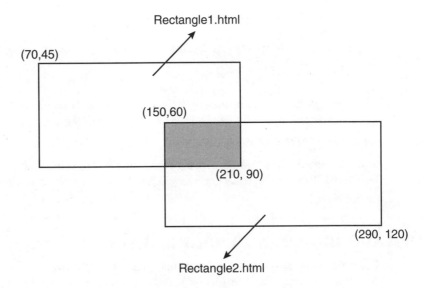

Rectangle1.html

(70,45)

(150,60)

(210, 90)

(290, 120)

Rectangle2.html

N O T E Why do browsers assume that you want to click an overlapping area to bring you to the first area listed? It's because when a click is registered on an image map, the browser starts logically reading through the <MAP> tag. It checks each area in turn to see if the coordinates that have been clicked fit within that shape. As soon as it finds a match, it whisks you away to the linked page, not bothering to look at the rest of the areas in the <MAP> tag. ■

Adding a Default Link

Another concern besides overlapping regions is the issue of what happens when a user clicks outside of all established regions on your image map. You can specify a *default link* that is activated in this type of situation. Default links are nice because they make sure that visitors to your Web page are always linked to *some* page, regardless of where they click the image.

To add a default link to your image map, all you have to do is add one final region to your image map—a rectangle that spans the entire width and height of your image. For example, the ACME Block Company image is 300 pixels wide and 400 pixels tall, so add the following line to the end of the image map definition:

```
<AREA SHAPE=RECT COORDS="0,0,299,399" HREF=default.html>
```

 The previous code line used 299 and 399 as the coordinates because the pixel count starts at 0,0. Thus, the 300th pixel across the screen is actually at X coordinate 299.

> **CAUTION**
>
> Make sure that this default area is the last item in your <MAP> tag. Otherwise, it will supersede any areas that might follow.

Of course, you might want nothing to happen when a user clicks outside of your designated areas. In that case, you still should add an all-image <AREA> tag, but use the NOHREF keyword:

```
<AREA SHAPE=RECT COORDS="0,0,299,399" NOHREF>
```

This informs your Web browser that any clicks outside of the other defined regions should be ignored. This tag isn't really necessary; it just makes your image map definition more complete.

Test the Image Map with a Browser

Once you're finished creating the image map, make sure that you test it thoroughly with either Netscape or Internet Explorer (or both). Test every region, one at a time, to make sure that your links have been created properly.

Many people overlook this step, assuming that there won't be any mistakes as long as they have followed the above steps exactly; however, typos, incorrect file names, and other mistakes can easily create flaws in your image map.

Providing a Textual Alternative

Although virtually all new Web browsers support client-side image maps, it's always a good idea to provide some sort of textual alternative. This accommodates visitors to your page who are using a browser that doesn't read client-side image maps, or who don't want to wait for the entire image to download before selecting a region on the image map.

Figure 8.19 shows how the ACME Block home page is updated to have textual links as well as graphical ones. Using a two-column table with the left column displaying the main image map, and the right column showing a simple list of links, this page balances Web graphics and text well.

FIG. 8.19
This simple table provides an alternative to using my image map.

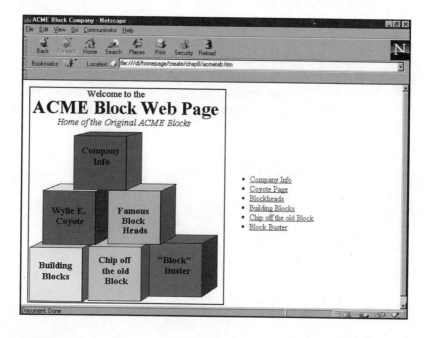

Image Map Design Tips

This section consolidates several important tips you should keep in mind when you begin using client-side image maps in your Web pages. Some of them are repeated information from throughout this chapter, and others aren't. Basically, this is a last-minute checklist you should run through before you let everyone on the Web have access to your image maps:

- **Choose the right type of image map.** Make sure that you understand the differences between client-side and server-side image maps. Although client-side maps may be more efficient, there are some situations where you don't want to use them—particularly, if you are afraid many visitors to your Web page won't use a browser with client-side capability.

- **Be careful of file size.** Images that are mapped tend to have larger file sizes because they usually appear larger onscreen. Make sure that your image's file size isn't outrageous (for instance, above 100K); otherwise, visitors to your Web page will become impatient.

- **Use interlaced images.** *Interlaced images* are those that load in multiple levels, starting out fuzzy and slowly becoming more detailed. Interlaced images are ideal for image maps, because as soon as visitors recognize which area they want to click, they don't have to wait for the whole image to appear. Learn more about creating interlaced images in *Creating Your Own Web Graphics*, also published by Que.

- **Define mapped areas clearly.** Make sure that you use an image that makes it easy for visitors to know which sections are mapped to other HTML files. It's easy for visitors to overlook small areas (or illogical areas) on an image map.

- **Test your image map at least twice.** I can't stress this enough. I've seen too many image maps that haven't been tested thoroughly. Usually, some regions link properly to files, but other regions don't. Nobody enjoys using an untested image map.

CHAPTER 9

Customizing Your Web Page

Remember when you bought your last car? You went to the dealer's lot, haggled over a few bucks, and drove off the lot. You had a nice car, but I'm sure you wanted to add a few personal (and cool) customizations to it. Some people add CD players or alarms, others add a sun roof or neon lights to their car—and don't forget about the fuzzy dice! These personalized customizations make every car different and unique.

Right now, you have a Web page driven straight off the lot. In this chapter, I'll show you how to customize your Web page to fit your own particular needs and wants. You can modify your standard Web page into your own customized vehicle.

Now, it's time to learn how to use some of these advanced HTML concepts to tailor your home page to your needs. This chapter introduces you to a potpourri of neat things you can do with your Web page once you master the basics. I cover a diverse set of topics, none too complicated for you to start using immediately. ■

Split your home page into a small set of integrated pages

Usually, a single page of HTML doesn't quite do the job. You'll learn how to create your own mini Web of pages all linking back and forth to one another.

Track how many visitors stop by and visit your Web page

Counting the number of visitors who stop by is an important and effective way of gauging how popular your Web page is.

Add an interactive guestbook for visitors to sign

Learn how to add a special HTML form that lets people enter in their own comments and opinions of your Web page.

Link to FTP, UseNet, and Gopher

You can integrate your site with all sorts of other Internet information with a simple twist on a tag you already know.

Let visitors send you e-mail directly from your home page

Unlike a guestbook, e-mail is a private link between you and visitors who stop by.

Expanding Your Web Page into a Web Site

When you left home, you probably moved into a small, single-room apartment—one where you could afford to pay the rent and utilities. You didn't have much furniture or decorations to arrange on the walls. Sooner or later, you realized that you would need to move to a larger apartment, and, eventually, to a house.

Compare that first messy, cluttered, and crowded apartment to the present situation of just too much information to fit on a single Web page. While a basic Web page might serve most of your needs, once you start adding all of your personal and professional interests, tossing in several images and multimedia clips, and creating links to WWW pages all over the Internet, you may notice that your Web page is both large and unwieldy. At that point, it is time to expand your horizons and change your Web page into a Web site.

Of course, remember that moving into that first home isn't always roses. Usually, homes require significantly more maintenance and there's always something that can be tinkered with and modified. Similarly, expanded Web sites come with some additional maintenance and baggage. It is more difficult to keep an entire Web site up to date and cohesive.

Your Web page is the main starting point for visitors looking for information about you—but now your Web page is linked to several other HTML documents pertaining to you. Combined, I call this set of HTML documents your Web site.

Expanding your Web page into different Web pages is a common practice as your HTML knowledge matures. For example, as you may have noticed, my home page had a lot of different pieces of information that I was trying to fit on one page. Eventually, I was at the maximum limit with what would logically fit onto a single page, and I still had more information to add. So, I split it up into about five different Web pages, all linked back and forth from my original page. Thus, you've created your own miniWeb of HTML documents.

Nowadays, my Web site is expansive. I have over 250 HTML files and 500 graphics making up the entire site at **http://www.shafran.com**. Without a good site plan, my Web presence would be cluttered, disorganized, and perpetually out of date.

Why Split Up Your Home Page

There are two important reasons for splitting your Web page into a Web site. The first reason is that splitting your Web page makes it easier for visitors to get the information they want. If a potential employer stops by your Web page, he or she does not really want to spend several minutes downloading text and images of your family; he or she wants to see your resume and work experience. Making all of these aspects separate documents, he or she can choose to see only the information sought. This gives your visitors more control.

The second, and more selfish reason (the reason for splitting here), is to add more "spiffy" graphics and personal information. This Web page, overburdened with graphics and multimedia files, would be unreadable for most WWW visitors with any more additions. When I split my pages up, I was able to double the amount of graphics and neat images I could use. Nearly every page has a graphic or a multimedia file of some sort.

Finally, the best reason to split up your home page is to make your entire site easier to manage and update. A well-organized Web site can quickly be updated with current information at any point.

Design Your Home Site Correctly

Before you split up your home page, design a plan. Remember that Chapter 2, "Weaving Your Own Web," focused on designing your single page appearance. This is the same process, except now you decide on the structure of your site and how your pages link together.

Below, I've sketched four possible ways you can choose to link your documents. Each of these methods has advantages and disadvantages in certain situations. Choose whichever method works best for your home page.

Standard—In this format, your Web page links to each of the other documents in your home site, and documents all link directly back to your home page. This is the easiest and most common way to create a Web site. Figure 9.1 shows a sample Standard way of splitting up your Web pages.

FIG. 9.1
Though not too exciting, the standard way is the most popular way of organizing Web pages.

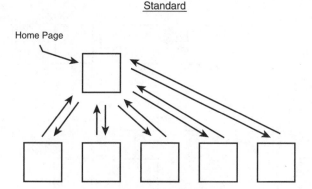

Standard

Home Page

Waterfall—Your documents are linked in a predefined order so that there is only one path through all of your pages. Figure 9.2 lets you see how a waterfall site might be set up.

Skyscraper—To get to room 2676 in the Empire State Building, you board the elevator and choose the 26th floor, before walking down the hall to the exact location. In the Skyscraper model, some of your pages can only be read if visitors follow the right path. Figure 9.3 should remind you of your local downtown.

FIG. 9.2
Water can only flow in
one direction, and so
can your visitors.

Waterfall

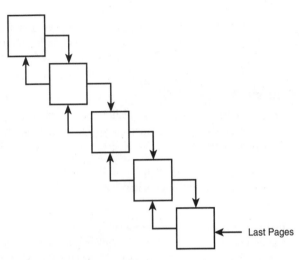

Last Pages

FIG. 9.3
Don't get off on the
wrong floor accidentally.

Skyscraper

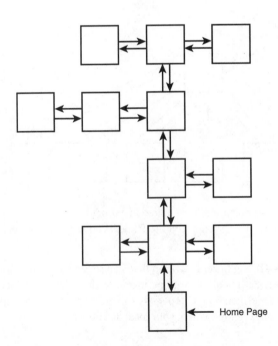

Home Page

Web—All of the pages in your Web site are linked to one another, allowing you to visit virtually any single page from another. This method is confusing when it gets out of hand, but it is popular when your document links are used with moderation. Figure 9.4 depicts a very small webbed design.

FIG. 9.4
Unorganized sites often follow the Web methodology.

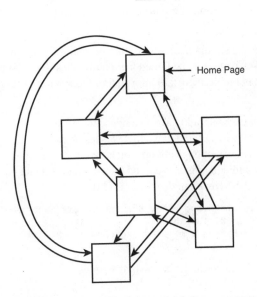

Web

Home Page

> **N O T E** Personally, I use a hybrid of these methods. If you combine the Standard and Web methods, you can see how my Web site is organized. While you can reach nearly all of the pages directly through the home page, several of the documents both reference and link to each other. ■

Splitting Your Page

Once you decide on a home site structure, it's time to actually split your pages. You can create new HTML files from scratch or based on your original Home page.

Try to give your files descriptive names so it's easier to make changes in the future. Naming files Page1.HTM, Page2.HTM, Page3.HTM, is far less useful than naming them academic.htm, personal.htm, and publish.htm.

> **N O T E** UNIX, Macintosh, and Windows 95 operating systems all support extended file names. For example, using Windows 95, you can name your three files **Academic Information.HTML**, **Personal Information.HTML**, and **Published Books.HTML**. Be careful when using spaces and special characters in your file names—not all operating systems recognize them universally.

continues

continued

Also, if you use Windows 95, you must use a 32-bit FTP program to upload your files, otherwise your extended file names will be automatically shortened during the upload and not what you originally named them. ▪

Make sure you add the <HTML>, <HEAD>, and <BODY> tags to each new page, as well as a new <TITLE> for the document. You must go through the same motions as you did originally creating your home page.

Each Web page you create should not assume that the visitor comes directly from your home page. Your separate Web pages can be linked from other sites. Each Web page should be self-contained, and should not omit important information (your name) that people who linked to it might want to know.

Also, each of your Web pages should have a standard footer at the bottom fully informing visitors about the Web page: who created it; when it was last updated, and whom to contact for more information. This information is not only included in your home page, but also on your other pages as well. In addition, it is also a good idea to include a link back to your home page to ease navigating your site. Here's my footer in HTML:

```
<A HREF="http://www.shafran.com">Andy Shafran's Home Page</A><BR>
<I> Last Updated April 28, 1997 by
<A HREF="mailto:andy@shafran.com">Andy Shafran</A><BR>
andy@shafran.com<I>
```

Figure 9.5 shows how the footer looks in one of my pages.

FIG. 9.5

It's a plain, but effective, standard footer; and it does the trick nicely.

My Standard Footer→

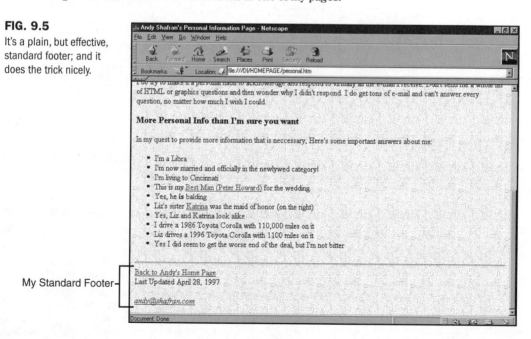

T I P Don't forget to remove your HTML targets. After you split your pages into smaller, easier chunks to read; targets are usually no longer necessary, because each section is now a separate file.

Linking Your Pages

With your pages split, it's time to link your home page to each one of the other Web pages. Make sure you link your pages in an order that makes sense to anyone visiting your home page.

For example, I have an online listing of all of my various jobs and one that describes all of my published books. I could have linked my published book page directly to my professional page because it is a result of my being gainfully employed. Even though this makes sense logically, most visitors would never even know I had a listing of published books unless they happened to visit the professional page first. Instead, I choose to make the published book page a direct link from **both** my professional and my central home page to make it easy for visitors to find this critical information.

You have several different options for linking your Web site. Personally, I use an unordered list on my page to depict each selection that visitors can choose, but you can use a table, or regular text just as successfully. Here's my unordered list:

```
<P>

You'll find a lot of information about me and my projects on this Web site.
Below, I've categorized some of the main topics of interest.

<UL>
    <LI>Photographs and more <A HREF="personal.htm">personal
information</A>?
    <LI>Corporate and <A HREF="profess.htm">Professional
information</A>.
    <LI><A HREF="books.htm">Books I've written</A>
    <LI><A HREF="links/links.htm">Lists of links</A>
</UL>
```

Additionally, I create a set of buttons that clearly labels each of these four main topics. Each button is linked to the same page as the corresponding unordered list I just described. For more information on using graphics as links, or working with links in general, see Chapter 7, "Linking Your Web Pages."

N O T E Notice how most of these HTML documents are located in the same directory as the original file. You can organize your HTML files into your choice of directory structure. Here you see a separate LINKS directory. Because the page includes a lot of different link pages, keeping them together, and organizing them in a subdirectory is an efficient and easy method. ▪

Figure 9.6 shows my home page now that it is linked to separate files.

Part
IV

Ch
9

FIG. 9.6
The links look the same as they did when all of my information was in the same file.

> You'll find a lot of information about me and my projects on this Web site. Below, I've categorized some of the main topics of interest.
>
> - Photographs and more personal information?
> - Corporate and Professional information.
> - Books I've written
> - Lists of links

Web Site Management

Splitting your Web page up into a well-organized site is just the first step. Creating and managing a larger Web site can be both difficult and time-consuming because you have to take care of many different links and constantly update them.

Fortunately, several powerful tools now exist that can make Web management a breeze. The best of these tools is WebMapper, published by NetCarta (recently purchased by Microsoft). You can download WebMapper at **http://www.netcarta.com** (see Figure 9.7).

FIG. 9.7
WebMapper is a shareware tool that maps an entire Web site.

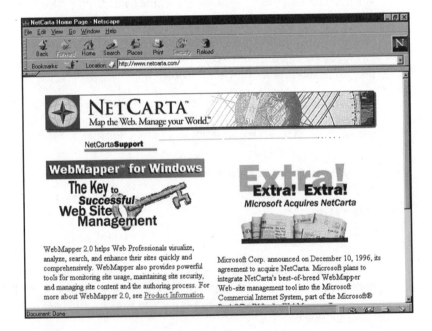

A shareware tool, WebMapper creates a graphic representation of how all the links and pages in your Web site work together. Once downloaded and installed, you can point WebMapper to any URL on the Internet. WebMapper will then visit every page and link at that site and create a compiled and graphical report. This report will show you the relationship of your Web pages, outdated links, erroneous IMG tags, and a host of other problems that can occur when managing a Web site.

Figure 9.8 shows **www.shafran.com** in graphical format after WebMapper has mapped through the entire site.

FIG. 9.8
WebMapper lets you browse through a site easily and identify how all the links work with one another.

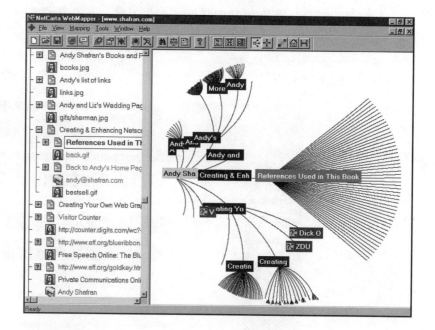

Part
IV

Ch
9

Tracking How Many People Visit Your Home Page

One of the most popular requests for a new Web page owner is how to determine the number of people stopping by his or her page. Without this information, you won't know whether your Web page is as popular as a Manhattan night club, or as barren as the Sahara Desert. If you run your own Web server, or if you have an unusually friendly Web provider, you may be able to get that information just by simply requesting it. The Web server software can automatically track such usage statistics.

In most cases, you've got to track your visitors yourself. There are several different ways to add an incremental counter to your home page. These counters keep track of every time someone visits your page, and add that increasing number to your Web page.

First, I'll describe a simple counter that anyone on the WWW can use and add to their home page in under five minutes. Then I'll talk about some advanced options you have if you're really serious about keeping track of your Web page visitors.

Adding the Simple Counter

There are several free services to home page creators which allow you to have an incremental counter on your Web site. Anyone who has a Web page can add an incremental counter to his or her page(s) by just adding a simple HTML link (like the kind you created in Chapter 7,

"Linking Your Web Pages"). Nothing fancy, this counter requires no time-consuming support or special knowledge of advanced HTML code.

Once you insert a link to the counter inserts into your Web page, the counter then increments "by one" each time a visitor stops by. This links your home page to a database which counts your home page visitors. Anyone can have his or her own personal counter added to his or her Web page. For more information, visit **http://www.freecounter.com** (see Figure 9.9), and you'll learn step-by-step how to add a link to your Web page with a single HTML tag.

FIG. 9.9

Here's the home page for one of the biggest free counter distributors out there.

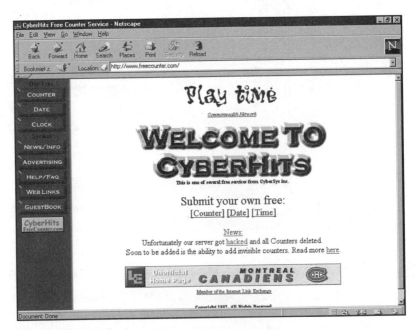

Basically, what happens is that you fill out a simple information form about yourself and your home page. Then you are given a simple HTML string to add to your Web page. Once added, a counter appears automatically—it is that easy. The counter site gives you all of the HTML code you'll need. To create your own simple counter, click on the link labeled "free counter" in Figure 9.9. You are brought to a new page where you enter your e-mail address, a password, and the starting number of your counter (see Figure 9.10).

Click on the Submit button, and you are given a simple listing of your counter along with all of the HTML required to add it to your Web page. Here's my simple HTML for the counter I just created:

```
<!--Start CyberHits Counter-->
<br><a href="http://www.freecounter.com/cgi-
bin/cybersys/stat.cgi?19030841"><IMG BORDER=0
SRC="http://www.freecounter.com/cgi-
bin/cybersys/counte.pl?counter=19030841"></a>
<br>Counter provided by <a href="http://www.cybersys.pp.se">CyberHits</A>
<br><!--End CyberHits Counter code-->
```

FIG. 9.10
Creating a counter requires only a few moments stop at this page.

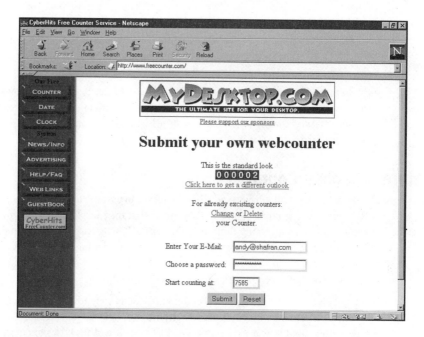

Figure 9.11 shows what this counter looks like on my Web page.

FIG. 9.11
Quite a few visitors since the last check!

Here's how it works. When a visitor stops by my home page at **http://www.shafran.com**, the browser loads all of the text and graphics. When finished, it then tries to load the image specified in my counter HTML tag. This is a simple image that sends back the current page count as a graphic. My counter is actually stored at **http://www.freecounter.com**.

Unfortunately, your counter is only as good as the Web site you are linking into. If for any reason **www.freecounter.com** goes down or becomes overloaded, your counter might be temporarily disabled. Don't worry, it'll eventually work again—after a few hours or so.

 You should place this link towards the bottom of your document. Browsers load your Web page from the top down, and it takes several additional seconds to link to the counter page and return with the current visitor number. Placing it on the bottom of your page makes it easier for visitors to ignore that short wait, because they can see the rest of your page.

N O T E There are several other free counter services on the Web. Two of my favorites can be found at **http://www.pagecount.com** and **http://www.digits.com**.

continues

continued

Also, some of these counters offer advanced services, which cost around $3–$5 a month, but offer some more information about the visitors who stop by and ensure that the counter is available 24 hours a day.

Businesses looking for a counter should read the following section. This simple counter is ideal only for home pages (businesses can have a Web provider add a counter, or make a customized company counter with a small charge). If you have more than 1,000 visitors a day to your Web site, you can't use this free counter, because it is mainly geared for individual users and for smaller businesses. ■

More Advanced Counters

There are several other, more advanced counter programs available free on the WWW. The advantage of these other counter programs is that they work locally, on your own Web server. Visitors don't have to wait to link to a counter halfway across the world to display the number of visits to your page. If you expect your Web page to get lots of visits (more than 250–1,000 a day), it is probably in your best interest to look into using a different counter than the previous one, based on these performance criteria.

Unfortunately, the other types of counters are not as easy to install as the previous counter. You must be familiar with computer programming, have advanced knowledge of HTML, and know a little about how a Web server works to use the other types of counters properly. I've listed several popular counter programs available for free. Each of these counters comes with instructions. Simply contact your Web provider with any installation questions. (That's why you pay them.)

- **http://www.yahoo.com/Computers_and_Internet/Internet/ World_Wide_Web/Programming/Access_Counts/**

  Here is a solid listing of many different access counters you can build into your Web page.

- **http://www.worldwidemart.com/scripts/counter.shtml**
  Add a counter to your Web Server with this all-purpose counter that works for just about anyone.

Getting Feedback from Visitors with a Quick Guestbook

In addition to adding a counter to Web pages, another popular request is having some way for visitors to easily add their own personal comments. This is called adding a guestbook to your Web page. A guestbook is an online registry where people can fill out a simple form of their own comments and leave their messages on your Web page. That way, subsequent visitors cannot only read previous visitors' comments but add their own.

Like simple page counters, guestbooks come in two basic flavors. The easiest to use are the free, public access guestbooks. These guestbooks work similarly to the free counters. Instead of running a special script on your Web site, you simply link into a publicly accessible guestbook created for you at another Web site.

Additionally, guestbooks also come as CGI scripts that can be installed on your Web server. In general though, unless you run an advanced Web server and are very familiar with CGI scripting, you'll want to use the free, public guestbooks. They are simple to use, powerful enough for most users, and add a great touch to a Web site.

There are several sites available to find free guestbooks on the Web. The best one can be found at **http://www.lpage.com** (see Figure 9.12). This site is similar to the previous counter site, where you can enhance your Web page in just a few moments with a single HTML link.

Part
IV

Ch
9

FIG. 9.12

Many Web developers like to have a guestbook, where people can stop by and leave comments.

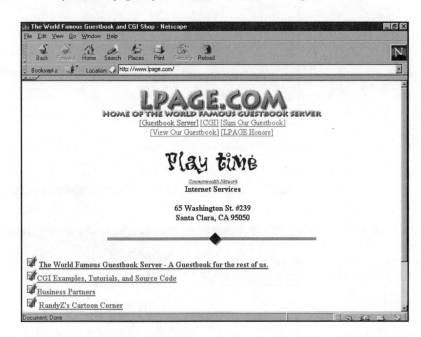

At the bottom of the page, click the link labeled The World Famous Guestbook. After following the online steps for registration, you have a complete URL to add to your Web page to include the guestbook.

Below are the two lines of HTML added to my Web page after I followed the online steps:

```
<a href=http://www.Lpage.com/wgb/wgbsign.dbm?
owner=creatingsecondedition>Sign My Guestbook</a>
<a href=http://www.Lpage.com/wgb/wgbview.dbm?
owner=creatingsecondedition>View My Guestbook</a>
<a href=http://www.Lpage.com/wguestbk>
<img src=http://www.Lpage.com/gif/lpagebutton.gif height=31
width=88alt="Guestbook by Lpage"></a><p>
```

The first link brings visitors a simple online form to fill out (see Figure 9.13). After filling out this form, visitors click the second link and see all the previous stored entries. Figure 9.14 shows one of the sample Web site's pages.

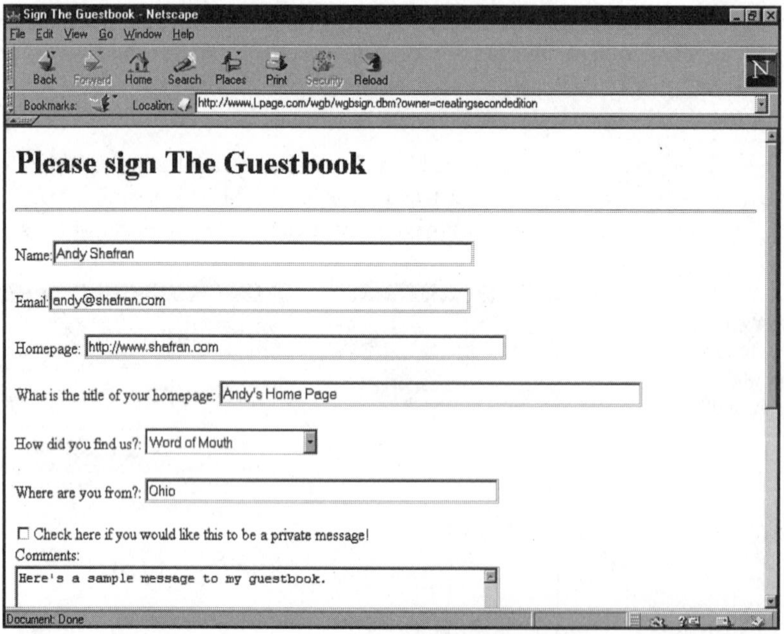

FIG. 9.13

This simple form makes it easy for people to add their comments.

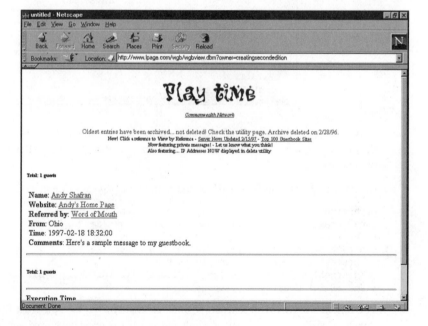

FIG. 9.14

Here's my running guestbook—I have only a few entries, not bad!

N O T E If you have trouble with this particular guestbook, you have several other options for this free service. Check out:

http://www.webpost.net/guest.html

http://www.dreambook.com/

Both of these sites focus specifically on creating and maintaining guestbooks for the general Internet public. ■

Linking to Other Internet Resources

When I was writing this book, I needed to stay in constant communication with Que, my publisher. I was on the phone with them daily and regularly exchanged e-mail messages as well. When simple words weren't enough, I would fax information to them immediately, while other times, Federal Express became an important crutch. All these types of communication were part of a normal day.

The Internet works in a similar way, only on a much bigger scale. Thousands of computers need to constantly talk to each other and exchange information. Using various communication standards, or Internet protocols, computers communicate with each other in several different ways. Each of these different protocols has its own special uses, features and advantages. I wouldn't use a fax machine to transmit a 100-page manuscript, and likewise, I wouldn't try to e-mail a huge file to my publisher—there are better, more efficient methods of sending that information.

In Chapter 7, "Linking Your Web Pages," I introduced links and showed you how to connect two HTML documents by using the HTTP Protocol. The HTTP Protocol was developed specifically for the World Wide Web, and was the first type of Internet communication that browsers, such as Netscape, Mosaic, or Internet Explorer, supported.

Since then, several other popular Internet protocols are now supported and can be integrated into your home page. They work the same way as the links I talked about in Chapter 7, "Linking Your Web Pages," only you need to know the correct URL to use the various Internet protocols.

In this section, I show you how to add HTML links to integrate FTP, Mailto, Gopher, and UseNet protocols into your home page.

FTP

There are millions of different files available on the Internet—everything from the latest shareware games to catalogs of recipes. All these can be downloaded directly to your home computer by using FTP (File Transfer Protocol).

Files accessible via FTP can be added directly to your home page. This convenience allows visitors the ability to download files without loading a separate FTP program. To add an FTP link to your Web site, you need to know the full FTP URL of the file you want to point to. Once you know the URL, you can add it just like any other standard http link you are familiar with.

Here's the FTP URL of HotDog, a very popular Web editor mentioned in Chapter 13, "Using HTML Editors and Other Web Tools:"

Here's how I added that address to my Web page:

```
<A HREF="ftp://ftp.sausage.com/pub/hdallinst.exe">
Download the HotDog Web Editor </A>
```

See, it's just like linking by using the HTTP protocol, only with a different URL. In your browser, **download the Hotdog Web editor** appears like any other link on your home page. When visitors click on that link, an FTP download connection is made automatically, and the browser starts retrieving that file. See Figure 9.15 for the window that appears when I click on the FTP link.

FIG. 9.15

Choose where to save the FTPed file to your hard drive.

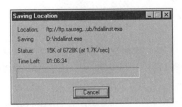

N O T E   This method works only for Anonymous FTP access. Anonymous FTP access allows anyone on the Internet to connect to a certain site and to download files. Most FTP sites allow anonymous access.

However, there may be times when you want to connect to a password-protected FTP site. If HotDog required a password to download the editor, your FTP URL would look like this:

ftp://userid:password@ftp.sausage.com/pub/hdgsetup.exe

You must specify the user ID and password (listed in boldface) when using a passworded FTP site.

Be careful when adding password-protected FTP sites to your Web page. Anyone who clicks the link can visit that FTP site by using your user ID and password. It is best to use links to nonanonymous FTP sites for Web pages that no one else ever sees. ■

News

Thousands of UseNet newsgroups exist on the Internet. These newsgroups cover every topic imaginable. Whether you want to talk about Bruce Springsteen or Windows 95, there is bound to be a newsgroup for you.

You can link your home page to as many different newsgroups as you like just by knowing the full newsgroup name. To add a newsgroup link to your home page, you need to know the URL to a specific newsgroup. Below is the URL to the newsgroup announcing new Web pages and tools:

Part
IV

Ch
9

Usenet News Protocol   Newsgroup to read

news:comp.infosystems.www.announce

To add this as a link to your home page, type the following HTML:

```
<A HREF="news:comp.infosystems.www.announce">USENET
Newsgroup:Comp.Infosystems.WWW.Announce</A>
```

After clicking the newsgroup link, a separate newsreader is initiated which connects with your Internet Service Providers NNTP (news transport protocol) server. A list of articles can be read in any order (see Figure 9.16). Click a message subject to read that particular newsgroup message.

FIG. 9.16

This high-volume newsgroup always has new messages to read.

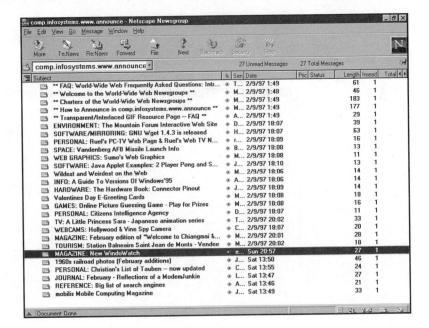

Gopher

Another popular Internet application is Gopher. Developed at the University of Minnesota (hence the name—Minnesota's mascot is the "Golden Gopher"), Gopher is a text-based menu system allowing Internet sites to sort and organize vast quantities of information. You must step through various levels of menus to find the information you want at a Gopher site.

Although most Internet sites use Gopher menu systems, these systems are increasingly less popular due to the increase in information migrating over to the WWW. Gopher is "text only" and less visually exciting than a colorful Web page. However, because there is still a lot of information and activity using Gopher, you may want to link some of that information to your home page.

The following is a sample Gopher URL that lists all of the most recent earthquakes (and relevant) information from around the world:

Gopher Protocol specification   Internet address of gopher information

**gopher://gopher.stolaf.edu:70/00/Internet%20Resources/
Weather-and-Geography/Earthquake%20Information**

Complete path to the gopher file

Below is the HTML code used to add this link to a home page. Figure 9.17 shows how the Gopher page appears in a browser.

```
<A HREF=" gopher://gopher.stolaf.edu:70/00/Internet%20Resources/
Weather-and-Geography/Earthquake%20Information">
Gopher report the most recent earthquakes around the world</A>
```

FIG. 9.17
Gopher may not be as pretty as the WWW, but it still has a lot of current information.

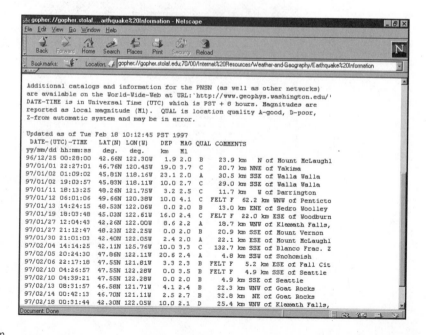

Part
IV
Ch
9

N O T E Do you notice the %20 in the Gopher URL? WWW browsers do not know how to interpret spaces in their HTML links. Bypass this shortfall by replacing spaces with the text: **%20**. Browsers automatically read and translates that special code.

If, by chance, you need to add an actual % into your URL, replace the actual % with the **%25** code. ▨

E-Mail

E-mail, or *electronic mail*, is the most popular way to communicate privately between users on the Internet. Usually, users must load a separate program to send e-mail across the Internet. However, you not only can embed e-mail addresses directly into your home page, but you can also send e-mail with a single click.

Most Web page designers add an e-mail link to themselves at the bottom of their page. This enables Web visitors to send questions or comments to the designers without switching back to an individual visitor e-mail program.

On my home page, I have an e-mail link to myself on every page. Here's my URL:

This URL tells the browser to bring up a blank e-mail message and address it to **andy@shafran.com** (see Figure 9.18). My HTML code appears below:

```
<A HREF="mailto:andy@shafran.com">E-mail to Andy Shafran</A>
```

FIG. 9.18
E-mail capabilities on to your home page is a welcome addition.

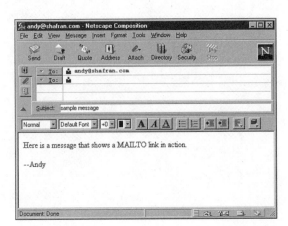

CHAPTER 10

Making Your Web Page Multimedia

Imagine making the movie "Star Wars." George Lucas started with a plain, old text manuscript (which you can download at **http://www.books.com**). That manuscript may have been thorough, but it wasn't nearly as much fun as the actual movie. The great soundtrack and cool special effects make the movie fun and enjoyable. Without them, Star Wars is just like any other movie about intergalactic war.

While we aren't going to create Star Wars (**http://www.starwars.com**), you are going to learn how to add all sorts of special effects to your Web page. Adding audio bites and video clips is within your reach, and these additions separate your page from all the other pages' blasé text and image-only pages.

So far, this book has taught you how to mark your own corner of the Internet quickly and easily by using a simple Web page. Now, it's time to take that extra step, and make your site truly spectacular.

Chapter 6, "Using Graphics to Excite Your Page," teaches you how to add all sorts of images to your home page. With images, your Web page becomes a multimedia page, because you combine graphics and text on one page. However, by today's terms, multimedia means including both cool audio and video clips in your home page.

Browse the WWW for how other sites use multimedia

Multimedia Web pages can be challenging to design and implement. Look at how other good multimedia sites work to gather ideas for your own Web page.

Recognize the different audio and video file types

Digital audio and video clips can be saved in many different file formats for your Web page. Learn about the standard formats you can use and the differences between them.

Start making your own audio and video clips

Creating multimedia clips can be fun and exciting. Learn what tools you'll need to create digital video and audio clips.

Find existing multimedia clips, both on the book's CD and on the Internet

I've included hundreds of megs of existing multimedia clips on the CD-ROM with this book. Learn how to incorporate them into your Web page immediately.

Add audio and video clips to your Web page

Finding the multimedia clips is only the first step. Next, you need to know the proper HTML tags so they work on your site.

In this chapter, you'll learn how to integrate audio bites and video clips onto your Web page to create a truly multimedia effect. ■

A Sampling of Multimedia Sites

Technically, your Web page is multimedia because you use text and images, but you won't qualify for a gold star unless you add audio or video clips to it (or possibly both). Today, particularly on the WWW, the word "multimedia" means using something in addition to both text and images. Before you learn to use these new multimedia formats on your Web page, first get some brainstorming ideas by taking a look at how some other multimedia Web pages are set up. Several places on the Web integrate text, images, audio, and video clips on the same page to achieve startlingly good effects. You quickly notice that most of these sites are professionally designed—that's because it is difficult to find good audio and video clips for Web pages, and even more difficult to create a cohesive site using them all.

Using all of these different media types presents several technical and design challenges. All of the design issues which emerged when adding images to pages are now back, threefold. You must worry about making these new aspects easy to use, and how to have them appear naturally in your home page. Adding too much clutter makes your page unreadable.

On the technical side, creating and adding audio and video clips is no walk in the park. The file size is a concern, as is multi-platform compatibility (will PC, Mac, and UNIX users all be able to use the clips?), and the quality of the clip.

This chapter focuses on these technical issues, plus how to correctly add audio and video clips to your Web page.

Politically Correct Bedtime Stories

One of my favorite pages on the entire WWW is the home page Buena Vista movies on the Internet. At **http://www.movies.com** there are many different multimedia examples of popular movies. This site includes video snippets and previews, sound bites, and many stills taken from the actual movies. Figure 10.1 shows me deciding which current movie to explore.

Great Multimedia Example—Independence Day

Another popular true multimedia site is the Independence Day home page (**http://www. id4movie.com**). This professionally designed page demonstrates what kind of Web a lot of time and effort can create. You'll find audio and video clips, interactive games, and in general, a true multimedia experience here. Stop by for a look. (See Figure 10.2.)

FIG. 10.1

Simple and easy to use, this site is a model for a basic multimedia home page.

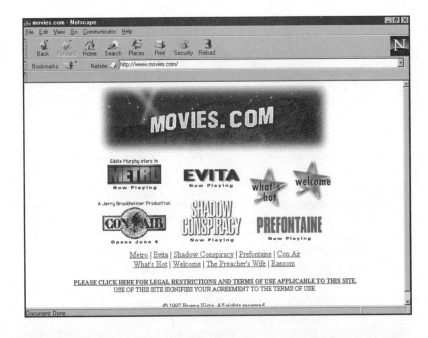

FIG. 10.2

Multimedia pages don't get much better than this.

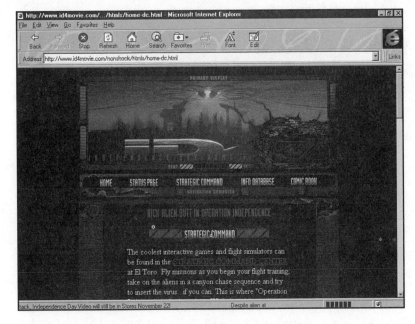

Understanding and Using Audio Clips

Audio clips, sometimes referred to as sound bites, add another dimension to your Web page. Not only can people see information you present, but they can hear it. Imagine watching "Raiders of the Lost Ark" without hearing the theme music. It just isn't the same. The music is so important to the entire theatrical experience. Similarly, sound is a welcome addition to Web pages because it makes exploring Web pages more fun and informative.

Unlike adding images, putting an audio clip on your Web page embeds an actual file that must be downloaded and played. Images appear alongside your text, while audio clips have to be downloaded in the background while you are browsing through a page.

N O T E To hear audio clips on your computer, you must have the correct hardware and software.
If you are using a PC-compatible machine, you must have a sound card (preferably a SoundBlaster or compatible) and speakers hooked up. Most multimedia kits accompanying CD-ROM drives include all the necessary hardware to hear sound clips. Often, PC users also need audio software to actually hear their files being played. You can find a handful of audio players on the CD-ROM included with this book. Macintosh users, on the other hand, have less work to do. Mac's multimedia capabilities are built in. ■

This section outlines the different types of audio file formats, and tells you where to find your own audio clips to add to your home page.

Explain Audio File Types and Formats

Throughout the WWW, you see a wide variety of audio clip file types and formats. These formats, representing the different methods used to electronically record the sounds into a computer, all have their own advantages and common uses.

Choosing from the different file types is like picking the right kind of film for your camera. You can use 35mm, disc, 110, or Polaroid instant film. Even though each film type works differently and requires a different type of camera, they all yield a similar result.

You need to be familiar with three audio formats. (See Table 10.1.)

Table 10.1 Common Audio File Formats	
Format	**Description**
AU	Developed by Sun, this file format, called mu-law, uses 8-bit sampling which makes the sounds crackle (like using a cordless phone), but does offer reasonably acceptable quality. Recently, an 11-bit version of the AU audio format has become more popular because it provides better quality. AU files tend to be small, compact, and easy to download. In addition, AU files work on all types of computers. This file type is the 35mm film of the audio world. It's international standard and works on just about every type of computer you can imagine. The software required to listen to .AU files is built into Netscape and Internet Explorer.

Format	Description
WAV	Microsoft Windows audio format. The .WAV extension is used for audio files created for use primarily under Microsoft Windows. While WAV files tend to be of higher quality than the AU format (and also significantly larger file size), there can be some problems with listening to WAV files on different types of computers. WAV files are ideal if you expect most visitors to your Web site to be using Windows. Nowadays though, WAV files are as popular as the AU format described above, and their use is ubiquitous. Netscape and IE both have built-in support for hearing WAV files.
AIFF	The Macintosh audio file format. Not very common on the Web, AIFF is also fully supported by most common browsers, so using them is a viable alternative.
MIDI	The MIDI sound format is popular because it works cross platform and stores sounds electronically without losing any quality. More Web sound files are being found in the MIDI format because of this versatility.
RA	RA is short for RealAudio (**http://www.realaudio.com**). RealAudio is the defining standard for streaming sound on the Internet. You can listen to a radio station sending its sounds as it broadcasts through RealAudio. RealAudio is usually only used for professional Web sites and those who can afford the money and skill for maintaining the special RealAudio software. You're more likely to use RealAudio than to embed these clips in your Web page.

Part
IV

Ch
10

The included CD-ROM comes with programs to let you record and listen to any of these three file types—preparing you for virtually anything you find on the Web.

One of the best is called CoolEdit. CoolEdit allows you to load a sound file in virtually any format and then convert it back and forth, depending on your needs. So, if you have a bunch of .WAV files you want to add to your Web page, consider using CoolEdit to convert them into mu-law, or .AU format first. You can download CoolEdit at **http://www.syntrillium.com/cool.htm**.

 TIP If you want to know more technical details about these audio-file formats (such as what 8-bit sampling really is), read the Audio File Format FAQ (Frequently Asked Questions) found on the WWW at **http:// www.cis.ohio-state.edu/hypertext/faq/usenet/audio-fmts/top.html**.

Where You Can Find Audio Clips

Now that you are familiar with the different types of audio clips, you probably want to add some to your Web page. Locating creative audio clips is not hard. Browse the WWW for audio clips that you like, or purchase the necessary equipment and digitize your own.

 On the CD-ROM Find literally hundreds of different digitized sounds and special effects that you can use immediately in your Web page on the CD-ROM included with this book. These audio files are meant to be used and played at your leisure, so have fun exploring them. Find animal sounds, special effects, and a variety of assorted treats for your ears.

Use Windows Explorer or File Manager to copy them to your own personal computer, or upload them to your Web site.

 Feel free to use the included AU and WAV audio clips in your home page however you like. You find a wide variety by clicking the Sound link from the main HTML page on the CD-ROM.

Finding Audio Clips on the Internet   The Internet is a fantastic resource for music and audio clips of all sorts. You can download everything from Jim Carrey ("Allllrighty then") to Martin Luther King Jr.'s "I Have a Dream" speech. The following is a diverse list of popular WWW sites where you can find, download, and listen to audio clips. These public archives allow anyone to download files:

■ **http://sunsite.unc.edu/pub/multimedia/sun-sounds/movies/**

This site has a fantastic set of movie sound clips from practically every movie you can remember. Some examples include snippets from: "Bladerunner," "Aliens," and "Raiders of the Lost Ark."

■ **http://www.dailywav.com/**

The Daily Wav Web Site. This site adds a new sound clip everyday and has many popular and contemporary sounds that may be useful on a Web page.

■ **http://Web.msu.edu/vincent/index.html**

Find famous people and speeches here. I found Martin Luther King Jr's "I Have a Dream" speech, among others, on this site.

■ **http://www.acm.uiuc.edu/rml/**

This is the most complete spot for digital audio and video clips that I could find. It contains links to hundreds of different multimedia sites around the Web—a great place to explore!

 When you click audio files at these sites, your browser automatically downloads them and plays them for you, without saving the file. Hold the shift button down when you click audio (and video) files to save them permanently to your hard drive. Once you save them, you can listen to them and add them to your own home page. Remember that only current Web Browsers support multimedia capabilities. Make sure you use Internet Explorer or Netscape Navigator 3.0 or better for full multimedia support.

CAUTION

Remember to keep copyright issues in mind when downloading these audio and video clips. Just because you found it on the Internet doesn't mean that all copyrights have been obtained to make them available. If you are dead set on using these clips on your Web page, it is best to obtain permission from the original creator first. Oftentimes companies will allow their likeness to be used for a fan club of a particular television show or series. For more information on how the copyright laws could affect you, see Appendix C, "Legal Issues with Web Sites."

Make Your Own Audio Clips   Finding neat audio clips on the WWW is fine for some people, but most of us want to have our own customized audio clips for our home page. Creating your own audio clips isn't too difficult or costly—it just requires a little bit of know-how.

Macintosh users have it easy. Today, Macs come complete with multimedia capabilities, their own microphones, and software. When you speak directly to your Macintosh, it records your speech, putting it on your home page within a few minutes. Make sure you save your audio file format in the AU or WAV file formats (instead of Mac's AIFF format). AU and WAV are the most popular formats on the WWW.

Don't fret if you are a PC owner. Practically anyone with a CD-ROM multimedia kit can create his or her personal audio files nearly as easily. Simply buy a cheap microphone (the Microsoft Sound System Kit comes with all the recording software and a microphone for under $50) to digitize your voice. For more advanced clips, connect your stereo directly into your sound card with a standard red/white cable.

> **CAUTION**
>
> Only record sounds that you own. If you like the new "U2" album, that's fine. However, digitizing it and making it available on your home page is illegal. Doing this gets you into legal hot water.

N O T E   This chapter just glosses over the process of recording your own audio clips. Make sure you consult your system and multimedia manuals to learn how to digitize sounds properly on your specific computer. If you have trouble digitizing in AU format, the sound programs included on the Web page CD convert practically any sound format into the AU format. ■

Adding Audio Clips to Your Web Page

Actually, obtaining the right clip is the hardest part to putting sound on your Web page. Once you have an audio clip in hand, you can easily add it to your home page. This section shows you several different popular methods for embedding audio clips directly into your Web page.

Each of these methods can be used interchangeably; they don't interfere with one another.

Adding Sounds via Hypertext Links

The first, and most common, way to add sounds to your Web page is by simply adding a link to the particular sound file. Simply use the same HTML tags used to insert a link into your page, `<A HREF=>` and `</A>` and you're all set.

On my home page, if I wanted to add an audio welcome to visitors who stop by, this is how I'd do it. My first step would be to digitize and record the greeting. For this example, I'll save a greeting called **WELCOME.WAV**. You can give your sound files any name you wish, but make sure that you add the appropriate file extension (WAV in this case) so browsers can recognize the file properly.

To add a link to this file on my home page, I typed in the following HTML:

```
<IMG SRC="images/sound.gif" ALIGN=LEFT>
<A HREF="audio/WELCOME.WAV">Listen to my greeting (130K) </A><BR CLEAR=LEFT>
```

The first line inserts a miniature sound icon telling visitors that the link next to it is an audio file (see Figure 10.3). The second line is an actual HTML link to the sound file. Clicking the HTML link to the sound file loads a separate audio player and plays the message; it does not display WELCOME.WAV in the browser.

FIG. 10.3
Now anyone can hear
my voice!

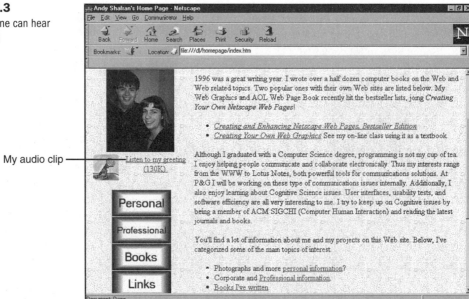

My audio clip

NOTE   Did you notice that the audio file size is placed in parentheses? This is done to allow Web
page visitors to estimate the time required to download the sound clip before clicking the
link. As a common courtesy, list the file size of every audio and video file that you add to your home
page. ■

Embedding Sound with Netscape

A recent phenomenon for multimedia Web developers is the `<EMBED>` tag which is used to incorporate audio and video clips into sites. Now, you can directly embed sound clips in your Web page, just as if they were text, or an image. When you embed a sound clip, your browser displays a set of audio controls, which lets you start and stop the sound clip at will, as well as rewind, and restart it.

This new method uses the HTML `<EMBED>` tag, which was designed especially for multimedia objects and files. This method is quickly becoming the most popular and efficient way to incorporate multimedia on most Web pages.

Here's how it works. You add the proper <EMBED> tag to your page. When a visitor stops by, your text and images are displayed first, then the browser starts downloading your sound file (or video clip, whichever is specified). Once the file is completely downloaded, sound controls appear and start playing the audio file—it's that easy!

Here's how I'm going to add the file LION.WAV (a lion roaring) to my Web page. The <EMBED> tag works similar to <IMG>. I've got to point to the embedded file by using the SRC keyword (see Figure 10.4):

```
<EMBED SRC="LION.WAV>
```

FIG. 10.4

The roaring lion is now embedded into my page.

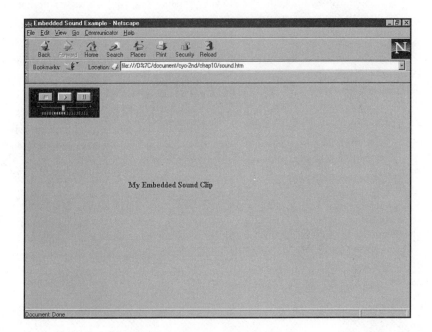

This tag embeds LION.WAV to my home page and assumes it is stored in the same directory as my page of HTML. However, when you add a clip to your Web page, you also need to specify the Height and Width of the Controls box which allows you to start, stop, and replay the sound clip. The default settings are HEIGHT=60 and WIDTH=140. So, now your HTML tag looks like this:

```
<EMBED SRC="LION.WAV" HEIGHT=60 WIDTH=140>
```

Additionally, there is one other keyword you can use when embedding audio clips into your Web page. By setting AUTOSTART=TRUE (the default is FALSE), your sound clip automatically plays as soon as Netscape downloads it. Otherwise, visitors must click the Play button in the controls box to hear your sound file. The following is my complete HTML for embedding the lion roar on my Web page:

```
<EMBED SRC="LION.WAV" HEIGHT=60 WIDTH=140 AUTOSTART=TRUE>
```

If you find yourself using the AUTOSTART keyword, you may be interested in the LOOP keyword as well. You can set LOOP=TRUE, LOOP=FALSE, or set LOOP equal to a positive number. This setting tells your browser whether it should automatically loop back and play the sound over and over again. By setting LOOP=TRUE, you set the sound to play over and over indefinitely, until the visitor goes to another page. LOOP=FALSE indicates that you want the sound clip to play only one time. You can also set LOOP to a number, like LOOP=5, which has the sound replayed for a total of five times.

One other keyword that may be useful when working with the <EMBED> tag is HIDDEN. By adding the HIDDEN=TRUE keyword to your <EMBED> tag, your browser automatically downloads and plays the specified sound, but no control panel appears. Your sound is now simply playing in the background for visitors, offering them no control over its duration.

```
<EMBED SRC="LION.WAV" HEIGHT=60 WIDTH=140 AUTOSTART=TRUE HIDDEN=TRUE>
```

Embedding Sounds with Internet Explorer

A unique feature to Internet Explorer is support for the <BGSOUND> tag. Using this tag, you can identify a default audio file that is downloaded and played automatically when a visitor stops by your Web page. You can add a welcome clip, a sound effect, or any type of audio experience you would like to incorporate as part of your Web page. Use the <BGSOUND> tag as follows:

```
<BGSOUND SRC="myaudio.wav">
```

When Internet Explorer stops by this Web page, it first loads all the text and images. Once finished, it starts downloading myaudio.wav (a windows sound clip) and plays it automatically on the visitor's machine. You can control how many times your sound is played by using the LOOP= keyword. By default, Internet Explorer plays a sound clip only once unless specified, as follows:

```
<BGSOUND SRC="myaudio.wav" LOOP=10>
```

Visitors to this Web site won't forget this sound clip: The preceding tag tells it to play 10 times.

 TIP If you want a sound clip to repeat endlessly, set LOOP=INFINITE instead of indicating a particular number.

CAUTION

Use this keyword sparingly. Visitors to your site may not want to hear long or inappropriate sounds. In fact, they may not want to hear anything at all. If you use this tag, keep it short.

Understanding and Using Video Clips

Adding audio clips to your Web page is just the first step to making your home page a true multimedia experience. The next step is embedding the video clips.

Video clips are combinations of moving pictures and sound, bundled up just like a movie. These video clips range from snippets of actual films to celebrity interviews. Although vast, this range is not nearly as large as the number of images and audio sounds available. Like adding audio clips to your Web page, video clips can be accessed via a hypertext link, or by directly embedding and playing them in your page.

Unfortunately, video clips have several drawbacks making them difficult to use. The main problem is file size. Video clips are gigantic, usually 1–2 megs in file size. Each video clip is a conglomeration of hundreds of images set to display one after another in rapid succession. Chapter 6, "Using Graphics to Excite Your Page," discussed image size. A one-minute video clip can have as many as 1,000 different image frames.

Downloading a 2-meg file, at the fastest speed your computer probably supports (28.8 baud) and in ideal conditions, still takes 10–20 minutes. Millions of WWW users use 14.4 or slower baud modems. For these users, the large file size often means they won't take the time to download a video clip. But, oftentimes they are worth the added trouble and value. Imagine visiting a movie's home page. You'd be disappointed if there wasn't a video clip or two of that blockbuster, regardless of the wait it takes to view.

Part
IV

Ch
10

N O T E Viewing video clips on your computer requires the correct hardware and software. This means having enough RAM (8 megs minimum) on a Windows-based computer to display the moving video images onscreen, plus a video viewing program (several of which are included on the home page CD). Again, Macintosh readers are luckier, because these video capabilities are built in. ■

Explaining Video File Types and Formats

You may run into several different types of video clips when browsing on the Web. Currently, none of these clips reign supreme as the default video standard, so you must decide which of the popular formats to use in your home page.

Primarily, there are three video file formats to be familiar with (see Table 10.2).

Table 10.2   Common Video File Formats

Format	Description
AVI	Similar to the .WAV audio style, this is Microsoft's Video for Windows file format. Windows users can use AVI video files easily, because AVI video files are optimized to be seen on a Windows computer. This video format is very popular and quickly becoming the video standard of choice because it is efficient and easy to create. Windows users will find this video format the most flexible and widely accepted.

continues

Table 10.2   Continued

Format	Description
VIVO	Also known as *compressed AVI* format, the VIVO video format significantly compresses the size of your video clips, drastically reducing the amount of download time required to view the clips. Unfortunately, they can't be seen automatically within a Web browser and need a special piece of software to view as part of a Web page. Visit **http://www.vivo.com** for more information on this exciting and useful video format.
QT	QT, or Quicktime, is the video format developed and licensed by Apple Computer (**http://www.quicktime.apple.com**). Taking the WWW by storm, most new video clips are released in Quicktime format because it is multiplatform, compact file size, and easier to record with. Personally, I suggest sticking with either the Quicktime or the AVI formats. Most home video cameras will save in Quicktime format directly onto your PC, making it another widely accepted standard. The Quicktime format also seems to be more efficient than the standard .WAV format.
MPEG	One of the oldest video formats around, MPEG is similar to the JPEG image file format, but optimized strictly for videos. The MPEG format is popular because video clips in this format tend to be of decent quality. Unfortunately, the MPEG format is hardware-intensive. It takes a lot of RAM and special hardware to create the MPEG format. You must buy a special piece of equipment used to encode videos, and make sure you have at least 16 megs of RAM. Although you'll see MPEG files around still, they are quickly becoming a rare find for multimedia users.

The Web page CD comes with programs letting you watch virtually any type of video or animation clip found on the Web.

TIP

If you want to know more technical details about these video formats, try the following links:

MPEG–**http://www.cis.ohio-state.edu/hypertext/faq/usenet/mpeg-faq/top.html**

QT–**http://www.cast.uni-linz.ac.at/st/staff/rm/QTquickcam/**

AVI–**http://www.microsoft.com**

Where You Can Find Video Clips

The same obstacles that were presented with creating, finding, and adding audio to your Web page comes back two-fold for video clips. Finding high-quality and useful video clips to add to your home page can be an extremely difficult task.

On the CD-ROM   Included on the CD-ROM, you find several different collections of digitized movies and sample video clips in QT and AVI format. Take a look at how they work to get an idea of what kind of video clips you can use in your Web page.

Although several collections of video clips are on the CD-ROM, the most impressive included here is a set of video clips (around 100 megs in all) from Four Palms software (**http://www.fourpalms.com**) (see Figure 10.5). Four Palms distributes stock video clips, offering over 10 different CD-ROM titles full of video clips. See a fantastic sample of its best on the CD with this book. Enjoy!

FIG. 10.5
Four Palms is a premier video clip provider.

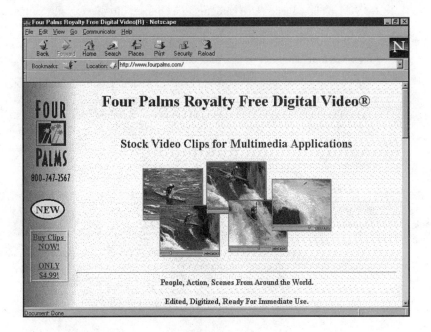

Finding Video Clips on the Internet   There are several different WWW sites that have large collections of MPEG and QT movies. Downloading all of them could take several weeks, but it's not a bad idea to stop by and pick up a few neat movie clips.

Here's a partial list of some hot spots to find good MPEG and QT files on the Web.

■ **http://members.aol.com/videolinks/index.html**

   Find a current collection of movies in several different categories here. These video clips range from episode shots of "Seinfeld" to popular commercials and trailers (quite a variety).

■ **http://film.softcenter.se/flics/**

   This is the most complete spot for digital video clips (Quicktime) that I could find. With over 1,300 clips available, this is the one-stop clearinghouse for video sites on the WWW.

■ **http://deathstar.rutgers.edu/people/bochkay/movies.html**

   An ever growing variety of Quicktime movies. You find different video clips that contain Kathy Ireland, Barney the Dinosaur, and "Star Trek" here.

Make Your Own Video Clips from Scratch   Just a year or two ago, if you wanted to make your own video clips and put them on your home page, I would have advised against it. At that point, the equipment required to digitize and store video in electronic format was far too expensive and difficult to use.

Today, it's a different story. You have several affordable low-cost alternatives to creating your own video clips. Basic video cameras that connect directly to your computer come with hardware and software for under $200. In addition, you can make video clips from VCR tapes you already have. For about the same price range, you can purchase a digital converter enabling your VCR and computer to talk to each other.

Stop by your local computer store to learn more about your digitizing options. One stop that you won't want to miss is the Connectix QuickCam. For $100, Mac and Windows users can buy grayscale video cameras that take still images and full motion video clips. These clips are digitized and saved automatically—ready for immediate use on your Web page. For around $199, you can also buy a color version of the bestselling Quickcam. Stop by **http://www.connectix. com** (see Figure 10.6) for more info.

FIG. 10.6

The QuickCam is the pioneer in personal PC video cameras.

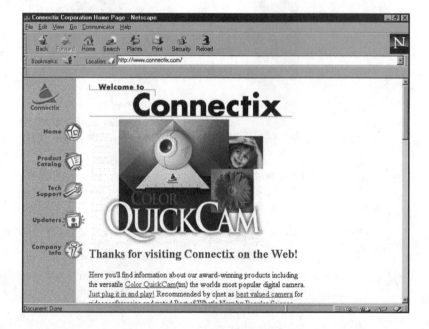

Another excellent low-cost camera is the WinCam. For around $200, you can order a color Wincam that looks much like an old Polaroid camera. It comes with a tripod and slide holder, as well as all the software you need. You can learn more about the Wincam at **http://www. wincam.com**.

Adding Video Clips to Your Home Page

Video clips are just as easy to add to your Web page as an audio clip and follow the same format. Like audio clips, you have a couple of different options and ways to add clips to your Web page.

One method is to add a hypertext link to the specific video file, while the other displays the video clip as part of the actual Web page. This section covers both popular methods.

Adding Video Clips via Hypertext Links

To add a link to a video clip, use the same tag, but specify the video's file name instead.

In addition to my audio greeting, I have also digitized a personal video welcoming visitors to my home page. After several takes practicing to be Steven Spielberg, I finally created a decent video clip and named the file WELCOME.AVI. Then I added a link to it in my home page with the following HTML:

```
<IMG SRC="images/video.gif">
<A HREF="video/WELCOME.AVI>A video welcome to my home page
(1.3 Meg) </A>
```

The first line inserts a miniature video icon telling visitors that the link next to it is a video clip. The second line is an actual HTML link to my video clip. A user clicks the HTML link, downloads the AVI video clip, loads a video player for his or her computer, and then watches the clip automatically. Figure 10.7 shows my video clip as part of the Web page.

FIG. 10.7
With a little more
practice, it's Hollywood.

My video clip link —

Part
IV

Ch
10

Embedding Video with Netscape

Similar to the new innovations for sound clips, you can also directly embed video movies as part of your Web page. Currently, the <EMBED> tag only supports movies in the AVI format.

When using this tag, your browser first displays the regular Web page, then downloads the complete video clip. Once the clip has been downloaded, it appears as an actual part of your Web page—it's pretty amazing! You can control the height and width of the video clip and whether it starts automatically. You can also display a set of controls which lets visitors pause and play the clip at their leisure.

This method also uses the HTML <EMBED> tag in the same way audio clips did. Specify the AVI file with the SRC= keyword. Additionally, you can indicate the HEIGHT and WIDTH the video clip should appear in pixel coordinates. This example embeds SPOR0061.AVI, a Four Palms video clip included on the CD-ROM:

```
<EMBED SRC="SPOR0061.AVI" HEIGHT=240 WIDTH=300>
```

This tag embeds SPOR006L.AVI to my home page and assumes it is stored in the same directory as my page of HTML. Figure 10.8 shows how this clip looks in a Web page.

FIG. 10.8

Here's a swimmer in action.

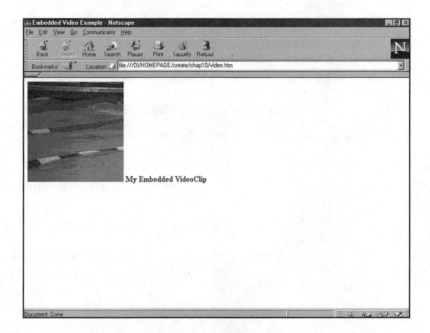

Additionally, there are a few other keywords you can add to control how your video clip works on the page. You can add AUTOSTART=YES to start playing the video clip immediately once it is downloaded.

Similarly, you can also add LOOP=YES which indicates whether the browser should keep repeating the video clip over and over until you link to another page. With these two keywords, your final HTML looks like this:

```
<EMBED SRC="SPOR0061.AVI" HEIGHT=240 WIDTH=300 AUTOSTART=YES LOOP=YES>
```

> **N O T E**   To pause your video clip while playing, click your mouse anywhere on top of it. To restart it, click again. ■

Embedding Video with IE

The most significant Microsoft multimedia extension enables you to directly embed video clips into your Web page. Using the <IMG> tag, you can tell Internet Explorer to display a video (in Microsoft .AVI format) instead of a standard image.

To add a video image to your Web page, use the DYNSRC keyword (short for *Dynamic Source*) in the <IMG> tag, as follows:

```
<IMG SRC="andy.gif" DYNSRC="andy.avi">
```

Internet Explorer first downloads andy.gif to be displayed on your Web page. Once all of the images and text have been downloaded, it starts downloading the animation file named andy.avi and plays it automatically in the same location where the original image was loaded. Pretty amazing, huh?

Don't worry about Netscape users. They'll only see the image pointed at by the SRC keyword; DYNSRC will be ignored.

Two other keywords that may come in handy are CONTROLS and LOOP. CONTROLS adds video playback controls to the bottom of the animation, as shown in the following tag:

```
<IMG SRC="andy.gif" DYNSRC="andy.avi" CONTROLS>
```

Additionally, you can set the number of times that the animation is to repeat by using LOOP (just like the background sound tag). By default, your animation will play one time.

Mixing Multimedia

One new aspect that desktop publishers haven't had to deal with is incorporating true multimedia in a single experience. In your Web pages, you can have text, images, sound clips, and video clips all being displayed (and heard) at the same time.

Working with multimedia is a new and difficult task to master. When you add a video clip to your Web page, you want to make sure it doesn't interfere with any audio plug-ins or background sounds. Here's a simple recipe that you should always follow when building a multimedia-enabled Web page:

1. Plan what the final "experience" should be like. Decide whether the sound, images, and video clips really go with one another. Consider the effect of the colors and styles of all of the images, sound, and video clips. Remember that you can change the color and appearance of any text as well.

Part

IV

Ch

10

2. Add all the text to your Web page. Format and colorize it properly. When using background colors and images, make sure that text is readable.

3. Add images next. Decide where to place the images, what size they should be, and make sure they are a reasonable file size to download so visitors don't wait forever to see your Web page.

4. Now add sound. Sound is easier to work with than video and animation because it's one-dimensional. Video clips often have their own soundtracks. If you use a background sound, make sure it's not too loud. Ensure that the sound clip you pick fits with the style of your Web page—for instance, don't add the Overture of 1812 to a Web page dedicated to Metallica.

5. Mix in video and animation. Often, you won't have audio clips on the same page with video clips and animations because they can interfere with one another. Check the performance of your video/animation clip to make sure it downloads quickly.

CHAPTER 11

Important Design Considerations

Now that you know all the basic mechanics behind building a Web page, this next section talks about slightly different topics. You'll learn how to shape and mold your Web page into a world-class and well-designed one. This section teaches you how to put the final touches on your home page before you make it available for millions of WWW surfers to see.

So far, I've mentioned many different tips and tricks for creating a high-quality Web page. Whether it's organizing your text with lists and tables, or linking your images properly, you've learned how important it is to properly present information on your Web page.

This chapter helps you put all those tips together. I introduce several different design concepts and show you how they make your home page look better and easier to take care of. If your Web page is the canvas, this chapter is the paint brush that you will use to create a masterpiece of a home page. ■

Make sure your Web page has a consistent look

Learn how important consistency is when making your pages and how you can practice those simple rules.

Keep your Web-page visitors coming back

All good Web pages need to know how to get visitors to keep coming back by piquing their interest and curiosity.

Make your HTML file easy to read and maintain

You'll want to use tabs and returns to make your underlying HTML code readable and understandable for future use.

Add comments to your HTML file

Add important HTML tags that let you leave messages for yourself when reading through the code that makes up your Web page.

Validate your Web page with an automated HTML checker

Ensure that your pages follow strict HTML standards by running them through a free online HTML validator.

Home Page Design Tips

As you've learned in this book, you can create a Web page in just a matter of minutes. Although creating a basic Web page isn't too difficult, you should keep several things in mind when designing the appearance of your Web page. In this section, I'll go over a couple of popular (but simple) design tips that will help your Web page look great!

Measure Your Page's Consistency

All telephones work the same. You pick up the receiver and dial the person you want to reach. When you finish, you hang up the receiver to stop your conversation. Sure, some phones require dialing a special number (like 9) to work, and other phones hide buttons in hard-to-find spots, but all phones generally work the same. This consistency lets you know how to use a phone worldwide.

Visitors to your Web site will appreciate that same type of consistency on your Web pages. All your Web pages should have a consistent style. Soon, your visitors will find that information on your Web pages without even looking.

Some examples of consistency are:

- Using the same headline format on every Web page. If you use the <H1> tag to label your home page, then you should use an <H1> tag to label every page in your site. Using different sized headlines on different pages looks odd, particularly when browsing from page to page.

- Add graphics and images in similar ways throughout your home page. If some of your graphics link to other Web sites, and others don't, visitors might not recognize which graphics are which and could get confused.

- Include the same information in the page's footer. At the bottom of every Web page you include important information about when it was created and who to contact for further information. Add this same default footer to every page in your site.

- Use the same background pattern and text colors. If you use background graphics or colors, and change the color of text on your pages, make sure you keep them consistent throughout the whole site. Visitors eyes adjust to reading colored text on a background and have to readjust every time you change the consistent look and feel of your site.

Brevity Is a Virtue

Some people like to compare the World Wide Web to a book that people can read and jump around from page to page. I prefer to liken the WWW to a glossy magazine—where people flip through the pages randomly. Every now and then a story or headline might catch their eye, but for the most part, pages are being flipped about as fast as their hand can move. With a short reader attention span, magazines have to present their information in a short and usable nature.

With this in mind, it's a good idea to keep your Web page concise and to the point. Using a mouse, people browse through Web pages quickly. If something looks long and boring to read, they keep going until they see something that catches their eye. Think of your own browsing techniques. It's easy to run out of patience when browsing the WWW. If there is too much information, or something doesn't jump out and grab you, you're more likely to jump to another page before slowly reading and digesting several paragraphs of text. Figure 11.1 shows you what a home page looks like when it has too much text on it.

FIG. 11.1
Nobody will bother reading this; it's boring and long winded.

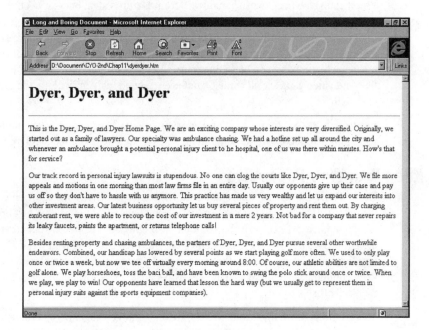

If you really have a lot of information to put on your Web page, consider splitting the information up onto several different pages (see Chapter 9, "Customizing Your Web Page"), letting a visitor link to the various pieces he or she wants to read. This protects your Web page visitor from information overload.

To keep readers interested, and my home page brief, I use a simple rule of thumb that I call the *three-by-three rule*. Basically, the *three-by-three rule* tells me not to ever place more than three paragraphs (each with three sentences) together on a home page. After three paragraphs, readers become bored and move on. Instead, I use lists and tables to bring out important information and catch visitors' eyes.

TIP Also keep in mind that every person that visits your Web page must download everything that's on it (including all the text and pictures) before reading it. The smaller your page, the less people have to wait, twiddling their thumbs, for your Web page to download. Remember that text downloads much faster than images. An entire page of text can download faster than a single image.

Part
V

Ch
11

Don't Overdo Your Web Page with Glitz

Along the same lines, don't let your Web page get out of hand with too much glamour and glitz. Everyone knows that you can add lots of pictures, sound clips, and clickable image maps to your home page, just don't overuse these neat and impressive aspects of HTML—otherwise, your site could look like a bad parody of Times Square in New York (a lot of hype but nothing substantial).

When your Web page uses so many different features all at once, it becomes difficult to read and hard to even look at. Don't try to add every neat HTML feature and trick you can think of to the same page. Although it's an impressive display of WWW knowledge and ability, it'll be gaudy to look at and impossible to understand. Keep in mind that this rule is even doubly important when mixing and matching more than images and graphics. Tables, counters, audio files and video clips are all fantastic but are tremendously difficult to add to Web pages without overdoing it.

In Chapter 10, "Making Your Web Page Multimedia," I provide several important tips and techniques for incorporating multimedia files alongside text, links, and graphics.

Keep Your Web Page Alive

Every Thursday night, a new episode of *ER* comes on. Every week, when you turn the TV on, you know that you aren't going to see the same episode you watched last time because that would be boring. Except for the summer, new episodes are weekly occurrences. Can you imagine if there was only one episode, and NBC played it over and over again? You'd watch it the first time, and maybe see the rerun once, but after that, you'd switch channels. The reason you keep coming back Thursday at 10 p.m. is because you know you'll see something new (and medically thrilling).

You should practice this same philosophy on your Web page. If you create a basic page and never update it or make changes, why would anyone come back? After one or two stops, they've seen everything there is to see on your Web page and will start visiting other WWW spots instead.

The key to getting visitors to come back again and again is to constantly update it to keep information fresh and new. One great example of a constantly updating site is the Weather Channel's home page (**http://www.weather.com**), as shown in Figure 11.2. Every time you visit, you can get current weather maps and information.

Once you build a basic Web page, keeping it fresh, new, and exciting is difficult; but the effort is well worth the trouble. For example, lawyers might keep a list of links relating to landmark precedents and decisions of interest to their clients. Accountants might note recent tax changes, offering regular tips on how to prepare for April 15th. If you think that your Web site needs infrequent updating, think again!

Figure 11.3 shows one zany example of a fantastic Web site—The Cologne Answer Guy (**http://www.cologneguy.com/**). The reason it is a good Web site is because the author clearly spends a lot of time always keeping the latest and greatest information online.

For example, you can stop by weekly and see what the most popular cologne is, where the latest smells are coming from, or read a timely review of the latest colognes and fragrances.

FIG. 11.2

Can you imagine if this page was never updated?

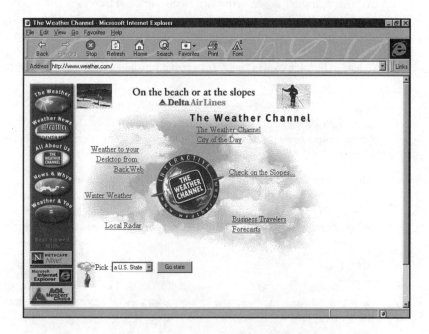

Part

V

Ch

11

FIG. 11.3

The Cologne Answer Guy's Web page keeps you coming back for another whiff.

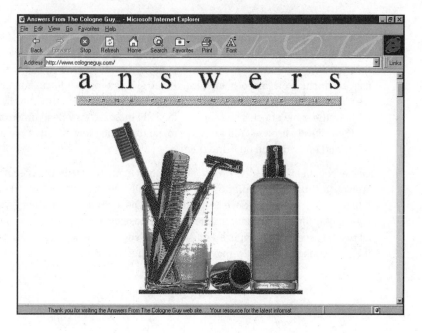

Be Aware of Creeping Featurism

Creeping featurism is one of the largest dangers that face Web developers and WWW pages. Creeping featurism is when you slowly add new and innovative features to your Web pages— one at a time (they creep into your Web pages) until eventually your Web page is full of gimmicks and features that don't look or work well together. The overall effect is that, while your Web page becomes full of "neat" features, it no longer is fun to visit, easy to use, or informative for visitors.

Because the Web is so exciting and has literally endless possibilities for Web pages, Web developers often fall into the trap of including *every* new innovation on their Web pages. Don't try to demonstrate a large reservoir of HTML knowledge but spend little effort creating a good site design.

You'll see the creeping featurism phenomenon pop up all over the Web—particularly in sites that use video and audio clips integrated into Web pages. Many times, people are impressed with how easy it is to add multimedia to Web pages, and all their carefully laid plans for a good Web page are ignored when they get the opportunity to add a "neat" new feature.

> **CAUTION**
>
> I'm not saying you should not take advantage of any or all of these new HTML enhancements; it's just important that you keep an aesthetic perspective when building them into your Web pages. Use them, but use them carefully.

Be aware that creeping featurism isn't necessarily a bad idea, as long as you take into account the new changes. For example, splitting your home page into several different pages which use multimedia clips and many graphics can be good—and bad. If you redesign your site into multiple pages, you could end up with a nice effect—a well-organized and easily-navigated Web page. Unfortunately, a poorly integrated Web site can make information difficult to find and what used to be an effective home page impossible to use. Multimedia clips and multiple graphics have the same effect. They can significantly increase download times and make Web pages painfully slow to browse. You just have to control which new features creep into your Web pages and how you end up using them.

One excellent example of a WWW site that had many new features creep in is the Walt Disney Web page (**http://www.disney.com**). Originally, this site was designed to offer visitors a peek into the world of Disney. Several months ago, Disney redesigned their entire site to take advantage of new multimedia enhancements made possible with the latest Web browsers. The overall result is spectacular. Figure 11.4 shows the current Disney home page—but who knows, by the time you read this, they may have redesigned yet again.

FIG. 11.4
You'll find just about every type of WWW feature imaginable here in the Magic Kingdom—and all used well.

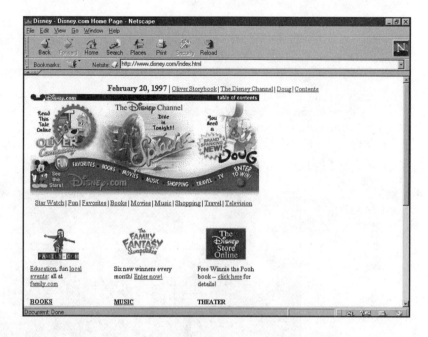

N O T E On a personal level, I get asked all the time why my own home page doesn't have spectacular animations, graphics that cover the entire rainbow of colors, multiple image maps, and other advanced features. The reason is that it is very, very difficult to build all of those features into a single Web page or Web site.

The goal of my page is to let people know who I am and provide them ample resources when they stop by after reading a book—not to impress people with my knowledge about the use of advanced HTML. I choose to limit the features that are placed in my Web page for simplicity reasons.

On top of that, creating a good Web site that has multimedia, image maps, tables, and graphics that truly work well together takes a lot of time and effort. ■

Don't Hide Links and Features

Another common sense strategy to follow is to make sure that your advanced features aren't difficult for visitors to find in your Web page. What's the point of building cool plug-in examples, interactive image maps, and advanced JavaScript applets if no one even knows they exist?

Image maps are particularly bad about hiding links to other Web pages because they aren't delineated well enough to describe what all the links actually are (see Chapter 8, "Image Map Education" for more information). The Warner Brothers home page—**http://www. warnerbros.com**—is a good example of this situation (see Figure 11.5). It's pretty easy to figure out where you visit if you click the shield labeled DC Comics; but did you know that if you click the Tazmanian Devil at the top of the building in the top-right corner of the image that you link to a spot that lets you send virtual greeting cards to people via the Internet? No? That's because it is a poorly laid out image map. If you look carefully in the bottom-left corner of the screen, you see a small icon that is labeled "Web Cards" and has Taz as the model.

Now you can put two and two together. Clicking the Taz in the icon is the same as clicking the Taz above the bulletin board. This is called a *hidden link*, one that is not intuitively obvious before being clicked. Some sites like to hide features and functionality like this, but in general it's not a good idea. Image maps are only useful if you know what Web page you are going to visit *before* you click an area in the picture.

FIG. 11.5
Although it's a great Web site, the image map makes it difficult to find all the possible links available.

Taz brings you Web cards

So does this icon

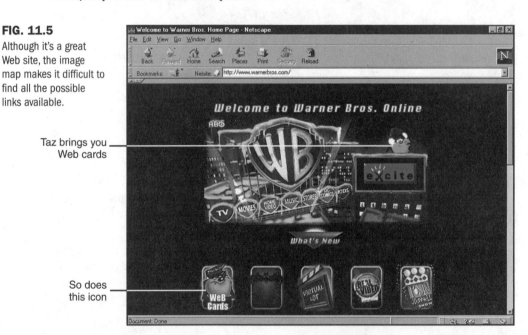

To get around this problem, many Web sites list each possible link beneath the clickable image map. This ensures that visitors won't miss out on one particular section of the image map that may not appear clickable. Warner Brothers follows this philosophy—to a point. At the bottom of their home page is a listing of all the main sites accessible from the image map (see Figure 11.6). You can almost match up the items listed with the various sections of the image map.

It's also important to make sure all of your textual links are easy to spot. Usually you want to link an entire word or phrase instead of a single character or number. Some people don't like hypertext links to appear all over their Web pages, so they link a single character, or the period of a sentence instead of an appropriate word. This is a bad idea and defeats the purpose of linking various Web pages together.

FIG. 11.6
Warner Brothers tries
to list all the links
available from the
image map.

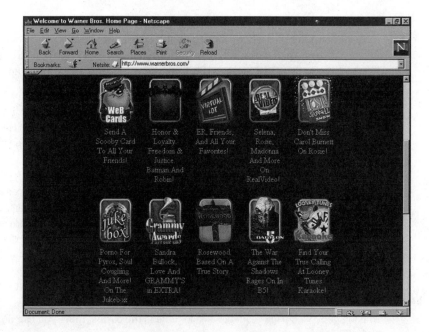

Explore Other Sites—Borrow Design Concepts

Although I try to point out many important design concepts, you will invariably find Web pages that you do—and don't—like on the WWW. One of the best parts about the WWW is that you can completely view the source code for all pages available with the View, Document Source command from your browser.

Whenever you are surfing the Web and exploring new sites, you should always make it a priority to keep your eyes open for new and innovative design and layout ideas for your Web pages. Feel free to borrow concepts from other sites on the WWW. The only way to learn and improve your Web site is through experience.

▶ **See** Appendix D (on the CD-ROM), "Legal Issues with Web Pages," for information on important laws concerning borrowing other site designs and concepts.

Improving Your HTML Code

One of the most common problems that I notice with Web pages are not even noticed by most people. I'm referring to how the HTML text (called source files) appears when you look at it as a straight text document. Since browsers like Netscape and Internet Explorer read HTML tags and formats based on tags, you usually never even see the underlying HTML file unless you've created it or are trying to see the HTML associated with a particular page.

While, technically, it doesn't matter what your HTML source file looks like, you'll find that it makes a big difference when you try updating and making changes to your Web page in the future. It doesn't take much time, or effort, to structure your HTML source file properly. You won't immediately reap many benefits from these few suggested improvements, but you'll be glad you did for future updates.

In six months, you may not remember why you used a table instead of a list to display your personal information, or spend six hours trying to decipher your cryptic HTML tags. That's why you should add comments to your home page. Comments never appear in a browser, they only show up when you are reading your home page as a text file.

N O T E In the world of computer programmers, these guidelines are strictly enforced as coding standards. That's because different people often work on the same program. So, everyone has to follow the same formatting standards, to make sure their work is readable. While no one else may be looking over your shoulder and grading your home page, following these guidelines is a must for formatting your HTML source code. ■

Make It Readable

Making your Web page readable as a text file is the easiest thing you can do with your Web page. There are only two exceptions to this general rule: tabs and returns. Returns and tabs do not affect layout of the Web page, but tags do. Web browsers ignore any and all tabs or returns. Therefore, you must separate paragraphs of text, make links easy to read, and align related information, such as lists and tables.

Take a look at Figures 11.7 and 11.8. Both of them look exactly the same when displayed through the eyes of Netscape (they are a version of my own home page). In Figure 11.7, the text is a confused, jumbled mess of text that is practically impossible to read. Just a simple use of tabs, returns, and spaces (shown in Figure 11.8) cleans up that mess. Which would you rather work with?

Your goal is to make your HTML code listing as readable as possible. Don't be afraid to use the tab or spacebar to align items or to separate paragraphs of text by hitting the enter key.

T I P   One popular way of formatting your source code is typing your HTML tags in all CAPS. This makes the tags distinctive and easier to notice when quickly scanning a document. Browsers aren't case sensitive, and don't care whether your <HMTL> tag looks like <html>, <Html>, or <hTmL>.

FIG. 11.7
HTML formatted like this is NOT fun, nor easy to work with.

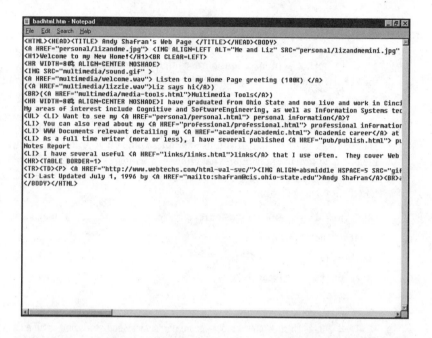

```
badhtml.htm - Notepad
File   Edit   Search   Help
<HTML><HEAD><TITLE> Andy Shafran's Web Page </TITLE></HEAD><BODY>
<A HREF="personal/lizandme.jpg"> <IMG ALIGN=LEFT ALT="Me and Liz" SRC="personal/lizandmemini.jpg"
<H1>Welcome to my New Home!</H1><BR CLEAR=LEFT>
<HR WIDTH=80% ALIGN=CENTER NOSHADE>
<IMG SRC="multimedia/sound.gif" >
<A HREF="multimedia/welcome.wav"> Listen to my Home Page greeting (100K) </A>
(<A HREF="multimedia/lizzie.wav">Liz says hi</A>)
<BR>(<A HREF="multimedia/media-tools.html">Multimedia Tools</A>)
<HR WIDTH=80% ALIGN=CENTER NOSHADE>I have graduated from Ohio State and now live and work in Cinci
My areas of interest include Cognitive and SoftwareEngineering, as well as Information Systems tec
<UL> <LI> Want to see my <A HREF="personal/personal.html"> personal information</A>?
<LI> You can also read about my <A HREF="professional/professional.html"> professional informatio
<LI> WWW Documents relevant detailing my <A HREF="academic/academic.html"> Academic career</A> at
<LI> As a full time writer (more or less), I have several published <A HREF="pub/publish.html"> pu
Notes Report
<LI> I have several useful <A HREF="links/links.html">links</A> that I use often.  They cover Web
<HR><TABLE BORDER=1>
<TR><TD><P> <A HREF="http://www.webtechs.com/html-val-svc/"><IMG ALIGN=absmiddle HSPACE=5 SRC="gif
<I> Last Updated July 1, 1996 by <A HREF="mailto:shafran@cis.ohio-state.edu">Andy Shafran</A><BR>
</BODY></HTML>
```

FIG. 11.8
Try formatting your home page's HTML like this. It's much easier to take care of.

```
goodhtml.htm - Notepad
File   Edit   Search   Help
<HTML>
<HEAD>
<TITLE> Andy Shafran's Web Page </TITLE>
</HEAD>
<BODY>

<A HREF="lizandme.jpg"> <IMG ALIGN=LEFT ALT="Me and Liz" SRC="lizandmemini.jpg" HSPACE=25></A>

<H1>Welcome to my New Home!</H1>

<BR CLEAR=LEFT>
<HR WIDTH=80% ALIGN=CENTER NOSHADE>

I have graduated from Ohio State and now live and work in Cincinnati, OH.
My areas of interest include Cognitive and Software
Engineering, as well as Information Systems technology. <P>

<UL>
   <LI> Want to see my <A HREF="personal/personal.html">
        personal information</A>?
   <LI> You can also read about my <A HREF="professional/professional.html">
        professional information</A>.
   <LI> WWW Documents relevant detailing my <A HREF="academic/academic.html">
        Academic career</A> at Ohio State
   <LI> As a full time writer (more or less), I have several published
        <A HREF="pub/publish.html"> publications</A> for Que and The
        Notes Report
   <LI> I have several useful <A HREF="links/links.html">links</A> that I use
        often.  They cover Web page creation, Broadway Musicals, and much more
</UL>


<HR>
<TABLE BORDER=1>

<TR>
```

Part
V

Ch
11

Comment Your HTML

Another popular way to enhance your HTML source code is adding comments. Comments are specially marked sentences and phrases that never appear inside a Web page, but are part of the HTML source code. In your HTML source code, comments are surrounded by <!-- and -->.

```
<!-- Here's a sample comment -->
```

Comments are particularly useful to record your thoughts or to explain complicated pieces of HTML code. For example, if you use an image map on your home page, you might want to include a comment explaining what choices the image map offers. Since you may not have the image handy when updating your source code later, this is useful information to have available. See the following example:

```
<!-- This image map lets people choose their different blocks.

Coyote Block > coyote.htm

Block Heads > blckhead.htm

Block Buster > buster.htm

-->
```

N O T E Although current Web browsers are particularly good at reading comments in your source file, sometimes older versions have trouble recognizing comments. If you want to ensure that your HTML source file is browser-proof, follow these rules when commenting your source code.

1. Don't use -- inside of your comment; the browser may be fooled and it may consider that the comment is complete.

2. Place "<!--" and "-->" comments at the beginning and end of every line. Some browsers don't recognize comments spanning multiple lines. (Why? I don't know.)

3. Don't use other HTML tags inside of comments. Doing this may cause other browsers to ignore the comment tags entirely. ■

CAUTION

Make sure you don't include private information in your home page comments because they can be read by anybody who visits your home page. Using the View, Document Source command, comments appear along with the rest of the source code. Passwords, personal phone numbers, and inappropriate language and remarks are examples of bad comment information.

Test Your Web Page

In college, before you submitted a term paper, you always gave it one final run-through and look-see. You'd break out the spell checker, and give it to friends to read before submitting it to your professor. Even though you spent a lot of time creating the perfect term paper, you almost invariably found small errors and silly mistakes that could cost you credit.

Can your Web page make the grade? Before you put your Web page on the WWW, announcing it to millions of visitors (see the next chapter), take a critical look at your home page. With a fine-toothed comb, check for common, easily preventable errors. This next section shows how to check your home page for common mistakes, and validate it according to HTML standards.

Preview Your Page

You can preview your HTML document anytime you wish. Simply load your HTML file into your favorite browser and see what it looks like.

Examine your Web page thoroughly. Here's a list of simple, but important, things to check when looking at your home page, plus tips on how to fix any possible problems you might find. You'll find a more complete list of last-minutes checks and hints in Appendix A, "Home Page Final Checklist."

Part
V

Ch
11

■ **Make sure your paragraphs are split properly.**

A common mistake is forgetting the <P> tag between paragraphs. Without this tag, your paragraphs of text bunch together, no matter how they appear in your HTML file. If your paragraphs are too far apart using the <P> tag, try using the <BR> tag. This tag adds no extra space between paragraphs.

■ **Ensure that images appear in the proper place.**

When you start adding images to your Web pages, it is easy to use the wrong keywords (accidentally aligning an image on the right side of the screen instead of the left). Make sure your image is properly placed and sized on your Web page and that text flows around the image correctly.

■ **Make sure all of your HTML tags are closed.**

A very common problem with home pages is forgetting a tag or not closing a tag properly. The home page shown in Figure 11.9 shows an omitted / to the </H1> closing tag at the top of the page. Oops, that one little mistake makes quite a difference. Web browsers try to help you identify problems like this by making erroneous and missing tags blink and stand out if you choose View, Document Source from the menu bar.

FIG. 11.9

This page is not for people who have bad eyesight, it's just a simple typo.

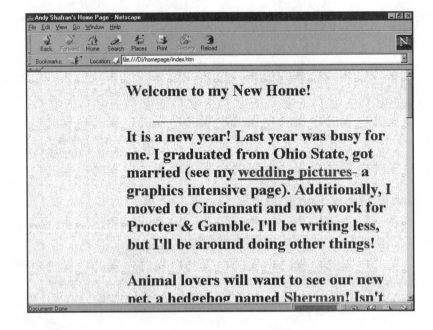

■ **Ensure all of your links work correctly.**

If you include HyperText links on your Web page, make sure they work correctly; otherwise, visitors see a screen that looks like Figure 11.10. Mistyping URLs is not only a common mistake, it is an easily avoided one. Several tools exist to check all of the links included in your Web page automatically. Try using the WebMapper, the program I talked about in Chapter 9, "Customizing Your Web Page," to check for broken links.

FIG. 11.10

Web Surfers hate to see this screen—it means a link has been broken.

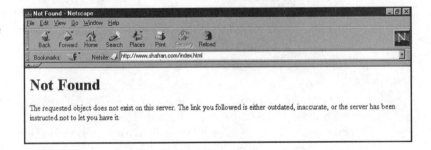

■ **Spell check your page.**

Spell checking your page is probably one of the easiest and most effective ways of improving your page's appearance. Misspelled words signify that you didn't take the necessary time to check out your page. If you purchase a professional caliber HTML editor, you'll likely get a spell checker along with it. Personally, I just copy and paste text from my HTML file into Microsoft Word and then run the Word Spell Checker from there. It is cost effective that way if you already own Word.

Use Another Browser

Although this book is geared to optimize your home page for visitors by using any browser, you'll likely only use one, either Netscape or Internet Explorer. Your visitors will stop by using all sorts of browsers and all sorts of versions. It is a good idea to check out your home page by using multiple browsers. Your Web page may look fantastic in Netscape, but it may be nearly impossible to read in Internet Explorer. Your goal is readability by any WWW user.

You may not want to take advantage of some of IE's advanced multimedia features that aren't supported by Netscape, and you want to know what visitors will see when stopping by. I recommend downloading current versions of both the Netscape and Microsoft Web browsers and ensuring that your pages are usable and readable in both.

TIP Older browsers typically don't support all of the new HTML extensions. They may display items such as tables in a jumbled fashion. For example, older versions of Netscape don't support all of the text underline and color features while Internet Explorer didn't support tables until version 2.0. Make sure you are always using the newest version of a WWW browser for this reason.

Part
V

Ch
11

Test and Validate Your HTML Document

After you run through your HTML code with the earlier checklist, you might think your Web page is spotless and in ship-shape condition. However, it's also worth your time to run an HTML Validation Tool over your Web pages. These validation tools look at your HTML source code and evaluate it according to the official definition of HTML usage. Since HTML is a world-wide standard, there is a very strict definition of how it is used. This definition is called a DTD (Document Type Definition)—it's the *Webster's Dictionary* of the HTML world. Find the official HTML standards for version 3.2 at:

http://www.w3.org/pub/WWW/MarkUp/Wilbur/

Validation tools do not consider the appearance of your Web page, the number of included links or graphics, or if the paragraphs of information are sensible. Validation tools only consider the proper use of HTML tags. Your eyes are the best tools to judge how your page *looks*. Validation tools are the best tools to judge how your page *works*.

HTML validation tools are important because they ensure that browsers and cool future WWW enhancements can read your home page.

For example, most browsers will interpret your HTML to the best of their ability. So, if you forgot to add the <HTML> and </HTML> tags to your Web page, it recognizes other HTML tell-tale signs and displays your document properly. A validation tool would recognize that you forgot the <HTML> tags and gives you a reminder that your Web page isn't official until it contains that tag.

In the future, other WWW tools might become available and not recognize your Web page if it doesn't meet official HTML standards. So while an HTML validator may not improve the way your home page looks, it's an important tool for future compatibility.

HTML Validator   Let's check your Web page with the easiest to use and most popular HTML validation service located at **http://www.webtechs.com/html-val-svc/**, as shown in Figure 11.11. You tell the WebTechs Validation Service the URL of the document you want it to check, and it will link there automatically. Within a few moments, you'll know whether or not your Web page meets HTML standards, and if not, what you can do to fix it.

FIG. 11.11
The WebTechs Validation Service checks to see if you have a technically correct Web page.

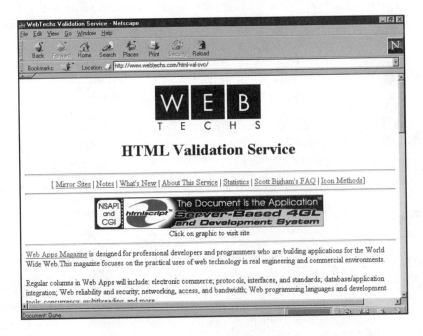

> **N O T E**   To validate your Web page, make it available on the WWW, not on your personal computer. Because the Webtechs Validation requires a valid URL to work properly, the service cannot evaluate HTML files on your local computer. ■

The first step in validating your Web page is selecting the level of HTML to use. The Webtechs Validation Service allows you to test several different levels/versions of HTML: Level 2 (the previous standard), Level 3.2, Mozilla (the nickname for HTML using special Netscape only extensions), Microsoft Internet Explorer specific tags, and several other similar flavors.

Since this book describes using all sorts of general HTML enhancements to make your page look better, choose Level 3.2 (Wilbur). Then, in the Check Documents by URL box, type in your home page's URL. Click the Submit URLs for validation button to validate your home page. Figure 11.12 shows my screen *before* I try to validate my home page.

FIG. 11.12
Getting ready to
validate the home
page.

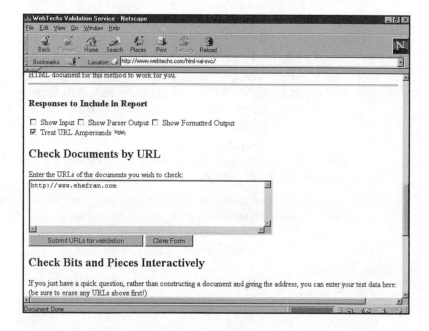

First the validation service clicks the button, then it retrieves your home page, testing it for a variety of HTML faults and problems. If your Web page fails the validation service, a screen appears informing you why you failed and helps to diagnose the problem. Once your Web page passes the validation tests, Figure 11.13 appears.

FIG. 11.13
I had better look
carefully at my HTML
mistakes!

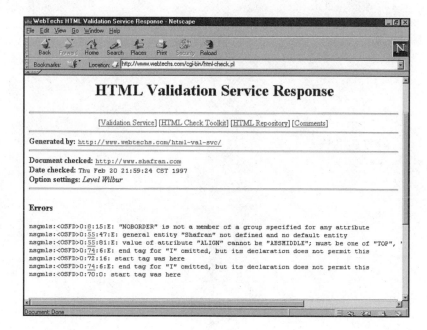

Other Validation Tools   Other tools exist, in addition to the WebTechs Validation Service to let you check your Web page according to HTML specifications. In the following, I've listed some of the more popular HTML checking programs, and given their URLs.

- Weblint (**http://www.cre.canon.co.uk/~neilb/weblint.html**): For UNIX fans, Weblint is an HTML version of Lint. This program checks HTML documents for proper syntax and good style. You must download and run this program on your WWW server to evaluate your Web pages.

- HTML Validator (**http://htmlvalidator.com/**): HTML Validator is a Windows 95 shareware program that runs on your personal computer and checks your files for complete HTML compatibility.

- Yahoo! List (**http://www.yahoo.com/Computers_and_Internet/Software/ Data_Formats/HTML/Validation_Checkers/**): A list of several other related tools and discussions related to validating HTML.

CHAPTER 12

Publicizing Your Web Page

Once your Web page is finished and available on the Web, hordes of people will stop by for a look because they want to see it. Right? Not if nobody knows about it. Without publicity and Web page advertisements, no one will even know that you have a Web page.

That's where this chapter comes into play. In it, you'll learn how to announce to the Internet and the World Wide Web that your page is up and raring to have visitors. I'll teach you how to create and place Web page advertisements in hot spots around the Internet. ■

Generate publicity for your Web page

Learn how to attract masses of Web surfers to see your Web page.

Add your Web page to several WWW catalogs

Several Web sites catalog the millions of Web pages in existence. To add your own listing just requires stopping by the biggest catalogs.

Use UseNet newsgroups to publicize your Web page

Take advantage of all sorts of Internet ways to publicize your Web pages. Learn how to use Internet Newsgroups to your own advantage.

Get other sites to link to your Web page

Cross referencing your Web site with another is a great way to increase the number of visitors who stop by.

Attracting Visitors to Your Web Page

We've all heard of the movie, *Field of Dreams.* Unfortunately, the "If you build it, they will come" philosophy doesn't work as well on the WWW as it does with baseball ghosts. You've got to do some legwork and spread the word about your Web page if you want to attract traffic.

Businesses understand this philosophy, and so should you. When a company creates a brand new product, it generally has to spend thousands (if not millions) of dollars advertising the product in magazines and newspapers and on television and radio. Fortunately, publicizing your Web page is generally free; your only cost is the time you spend telling other WWW surfers about it. But the time is well spent.

Before you start advertising your Web page on the WWW, you should first think through why you are publicizing your Web page, who you are announcing it to, and what kind of results you expect. You will, therefore, have a better idea of your overall goal.

N O T E   Before you can publicize your Web page, you've got to upload it to the Internet. See "Connecting to a Web Provider" in Chapter 2, "Weaving Your Own Web," for more information about finding the right spot on the WWW for your page. ▪

Why Publicize Your Web Page?

For your Web page, you're probably advertising for personal satisfaction. Since you installed a counter (see Chapter 9, "Customizing Your Web Page"), you want to see how many people visit your Web page—it's almost like a contest. Another reason might be that your Web page revolves around a particular hobby. You want to publicize your page so other like-minded individuals will stop by. On my home page, for example, I have an entire section on Broadway musicals. When I advertise my Web site, I always mention my musical section so other people who love *The Phantom of the Opera* (and others) can see my efforts.

Business home pages usually have additional reasons to get you to stop by their site. They might advertise their products or services or simply try to impress visitors. Chrysler's home page (**http://www.chrysler.com**) is a prime example of this (see Figure 12.1). You're not going to buy an automobile without test driving it (and smelling the new interior), but just having a WWW presence is good publicity.

Before you go out and scrawl your Web page's URL all over the world, make sure you really want to advertise your Web page. Some Web providers charge based on how many times your Web page is accessed. You might get thousands of people visiting daily, but it may not be worth the cost. Instead, you might want to tell only a select group of people about your Web page.

In fact, many people don't even care about advertising their Web pages. They use their Web pages as personal starting points on the WWW, and customize them for their own purposes. They create lists of links that interest them and spots they like to visit. Such a Web page is more like a home base, where the owner just checks in every now and then. If this is you, why spend a lot of time publicizing your home page if you don't care who visits it?

FIG. 12.1
You can't test drive a minivan in cyberspace, but this Web site really moves!

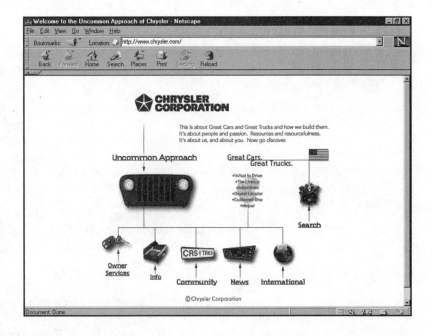

Set Reasonable Expectations

Most likely, advertising your Web page will increase the number of visitors you get. Originally, my home page was getting about five visits a day, ranging from my friends to random visitors. Once I publicized my home page all over the Internet, my daily tally started increasing rapidly. Eventually, I was averaging around 40 visitors a day. That may not sound like a lot, but I was very happy with these results. Of course, I have no idea whether they liked my home page, found it useful, or ever came back.

 Your Web provider should be able to furnish advanced statistics for your Web page, and should know how many visits you get, who the visitors are, and whether or not they used any links on your page.

After awhile, the daily visitor count started to taper off to about 10 to 15 visits a day. Don't expect basic advertising techniques to attract millions of visitors; set reasonable expectations so you're not disappointed. And of course, no one is going to top the king of all Web sites, Netscape, which receives over 5 millions hits a day!

N O T E Although you may be lucky to get a couple of hundred people to visit your home page, some sites get thousands of visitors a day. That's because they offer unique services that pique the curiosity of many people, which keep them coming back again and again. For example, the Worst of the Web site(**http://www.worstoftheweb.com/**) lists a handful of bad Web sites (mine hasn't made it—yet) and gets thousands of people daily because it is a creative and constantly updated site. ∎

Using WWW Catalogs and Announcement Services

The easiest and most popular way to advertise your Web page is by using existing WWW catalogs, announcement services, and indexes. These places exist to publicize new and popular WWW sites all over the world.

Announcement services are like a town crier standing on the corner. They list loads of new Web pages constantly for all of the WWW public to read and see. Every type of Web page imaginable is listed in these public pages. Related to announcement services, WWW catalogs create searchable lists of Web pages. You can search a WWW catalog for a specific topic or keyword. Finally, WWW indexes actually go out on their own and search the Web for new pages. They add every page they find to a huge database and let WWW surfers search for different Web sites.

In this section, I have listed several of the most popular announcement and catalog services, and indexes available, and you'll learn to include your home page in their listings.

Announcement Services

Announcement services, such as the Netscape or the What's New listing pages are publicly available sites that anyone can use to announce a Web page. You submit a blurb about your Web page, and your information will soon appear on the What's New pages for thousands of WWW surfers to see.

These services receive thousands of submissions weekly. Typically, any type of Web page is accepted and listed in announcement services. They're a great place to start your Web page publicity.

The What's New Listing Pages   Conveniently located at **http://www.whatsnew.com**, this site is a huge clearinghouse for people to announce their newly created sites to the entire world. This Web site is run by the publishers of *Internet World*, a monthly magazine for Internet and WWW users. With nearly 200,000 submitted sites, What's New is the center of all major announcements services.

Figure 12.2 shows the main page with new listings. You'd have to stop by two or three times a day to see all the new listings!

NCSA What's New Home page is located at:

> **http://www.whatsnew.com**

Add new submissions at:

> **http://www.emap.com/whatsnew/addyours.shtml**

Submitting your Web page to the What's New listing is, and always has been, free. It only takes a few moments. Stop by and fill out the online form displayed in Figure 12.3. All you have to do is type in the name, URL, and a short description of your site. Typically, there is a short delay between submitting your entry and its appearance in the What's New pages.

FIG. 12.2
This is a huge announcement service site.

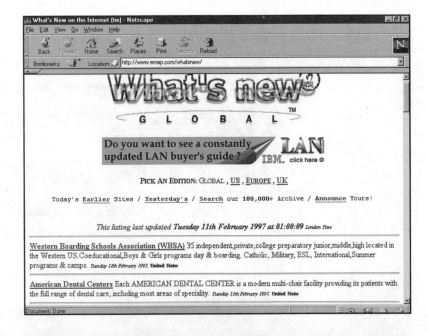

FIG. 12.3
This entry form is for all Web sites out there.

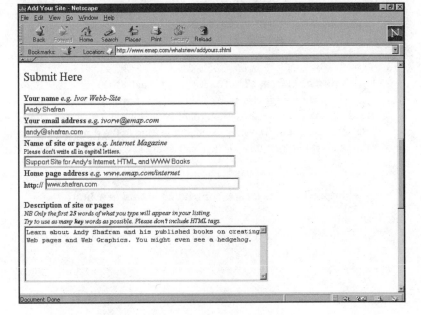

Once you submit your info, you are asked to confirm everything you typed in (see Figure 12.4). Click on the Confirm button and you are all set. What's New will send you an e-mail letting you know when the page appears in this listing.

FIG. 12.4

Your listing needs to be confirmed and you're all set.

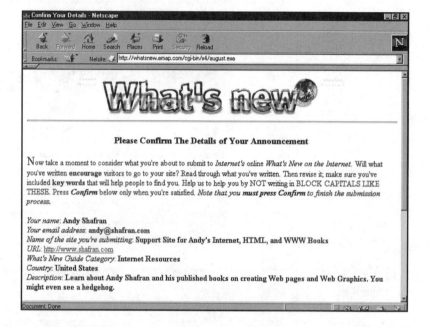

What's New at Netscape? The Netscape What's New page (see Figure 12.5) is known for listing creative and innovative Web sites. If you have a particularly exciting Web site or use HTML in some previously unthought-of or useful fashion, you could be listed here. Netscape limits the amount of Web sites listed, but getting in the directory can bring you a lot of traffic. Some sites report getting 100,000 plus visitors just by being listed in this index!

Netscape's What's New? page is located at:

http://home.netscape.com/home/whats-new.html

Submitting new entries is easy, but don't bother unless your site has something extremely special to offer. Netscape receives thousands of entries, and only a handful make it to its list.

FIG. 12.5
Stop by to see some of the hottest WWW spots available.

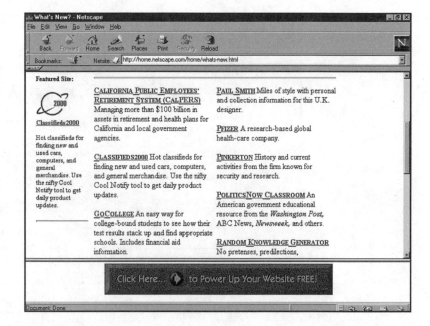

WWW Directories

Unlike announcement services, WWW directories are catalogs of thousands of Web pages. Some, such as Yahoo!, are organized by category. Others are huge listings of Web pages that read more like the White Pages than anything else. You can stop by these directories and browse or search for a specific entry.

WWW directories are great places to advertise your home page because once your entry is accepted, it will always be listed in the pertinent category. For example, if your home page centers around baseball, you can add it to the Yahoo! catalog. Then anyone who searches through the catalog looking for America's favorite pastime will find your home page. You don't have to rely on their reading an announcement page on the right day to spot your site.

Yahoo!   Yahoo! is the biggest, best, and most-used WWW index. Started a couple of years ago by two Stanford University students, Yahoo! has grown to become the best spot to find Web sites. It is my personal favorite Web directory, and I use it almost every day. With over 1 million entries, if a subject isn't listed in the Yahoo! directory, you'll likely have trouble finding it elsewhere on the Web.

Yahoo! is located at (see Figure 12.6):

   http://www.yahoo.com

Part
V

Ch
12

FIG. 12.6
Yahoo! is the biggest and best index out there.

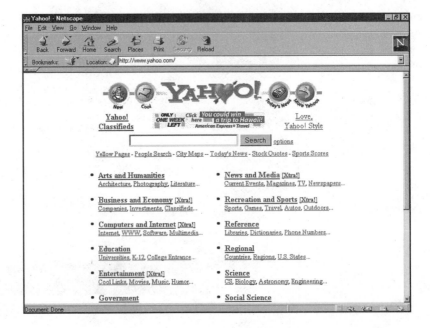

You can add new entries in any category. Simply go to the Yahoo! category you want to add your Web page to and click on the Add new entries link at the bottom of the screen. Anyone can submit entries for their home pages (see Figure 12.7).

FIG. 12.7
Once you're listed in Yahoo!, you've increased the chances of getting a consistent stream of visitors to your Web page.

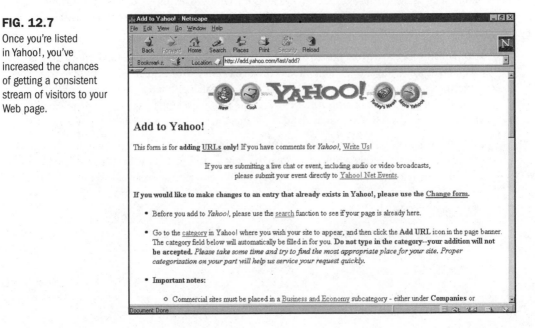

Excite   Excite has really taken the WWW by a storm. Instead of being a general clearing-house for thousands of different URL's indexed purely by matching a specific word or phrase in a query, Excite uses an advanced Context Based database. When a search is performed, Excite searches its databases for entries that most closely matches the concept of the item you are searching for. Excite rates each page according to what information is actually present in your Web page—in a sense it reads your page automatically, gets the gist of what your page talks about, then saves that impression in a database for future reference. This is a really powerful concept and allows for some fantastic and high-level searches. In addition, there are over 50,000 Web sites reviewed and rated by Web surfers.

Excite is located at:

http://www.excite.com

You can submit a URL to Excite and have Excite rate and save a concept of your Web page. You can be sure that search results here truly match what you wanted to find (see Figure 12.8).

FIG. 12.8
Getting your Web site listed in Excite will certainly "excite" the number of visitors who stop by.

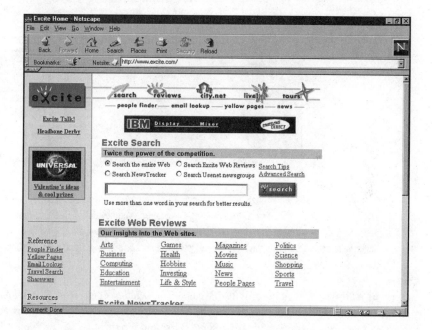

Part
V

Ch

12

Four11   Four11 is *the* Internet clearinghouse for listings of individuals on the WWW. There are literally millions of people listed in this gigantic electronic white pages. One stop here, and I can practically guarantee you'll find who you are looking for. It only makes sense for you to register yourself and your own Web site here as well.

Four11 Directory Services is located at:

http://www.four11.com

It is likely that Four11 already has your e-mail address listed. By becoming a registered user (free), you can add a little bit of information about yourself and a link to your Web page. As a general rule, *everyone* should register here at Four11 so that people who are searching for you, or topics that are related to you, can find that particular information. Figure 12.9 shows the main Four11 screen.

FIG. 12.9

The Four11 white page directory would be about a mile thick if it were printed out.

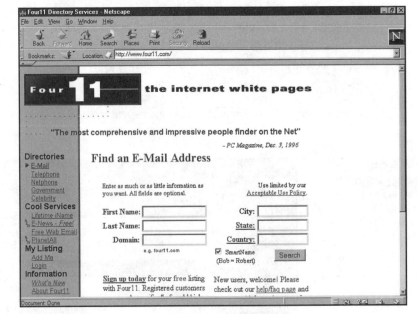

N O T E   Interestingly enough, when I registered at Four11, I saw a noticeable difference in the number of visitors to my Web page. I also received several pieces of e-mail from other people with my last name (Shafran, which is not very common), wondering if we were somehow distantly related. Of all the places I have registered, Four11 ranks right up there with Yahoo! as being the most fruitful. ■

Official World Wide Web Yellow Pages   *The Official World Wide Web Yellow Pages* is sponsored by New Riders Press (a sister publisher of Que Corp.). You can buy an actual hard copy of *The Official World Wide Web Yellow Pages* and flip through the organized listings of WWW sites, or search through the online version (whichever is your preference). Remember that the online index is constantly updated and will likely contain more current information.

Official WWW Yellow Pages is located at:

http://www.mcp.com/nrp/wwwyp/

Add new entries at:

http://www.mcp.com/nrp/wwwyp/submit.html

Shown in Figure 12.10, this site resembles your friendly phone book. Users can search for Web pages by keyword or category, and even add their own home pages to the list. I recommend including your Web page in this directory because of its ever-increasing popularity. (And on the next printing, it will even appear in the book!)

FIG. 12.10

A cyberspace phone book, *the WWW Yellow Pages* is one of the best directories on the Web.

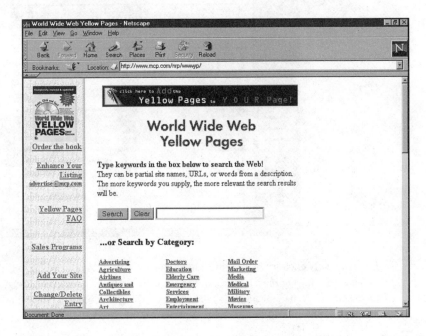

Searching the WWW

Similar to WWW directories, several available WWW search tools will reach out and search thousands of different WWW sites for information. Nicknamed WWW Spiders, these search tools crawl from Web page to Web page looking for queried information. They use the links found on one page to bring them to new and different links, thus traveling the WWW like a spider.

I've listed two popular WWW search tools. You can add your site to these tools and let their WWW spiders creep into your home page!

Lycos The Latin word for wolf spider, Lycos boasts that it is the catalog of the WWW. Indexing almost 6 million Web documents, Lycos is constantly traveling the World Wide Web looking for new pages to add to its index (see Figure 12.11). Users can submit a search query, and Lycos will return WWW pages according to how well it matched your query.

Lycos WWW page is located at:

> **http://www.lycos.com/**

Add new entries at:

> **http://www.lycos.com/addasite.html**

Part
V

Ch
12

FIG. 12.11

Lycos never gets tired. It explores the Web day and night.

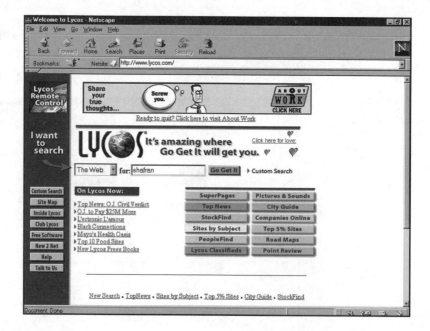

Lycos actively encourages anyone who creates a WWW page to add it to the index with the aim of being the most comprehensive index available. In fact, Lycos may already have your Web page listed. Because its spider is constantly crawling through the Web, it adds new Web pages as they are found, whether or not you request to be listed.

T I P If for some reason you do not want to be included in the Lycos catalog, but the spider has already found you, choose to delete your pages from the Lycos home page.

N O T E The Lycos index is updated weekly. Don't worry if your home page doesn't immediately appear in the searchable index. Give it some time to crawl over to your Web page. ■

WebCrawler   Owned by America Online (AOL), WebCrawler is another popular WWW Search Service (see Figure 12.12). It fields nearly 450,000 searches every month and has visited hundreds of thousands of WWW pages.

WebCrawler is located at:

http://Webcrawler.com/

Add new entries at:

http://Webcrawler.com/WebCrawler/SubmitURLS.html

You can add your Web page to WebCrawler's list of URLs to visit, explore, and index.

FIG. 12.12
Although WebCrawler is smaller than Lycos, it's used extremely often.

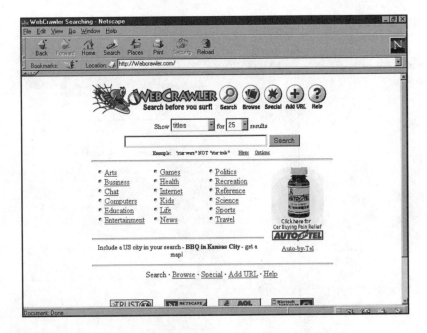

Submit It!—16 WWW Catalogs in One

The fastest and easiest way to publicize your home page on the WWW is by using Submit It! This one-stop publicity site enables you to fill out one form and submit your home page to 15 of the most popular indexes and catalogs of Web sites (including Yahoo!, Lycos, WebCrawler, and the Official WWW Yellow Pages).

Submit It! is located at:

http://free.submit-it.com

Here's how it works. You fill out an entry at the Submit It! site. Automatically, your home page information is sent to all of the WWW indexes and catalogs shown in Figure 12.13. Each site then reads your request and decides whether or not to add your entry.

Unfortunately, using Submit It! has several drawbacks. You only get to choose your category once. Each of the catalogs has a slightly different set of categories, so you never get to choose the optimal category for any of them (which is extremely important for such catalogs as Yahoo!).

Additionally, no records are kept letting you know where you have submitted your Web page, and you might not know whether your submission has been accepted. You have to check most of the services individually to see if your submission made it. Still, Submit It! is a great place to start publicizing your Web page.

Part
V

Ch
12

FIG. 12.13
Submit It! enables you
to add your Web page to
many WWW catalogs in
one shot.

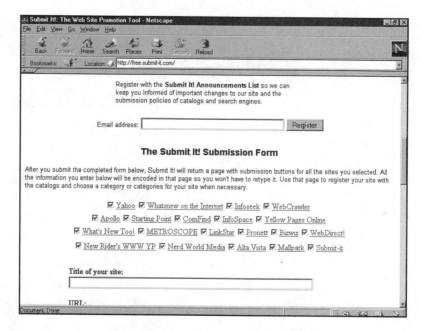

Also, if you are willing to pay for your publicity, Submit-it! also has a subscription service which costs $69.95 a year and registers your Web site in literally 300 different Internet search engines across the world. Visit **http://www.submit-it.com** for more info on this subscription service.

Using UseNet Newsgroups

Besides the WWW, newsgroups are one of the most popular applications available on the Internet. Organized into many different categories, newsgroups enable people from all over the world to hold virtual conversations. I could post a question from my home in Cincinnati, Ohio, and receive responses from California, Mexico, and Australia.

There are literally thousands of different newsgroups, ranging in interest from Microsoft Windows to automobiles—and covering everything in between. Posting messages to newsgroups is a great way to publicize your home page because it's cheap and reaches a large audience.

comp.infosystems.www.announce

The sole purpose for this newsgroup is to announce new Web pages and HTML services and tools. This is a high-traffic newsgroup (several hundred posts a week). It is a moderated newsgroup, meaning someone reads every message before it is posted throughout the world, and messages must follow a strict format, or they'll be rejected.

You can post to comp.infosystems.www.announce directly through the news reader in your browser. Go to the following URL:

news:comp.infosystems.www.announce

Click the Post New Article button at the top of the screen to bring up the Send Mail/Post News dialog box. Type in the message subject and body. Your messages subject should contain one of the words listed below in all caps, followed by an accurate description of what can be found there:

ARCHIVE ENTERTAINMENT MAGAZINE SCIENCE

ART ENVIRONMENT MISC SERVER

BOOK FAQ MUSIC SHOPPING

BROWSER GAMES NEWS SOFTWARE

COLLECTION HEALTH PERSONAL SPORTS

ECONOMY HUMANITIES POLITICS TRANSPORTATION

EDUCATION INFO REFERENCE

EMPLOYMENT LAW RELIGION

If the message's subject is not correct and accurate, the newsgroup posting will be rejected. Here are some examples of good message subjects:

PERSONAL: Andy Shafran's home page about musicals and writing books

SPORTS: The Cincinnati Reds Baseball Team Page

BOOK: Creating Your Own Web Pages, Second Edition

Likewise, here are some bad message subjects (these would certainly cause messages to be rejected):

PERSONAL: My home page

A simple Web page for my alma mater

Software: Playing games

In your message body, it's important to include the full URL to the page you are announcing. Also, limit the message body to 75 lines (no one will read a message that long anyway). When you're ready, click the Send button. Your posting will appear within 48 hours. Figure 12.14 shows my sample submission.

TIP   If you have trouble posting to newsgroups, you can also submit announcements via Internet mail. Include all of the same information in the subject and body, and address the message to **www-announce@boutell.com.**

FIG. 12.14

I'm ready to announce my Web page.

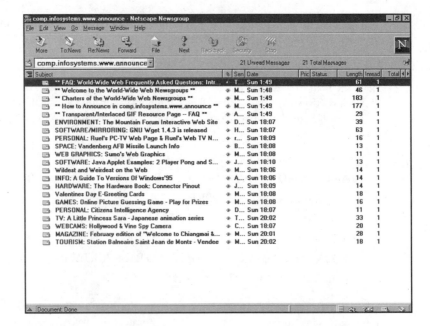

Personal Newsgroup Interests

Comp.infosystems.www.announce is only the first newsgroup you want to post an announcement message to. Most likely, several other newsgroups will also be interested in knowing about your home page.

Search through your available newsgroups to find others that are related to your home page. Because my page has a lot of information about musicals, I might want to post an announcement to **rec.arts.theatre.musicals** or **alt.stagecraft** to attract like-minded individuals.

Don't forget to check out newsgroups that are local to your city, state, or information provider. The University of Cincinnati, Hamilton County, the City of Cincinnati, and the State of Ohio all have their own local newsgroups, and because that's where I live, it would be appropriate for me to post a message to them.

> **CAUTION**
>
> Make sure you don't go overboard in advertising your home page to lots of different newsgroups. Notifying people who might be interested in stopping by is acceptable, but posting a message about your home page to every single newsgroup that you can find—regardless of its subject—is considered poor *netiquette*. You'll likely be reprimanded by newsgroup participants.

Other Ways to Advertise Your Home Page

Using WWW catalogs and Internet newsgroups is not the only way to publicize your Web page. These methods may attract a lot of initial attention, but to keep visitors coming to your home page, you've got to continually plug it wherever you can (and when it is acceptable).

Resumes and Business Cards

I include my home page's URL on my resume and business cards. Because I'm proud of the work that I've done, I invite clients and prospective business associates to stop by for a visit.

Because home pages are so flexible, I can arrange mine however I like. When people stop by, it gives them a chance to learn a lot more about my interests and even enables them to send e-mail to me directly.

Figure 12.15 show's what my business card looks like.

FIG. 12.15
Check out my business card.

Andy Shafran
http://www.shafran.com

Phone number   Address

Signing Your Mail and News Postings

Another popular way of getting the word out is to include information in all of your e-mail messages and newsgroup postings. At the bottom of every message that I send out, I include my name and the URL of my home page:

—Andy Shafran

http://www.shafran.com

This lets my correspondents know that I have a home page, and it informs them of its location should they want to pay a visit.

Ask Other WWW Sites to Link to You

Another way to attract visitors is by asking people who maintain other pages on similar topics to include a link to your page. For example, there are a lot of other Broadway musical pages out there—mine isn't the only one. Because people who visit one musical page might be inclined to visit others, it only makes sense to try to link all of these related pages.

Send e-mail to other Web page creators who have pages related to yours. Tell them about your Web page and give them your URL. Ask them (nicely) to include a link to your page and tell them you will reciprocate. Most likely, they'll be as excited as you are about linking their pages to a new site. This type of exchange advertising is very common and useful to both you and the visitors to your site.

WWW Advertisements

Adding your WWW pages to the large indexes isn't often the best way to publicize them because your Web site is just one among the masses listed—but it's usually a free service.

To attract more people to their Web sites, some developers have turned to paid advertising at popular sites. These advertisements usually consist of simple images that, when clicked, bring visitors immediately to a specific Web page. Figure 12.16 shows an advertisement as it appears on the Que home page (**http://www.mcp.com/que**).

FIG. 12.16

With thousands of hits a day, the Que page is an excellent example of where an ad gets good exposure.

Here's a sample ad for Columbia House

Unfortunately, advertising on popular Web sites can be expensive. For example, a week long advertisement at Yahoo! starts at $1,000. Many advertisements are significantly more expensive, and most businesses can't afford them. Figure 12.17 shows WebLaunch: the costly, but effective, advertising service of Yahoo! (**http://www.yahoo.com/weblaunch.html**).

FIG. 12.17
WebLaunch is one of my favorite advertising locations on the Web: it's well designed and easy to use.

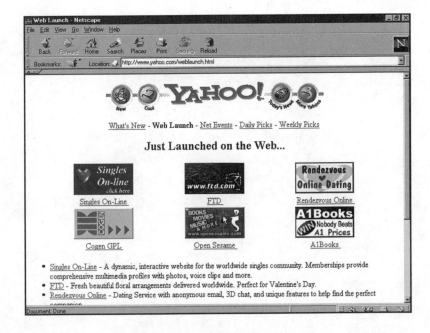

Many popular Web sites allow advertising, usually ranging from $50 to $1,000 for any period of time ranging from a week to a few months. Any spot on the WWW that sponsors advertising should be able to give you detailed information about the number of visitors that stop by (thus seeing your advertisements). If not, you don't want to advertise there.

Advertising Web pages is usually left to businesses who are willing to make a financial investment to get people to visit their pages. This usually means that they are selling a product or service. If you don't fit in this category, your best bet is to stick with the free catalogs and indexes of Web sites.

As you can see, there is more to creating a successful Web site than programming acumen and design skills. Learning how to intelligently promote your WWW page is an important ingredient in making your presence felt on the World Wide Web.

Part
V

Ch
12

CHAPTER 13

Using HTML Editors and Other Web Tools

Understand HTML editors

HTML editors are special tools that are used in creating Web pages. There are several different flavors of HTML editors out there and this chapter highlights some of the best.

Take advantage of the easy-to-use HotDog HTML editor

Making Web pages is easy when you use the right tools for the job—in this case HotDog, the best all-around HTML editor around.

Use other Web tools as needed

Besides HTML editors, you'll also find useful tools in creating graphics, animations, and interactivity on your Web site.

Imagine you're building your own home—but only using a screwdriver. You've got all the wood, steel, and concrete you can imagine to become the new Frank Lloyd Wright. A screwdriver is a flexible tool. Besides its obvious uses, you could use it as a hammer (if the handle was strong), to spread cement out (with the flat blade), even to dig a hole if you were really patient—and desperate. Instead of forcing your single tool to do every job, you'd likely purchase at least a few other tools when building a house—maybe a saw, wheelbarrow, shovel—who knows? The point is that for any given job, there is likely to be a special tool optimized for that purpose.

Similarly, on your computer, you've got a vast array of software tools available at your disposal—word processors, spreadsheets, finance management programs, the whole works. And for creating Web pages (according to this book), as you can likely imagine, there are several useful tools geared specifically for that purpose.

I'm going to change gears slightly and talk about some of these important tools which will make it easier and more exciting when making Web pages. In Chapter 1, you learned there are several ways to create HTML files. You can type in each tag, or use a special program, called an HTML editor, to do much of the work for you.

This chapter introduces you to several popular and useful HTML editors that will make building Web pages a breeze. I'll show you what kinds of tools exist for building Web pages and give you some detailed information about a handful of them. ■

Choosing Your Web Publishing Tools

The next step to successful HTML development is picking the right tools for the task. As HTML becomes a popular pursuit, there are more and more programs and utilities being developed to help you get a head start in HTML. Sifting through them can take some time, but you may find a gem that really is a considerable help.

Many popular HTML editors work a lot like a simple text editor. There are simple screens of text and the editor has built in commands and functions that allow you to add HTML features automatically. But, you still are editing a plain HTML file, and to see your Web page, you must load it into a browser, like Netscape or Internet Explorer.

The other main flavor of HTML editors is called a WYSIWYG Editor. WYSIWYG stands for: "What you see is what you get." A WYSIWYG HTML Editor shows a Web page as it would appear in a browser. So, if you mark text to appear as bold, the text appears darker on the screen. When you add an image to your Web page, you don't just see the `<IMG SRC>` tag, but you observe the actual graphic. WYSIWYG HTML editors are popular because you see what your page looks like as it is being built.

Unfortunately, WYSIWYG editors don't offer as much flexibility and customizations of your file. Of course, the trick to using a standard editor is that you need to know HTML pretty well just to create Web pages. In reality, you're likely to use both types of HTML editors, so I mention a few of each in this section.

Using HotDog Pro

HotDog Professional is shareware, and comes in both 16- and 32-bit versions. You can evaluate HotDog for 14 days before deciding to purchase it. There is also an advanced version, HotDog Pro, which is costlier but has many Web management tools, a spell checker, and other HTML enhancements, built in. You can download HotDog from the Sausage Software Web site at **http://www.sausage.com** (see Figure 13.1).

Included on the CD-ROM in the back of this book, HotDog makes it easy for you to create your own home page. HotDog is geared toward creating effective-looking HTML documents.

TIP   *Shareware programs* are software packages that you are permitted to evaluate and use for free for a limited period of time. After that evaluation period is over (usually around 30 days), you must purchase the program to legally continue using it.

FIG. 13.1

The HotDog home page is fun, whimsical, and informative to visit.

 TIP The version of HotDog included on the home page CD is a shareware version which is only good for 14 days. To use HotDog after that, you need to purchase it for $99.95. You can purchase it directly online at **http://ssr.sausage.com.au/**.

Although not a WYSIWYG editor, HotDog Pro remains an overwhelming favorite of folks all over the Web. With support for advanced HTML features, including true HTML 3.2 elements, HotDog is especially popular with folks on the cutting edge of Web design, because it allows you to incorporate many multimedia special effects and works hand in hand with several other Web development products released by the same company.

One of the more impressive features of HotDog is its built-in support for more easily creating tables and graphics by using dialog boxes that guide you through the process. Just click the Table or graphic button on HotDog's button bar, and you're presented with a dialog box to help you create the element. This lets you avoid some of the tiresome, detailed HTML coding usually required.

Figure 13.2 shows HotDog Pro Version 3 for Windows 95.

HotDog will walk you through the installation process and set itself up on your hard drive. Once installed, HotDog allows you 30 days of free use until your license expires.

Once HotDog is installed on your computer, you've got to customize it so it can use your favorite browser to preview your HTML documents. From the menu bar, choose Tools, Options to bring up the Options dialog box. Click the tab labeled File Dirs to set your HotDog options (see Figure 13.3) to link HotDog with your favorite browser—in my case Netscape.

Part
V

Ch
13

FIG. 13.2

Sausage has many entertaining and innovative tools built into its editor.

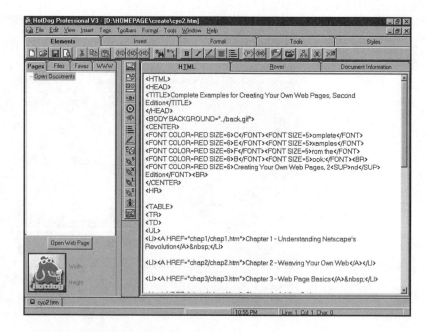

FIG. 13.3

Link Hotdog to your favorite Web browser.

Make sure you stop by the HotDog home page at **http://www.sausage.com** to see if a newer version of HotDog is available for downloading.

Once you install HotDog, take it for a test drive. On Windows 3.1, double-click the icon labeled "HotDog Editor" to begin the program. To run HotDog from Windows 95 you have to use File Explorer (or use the Find option) to locate the HotDog program. Once you find it, double-click the HotDog program to start up the editor. A shareware notice appears, and then the main editor window appears. The first time you use HotDog, a dialog box will come up asking you for your next action.

TIP If you're using Windows 95 and HotDog a lot, you might want to create a shortcut for it. To create this shortcut, simply find the HotDog program when browsing through the "My Computer" icon in Windows 95 and click the right mouse button. From the pop-up menu select Create Shortcut. A shortcut to the HotDog editor will appear on the desktop, so you can run it whenever you feel like and not have to look around for it. Alternatively, you can drag the icon to your desktop.

You'll use the buttons lining the top of the screen to add new HTML elements to your home page. All you have to do is type your home page information into the main window. Then, using your mouse, highlight the different parts of the text you want to add an HTML tag to. Click the appropriate button and—Voilà!—your text is marked automatically.

CAUTION

You might not see the last three icons on your computer screen depending on your monitor's resolution. Mine is set to 800×600 (Super VGA). If yours is set at a smaller VGA resolution, HotDog looks slightly different.

For example, type the following text in your main window:

Extra! Extra! Read all about it!

According to Fortune Magazine, Bill Gates is the second richest person in the world, second only to royalty who inherited his money from his family and past generations. Not to be outdone, Gates intends to buy his own country and set himself up as monarch for life.

Now take your mouse and highlight "Fortune Magazine." We want to italicize that text because it is a magazine's title. So click the Italics button and watch HotDog add the <EM> and </EM> tags automatically for you. Now boldface Gates' name wherever it appears in the paragraph by selecting the text and clicking the boldface icon. Finally, let's make the first line look like a headline. Select it and click the H1 button. The H1 button tells Netscape to add <H1> and </H1> tags around marked text. H1 is short for heading, size 1 (the biggest). Alternatively, you could choose H2, H3, and so on to make a smaller headline.

When you are finished, your text should look like this:

<H1> Extra! Extra! Read all about it! </H1>

According to <EM>Fortune Magazine </EM>, <STRONG>Bill Gates </STRONG> is the second richest person in the world, second only to royalty who inherited his money from his family and past generations. Not to be outdone, <STRONG>Gates</STRONG> intends to buy his own country and set himself up as monarch for life.

Now click the Preview button. Netscape appears (since I associated HotDog with Netscape) and shows you how the text would look to people browsing on the Web (see Figure 13.4).

Part
V

Ch
13

FIG. 13.4

Not too complicated, but pretty neat for 10 seconds of work.

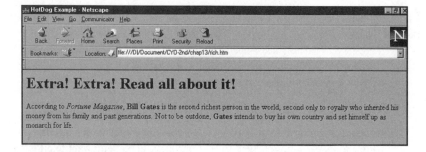

CoffeeCup

CoffeeCup is another standard HTML editor that follows the same veins as HotDog. With a slightly irreverent attitude, the Coffeecup HTML Editor is text based and allows you to quickly and easily mark up your text and make good-looking Web pages.

Figure 13.5 shows the CoffeeCup home page at **http://www.coffeecup.com**, where you can download the shareware software. Of course, I've also included a version of CoffeeCup on the CD-ROM with this book.

FIG. 13.5

CoffeeCup is the up and coming HTML Editor.

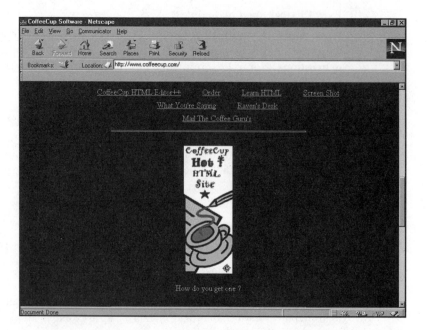

Not only is CoffeeCup a fantastic editor, but you just can't beat its price—$20. Nowadays, most of the good HTML editors are upwards of $100, and CoffeeCup is trying to put out a quality product for a very reasonable cost. You can purchase CoffeeCup securely at **http://www. encrypted.com/clients/coffeecup/orderform.html**.

In addition to HTML editing, there are also several great features built into CoffeeCup, including:

- A collection of animated GIFs that are prebuilt and ready to use on a Web page.

- A collection of JavaScript applets that perform interactive tasks with visitors who stop by.

- Background color-code hunting. This allows you to choose from 16.7 million colors by pointing and clicking at a virtual rainbow of colors.

- Multiple Web page management and creation.

Figure 13.6 shows a sample screen shot of CoffeeCup in action, building my own Web site.

FIG. 13.6
CoffeeCup is the hippest and most popular HTML editor under $50.

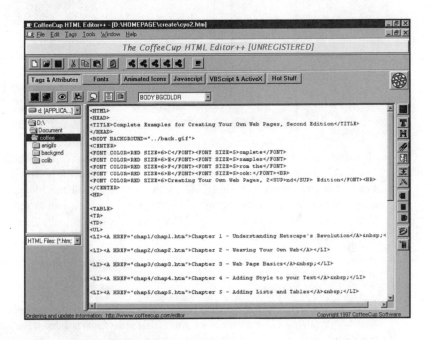

HoTMetaL Free and HoTMetaL Pro

HoTMetaL Free and HoTMetaL Pro take a fundamentally different approach to HTML creation. In a nutshell, you don't have to understand HTML. HoTMetaL is a completely WYSIWYG environment that is designed to shield you from the underlying HTML codes; it is a phenomenon that, earlier in this chapter, I suggested we would begin to see more frequently in Web design tools.

Instead of inserting HTML commands, HoTMetaL users simply enter text onscreen, select it, and choose the formatting or linking elements from the program's menus. HoTMetaL then allows you to either hide or display the resulting HTML tags. Hidden, they provide you with a WYSIWYG representation of your page—even including graphical elements (see Figure 13.7).

FIG. 13.7
HoTMetaL Free allows you to view HTML in a WYSIWYG environment, with or without HTML codes.

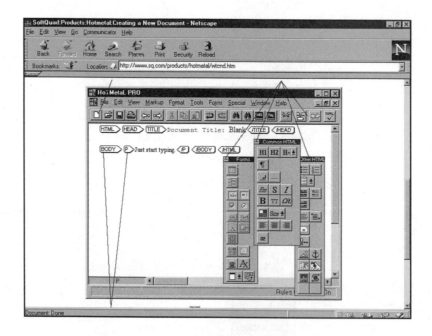

HoTMetaL Free is a scaled-down freeware version of the commercial application HoTMetaL Pro, which retails for an astounding $195. The Pro version does, however, offer just about everything you'd need to create HTML pages, including spell checking and thesaurus, search-and-replace, inline graphics display, tables support, templates, and forms support. Plus, an added bonus over many editors is the HTML parser, which actually checks to make sure your HTML documents are valid and correctly formatted.

Both are the work of SoftQuad, Inc. HoTMetaL is one of the most successful commercial HTML editors and can be downloaded at **http://www.sq.com**.

N O T E   Web Weaver for Macintosh is a popular editor for Mac users. It's considered semi-WYSIWYG, meaning it shows you a good deal of the formatting that will appear in your browser, but not necessarily all of it. Web Weaver uses floating palette windows to give you access to common HTML tags, while the rest are available as menu commands. You can also create your own custom palettes for getting at your favorite or most used elements. ■

Netscape Composer

Another extraordinarily popular HTML editor is Netscape Composer, which comes as part of the Netscape Communicator suite. Netscape Composer is like HoTMetal in that it is a WYSIWYG HTML editor, but it offers several advantages.

The best reason to use Netscape Composer is that it is directly built into the browser. You always know exactly what your pages are going to look like in Netscape because you are seeing the changes as they're being made.

Unfortunately, because of its simplicity and ease of use, Netscape Composer can sometimes make it difficult to create advanced-looking HTML pages because it doesn't support all of the latest and greatest tags. This limited functionality keeps Netscape Composer as primarily an editor used for beginners and those of us who create simple Web sites.

Another great feature of Composer is its price—free. Since it comes as part of the Netscape Communicator suite, it can be downloaded by anyone in the world, and for nearly any computer type at **http://home.netscape.com**.

Figure 13.8 shows me working on a Web page by using Netscape Composer.

FIG. 13.8
Composer makes creating simple Web sites a breeze.

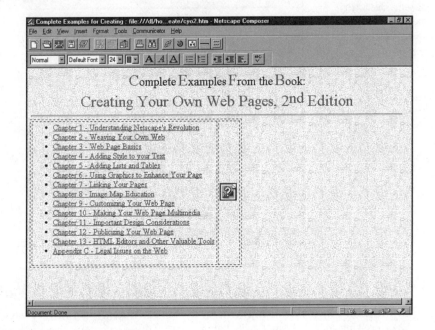

HTML Tools for Microsoft Users

Recognizing the popularity in converting data into HTML format, Microsoft has an entire suite of tools which works with its office applications and converts information into Web format. Called Internet Assistants, these free add-in programs allow you to incorporate Office information into a Web site with the click of a few buttons.

You can download Internet Assistants for:

- Word
- Excel
- PowerPoint
- Schedule+
- Access

Part
V

Ch
13

Visit **http://www.microsoft.com/msdownload/** for more information on downloading Internet Assistants.

Figure 13.9 shows Internet Assistant for Microsoft Word 7.0 being used to compose an HTML document.

FIG. 13.9

Internet Assistant is a great free tool which allows Web developers powerful creativity tools when building Web pages.

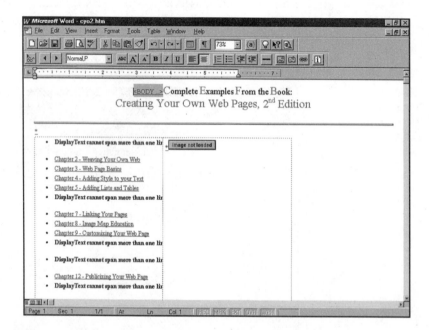

Other Programs Useful for Building Web Pages

Aside from HTML editors, there are several other programs you'll probably find useful for creating your Web site. I talked about most of these in various places throughout this book, but I wanted to include a summary of these important tools and how they can be used to build Web pages.

PaintShop Pro

Since graphics tend to be a focus on the Web, you'll want programs to deal with those. If you have access to professional graphics programs like CorelDRAW! or Adobe Photoshop, you'll definitely find good reasons to use them. There are powerful shareware alternatives for graphics that are cheaper, easier to use, and often have special features built in for Web developers.

The best of breed graphics program for Web developers is PaintShop Pro (PSP for short). Created by JASC software, you can download PSP at **http://www.jasc.com** (see Figure 13.10).

FIG. 13.10

JASC makes all sorts of impressive image and graphics products.

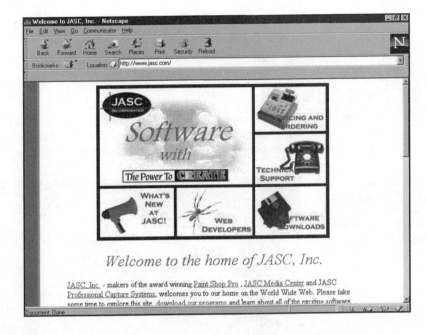

PaintShop Pro lets you manipulate and create all sorts of different images and graphics and has several special features which enable you to create special Web backgrounds and buttons. Figure 13.11 shows PaintShop Pro 4.1 editing an image. Visit the JASC Web site at **http://www.jasc.com**.

FIG. 13.11

PaintShop Pro is the tool of choice for graphics developers across the world.

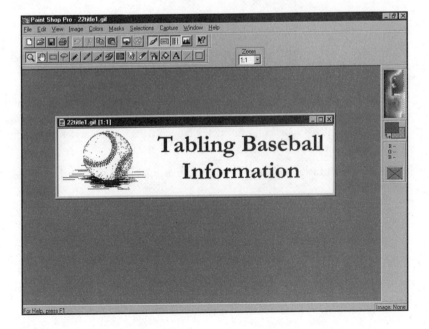

Part
V

Ch
13

> **N O T E**   For more information on creating graphics with PaintShop Pro see *Creating Your Own Web Graphics*, by Andy Shafran and Dick Oliver. This book steps you through building robust images with PaintShop Pro and integrating them into Web pages. ■

GIF Construction Set

Another extremely popular graphics tool used in creating graphics is the GIF Construction Set. Created by Alchemy Mindworks, this tool can be downloaded at **http://www. mindworkshop.com/alchemy/alchemy.html** (see Figure 13.12).

FIG. 13.12
Alchemy Mindworks is a center for graphics programs and reference books.

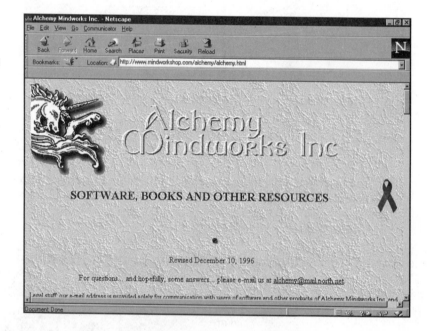

GIF Construction Set is a specialized tool that allows you to combine multiple images into one file, and display them as if they were animated. This technique, called animated GIFs, works like thumbing your finger through a flipbook; each cell has to be individually drawn and coordinated together.

Figure 13.13 shows how to create a simple animated GIF by using the GIF Construction Set.

FIG. 13.13
This animated GIF only
has a few cells.

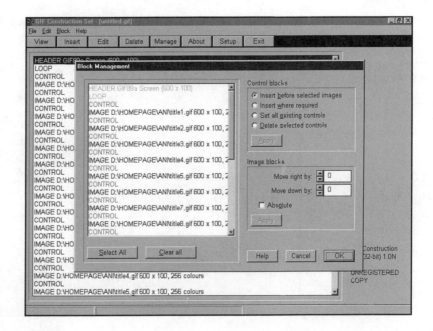

Staying Current

New software is constantly being released; it's an evolving process of companies around the world trying to improve on their products before the competition beats them to it. Since Web development is a relatively young field, there isn't an overabundance of high-quality tools out there to make creating Web pages as easy and fun as it should be.

Of course, there's always going to be a new tool or version available—it's hard to keep up to date. If you are unable to find the tools that you want for your Web page, or just want to browse through a list of the latest and greatest, stop by the TUCOWS Web site (The Ultimate Collection Of Winsock Software) at **http://www.tucows.com**. Figure 13.14 shows the list of software available for Windows 95.

Part
V

Ch

FIG. 13.14

Tucows is the best place to look for current shareware Web development tools.

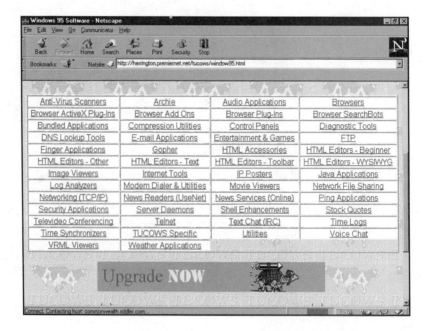

What's on the CD-ROM

The CD-ROM bundled with this book has been carefully prepared and researched so you'll have a variety of tools and examples to assist you in enhancing your Web pages. The entire CD has been linked with HTML Web pages so it can be accessed via your favorite browser. You'll find that the Web pages have links to the software programs on the disc, the graphics files and examples, and to actual Web sites on the World Wide Web. (You'll need an Internet connection to use these.)

Starting up the CD is simple. From within your browser, load the file LOADME.HTM. The first page will lead you to the next pages where you can choose what you'd like to see next.

I've highlighted several special programs and examples on the CD-ROM that I think you'll find particularly useful. At the end of this appendix, there is a list highlighting some of the files and programs that are on the CD-ROM.

This CD-ROM contains hundreds of megabytes of files, programs, and examples, all designed around creating Web pages. Enjoy the collection; I've spent a lot of time making it the best it could be. ■

N O T E Many of the software on the CD is shareware, offered free for a period of time so you can evaluate them. If you decide to use any of this software, you can register with the software company, pay a fee, and receive a fully working version and possibly other perks. Please respect the efforts of the software authors who have toiled over a hot monitor late into the night to bring you a quality program at a reasonable price. ■

Programs and Examples Used in This Book

This collection—including programs, samples, and information—is the cream of the crop on this CD-ROM, and you should take some time exploring it and looking in the relevant sections of the book.

CoffeeCup HTML Editor

CoffeeCup is a wildly popular, irreverent HTML editor that is robust, easy to use, and afford-able. Another shareware product, CoffeeCup is significantly cheaper than HotDog and will likely fulfill all of the Web creators' standard needs.

You can reach CoffeeCup by clicking the Software link from the main HTML page that refer-ences the entire CD-ROM. Its location on the CD-ROM is \SOFTWARE\COFFEE\

HotDog HTML Editor

HotDog is one of the leaders in HTML Editors. I mentioned it in Chapter 13, "Using HTML Editors and Other Web Tools," as an easy-to-use and friendly editor. This shareware product may well be worth the registration if you find yourself building and maintaining many Web pages.

You can reach HotDog by clicking the Tools link from the main HTML page that references the entire CD-ROM. Its location on the CD-ROM is \SOFTWARE\HOTDOG\.

MapTHIS!

Those lovely image maps you see on other Web pages can be difficult to create unless you have a program such as MapTHIS! It's an excellent utility for setting up the links from different areas of your image. MapTHIS! is freeware and can be run directly from the CD-ROM.

You can reach MapTHIS! by clicking the Tools link from the main HTML page that references the entire CD-ROM. Its location on the CD-ROM is \SOFTWARE\MAPTHIS\.

Collections of Images and Graphics

When creating Web pages, one of the most valuable weapons in your arsenal is a robust collection of creative images, buttons, bars, and graphics. I've literally scoured the whole world to find impressive samples and collections of graphics that you can use on your Web page. All of the images found on this CD-ROM are royalty free and can be used and modified however you like for your Web page.

There are hundreds of images for you on this CD, including the following types:

- Backgrounds
- Bullets
- Buttons
- Lines
- Pictures

In fact, I have so many different collections of graphics, I can't even name them all here. You can see all of them from the CD-ROM by clicking the Graphics link from the main HTML page that references the entire CD-ROM.

Sound Clips

Choose from hundreds of audio files. You'll find the following general categories of sounds on the CD:

- Animal sounds
- Special effects
- Sounds from around the house
- Instrument sounds
- Sounds from nature
- Voices

Links to sound archives on the Internet are included.

Video Clips

One of the crown jewels of this CD-ROM is the over 90M of impressive video clips (in Windows AVI format) that you can use however you like. Put together by FourPalms Software, there are over 20 different video clips in two different resolutions. Besides the sample FourPalms clips, there are also several other Quicktime and MPEG video clips on the CD-ROM just for your enjoyment or for your Web page.

You can watch and use these video clips directly from the CD-ROM by clicking the Video link from the main HTML page that references the entire CD-ROM.

Example Files

Throughout this book, you have probably noticed the many practical and useful examples that I created when discussing a new topic. Whether it is working with lists or multimedia clips, I have included virtually all of my sample files on the CD-ROM.

Each chapter that has examples has its own index of examples. You can see how the examples look in your Web browser for yourself, pick apart the HTML files, and look behind the scenes.

You can reach the example files by clicking the Examples link from the main HTML page that references the entire CD-ROM.

References Used in This Book

Appendix B, "References Used in This Book," is a useful collection of links that any Web developer, new or experienced, will find useful. It is a list of all the sites on the WWW that I mention somewhere in this book. I've converted it to HTML format so you can directly reference each of those sites—without typing an URL for every spot you want to visit—while browsing.

Click the References link from the main HTML page to see the list of references online.

A Complete Listing of Software on the CD-ROM

For those of you who would like to know what else is available, we've put a lot of other software packages on the CD-ROM. You might find that you prefer some of them to the programs mentioned in this book. Many are useful WWW tools and browsers, and you'll also find important file management and general Internet tools.

Software on the CD-ROM

- Adobe Acrobat Reader
- View PDF files

- AANT HTML
- Word to HTML and HTML to WYSIWYG conversion
- Home page: **http://telecommunications.com/ant/antdesc.htm**

- AppletAce
- Configure and test Macromedia's Java PowerApplets
- Home page: **http://www.macromedia.com/software/appleace/**

- Clickette
- Easy Java button effects
- Home page: **http://www.sausage.com/**

- CoffeeCup
- Easy and powerful HTML editor
- Home page: **http://www.coffeecup.com**

- Color Manipulation Device
- Color picker utility
- Home page: **http://www.meat.com/software/cmd.html**
- CoolEdit
- Audio editor

- CrossEye
- Generate client side image maps
- Home page: **http://www.sausage.com/**

- CuteFTP
- Windows FTP

- EasyHelp/Web for Word
- Easy Java animation and sound

- Egor
- Easy Java animation and sound
- Home page: **http://www.sausage.com/** **<Picture: *>**

- Flash
- Animate the browser status bar
- Home page: **http://www.sausage.com/**

- FrameGang
- Easy HTML Frame Creator
- Home page: **http://www.sausage.com/**

- Free Agent
- Online/offline newsreader
- Home page: **http://www.forteinc,com/forte**

- GoldWave
- Audio Editor

- HAHTSite
- WYSIWYG editing, site management and more
- Home page: **http://www.hahtsite.com/**

- Hot Dog
- Powerful HTML editor
- Home page: **http://www.sausage.com/**
- HotDog for Win 3.x helper files

- HTML Assistant for Windows
- HTML editing software

- HTMLed

- HTML Notepad
- Simple, easy-to-use HTML editor

- HTML Writer
- Home page: **http://www.public.asu.edu/~bottger/**

- MapTHIS!
- Create image maps
- Home page: **http://galadriel.ecaetc.ohio-state.edu/tc/mt**

- Mod4Win
- Digital music module player
- View the Readme File

- MS ActiveX Control Pad
- Development tool

- MS Internet Assistant for Access
- Access to HTML converter

- MS Internet Assistant for Excel
- Excel to HTML converter
- Home page: **http://www.microsoft.com/**

- MS Internet Assistant for PowerPoint
- PowerPoint to HTML converter
- Home page: **http://www.microsoft.com/**

- MS Internet Assistant for Word
- Word to HTML converter

- MS Internet Explorer 3.02
- Full-featured Web browser

- PaintShop Pro
- Image-editing software

- ■ ScriptActive
- ■ ActiveX Plug-in for Netscape Navigator 3.0
- ■ Home page: **http://www.ncompasslabs.com/**

- ■ Swami
- ■ Java text effects
- ■ Home page: **http://www.sausage.com/**

- ■ UUCODE
- ■ UUencoder/decoder

- ■ VDOLive Video Player
- ■ View live and on-demand video
- ■ Home page: **http://www.vdo.net**

- ■ Visual Intercept
- ■ Project-oriented incident management system
- ■ Home page: **http://www.elsitech.com**

- ■ VuePrint Pro
- ■ Multiformat image viewer
- ■ Home page: **http://www.hamrick.com/**

- ■ Webber
- ■ HTML Editor
- ■ Home page: **http://www.csdcorp.com/webber.html**

- ■ Ken Nesbit's Wed Edit
- ■ Popular HTML editor
- ■ Web Forms

- Create forms for your Web pages
- Home page: **http://www.q-d.com**

- Web Mania
- Create your own WWW documents quickly and easily
- Home page: **http://www.q-d.com**

- WinCode
- MultiPurpose Encoder/Decoder

- WinJPEG
- Image utility

- WinZip
- File compression utility
- Home page: **http://www.winzip.com/**

- WIRL
- Enables virtual reality on the Web
- Home page: **http://www.vream.com**

- WS Gopher
- Windows gopher
- Home page: **http://www.mstc.com/wsgopher**

- WS FTP Limited Edition
- Windows FTP

Index

Symbols

/ (forward slashes), 53

3-D graphics (enclosed CD-ROM), 109

A

<A> (anchor) tags, 138-139, 146-150
  anchors
    creating, 148-149
    linking, 149-150
    naming, 148-149
    placing, 149
    Web sites, 146
  audio clips, adding, 201
  HREF keyword, 150
  links, adding, 140-141

ABSMIDDLE keyword (images), 124

Accent browser, 23

Accent Software Web sites, 23, 81

Access (Internet Assistants), 259

accessing FTP sites, 190

ActiveX, 23

<ADDRESS> tags, 53-55
  adding, 54
  Explorer, 23

Adobe Photoshop, resizing images, 121

advertising
  businesses, 249
  cost, 248
  Web pages, publicizing, 248-249

AIFF file format, 199

Alchemy Mindworks Web site, 262

ALIGN keyword
  bullets, adding, 127
  <IMG> tags, 123-125
  tables, 101

ALINK keyword links changing color, 144

ALT keyword
  images, 123
    linking, 145

Amaya browser, 23
  Web site, 23

America Online, see AOL

anchor tags, URLs, 147

anchors
  creating, 148-149
  linking, 149-150
  naming, 148-149
  placing, 149
  Web sites, 146
  see also <A> tags

animated GIFs (GIF Construction Set), 262

announcement services Web pages, publicizing, 234-236

anonymous access (FTP sites), 190

AOL (America Online), 47
  WebCrawler, 242

Apple Computer Web site, 206

applets (JavaScript CoffeeCup), 257

<AREA> tags (image maps), 168-170

Area List dialog box, 165

ASCII (HTML), 24

AU file format, 198

audio clips, 198-201
  adding, 201-204
  CD-ROM (enclosed), 199, 267
  converting file formats, 199
  copyrights, 200-201
  creating, 201
  embedding
    Explorer, 204
    Netscape, 202-204

file formats, 198-199
finding, 199-201
Internet, 200
links, adding, 201-202
saving, 200
Web sites, 200

**Audio File Format FAQ
Web site, 199**

author
home page, 35, 84
Web site, 72

AUTOSTART keyword
audio clips, embedding,
203
video clips, embedding,
210

AVI file format, 205
Web sites, 206

B

<B> tags, 68-69

**BACKGROUND keyword,
130-131**

backgrounds
CD-ROM (enclosed), 109
color-code hunting
(CoffeeCup), 257
colors
default, 129
Web site, 130
design tips, 214
images, adding, 130-131
tables, selecting color,
102-103
text, 129-131
troubleshooting, 131

**bad-image pointer icon,
119**

bars, adding, 127

**BGCOLOR keyword,
129-130**
tables, 102-103

**<BGSOUND> tags,
adding audio clips, 204**

<BIG> tags, 70-71

<BLINK> tags, 69-70
Explorer, 70

**blinking text, formatting,
69-70**

<BODY> tags, 53-54
images, adding, 118
links, configuring color,
144
text, coloring, 79
Web pages, splitting, 180

**bold text, formatting,
68-69**

**BORDER keyword
(tables), 96**

**BORDERCOLOR
keyword, 103**

**BORDERCOLORDARK
keyword, 103**

**BORDERCOLORLIGHT
keyword, 103**

**borders (tables),
selecting color,
102-103**

**
 tags, 60**
icons, 127
images, aligning, 125
lists, 85

browsers, 21-23
Accent, 23
Amaya, 23
comparing, 23
Explorer, 21-23
ActiveX, 23
audio clips, 204
<BLINK> tags, 70
horizontal lines, 62
images, 111
PNG images, 116
text, 59
URLs, 113

video clips, 211
Web site, 22
GIFs (transparent),
132-133
HTML extensions, 26
image maps
client-side, 173
testing, 172
Mosaic, 18, 23
Netscape, 21
audio clips, 202-204
color settings, 144
history, 18
image maps, 167
images, 110
PNG images, 116
tables, 104-105
text, 59
video clips, 210-211
status bars, 142
tags, displaying logical,
69
URLs, 141
Web pages, testing, 227
Web sites, 23

**BrowserWatch Web site,
23**

budgetweb Web site, 45

**Buena Vista movies Web
site, 196**

**bulleted (unordered)
lists, adding, 88**

bullets, adding, 127

business cards
home pages, 32
Web pages, publicizing,
247

businesses
consulting charges (Web
providers), 45
home pages, 32-33
Web pages
advertising, 249
counters, 186
publicizing, 232-233

Web sites (Forman Interactive), 47

C

cameras, video, 208

<CAPTION> tags, 95

Cascading Style Sheets (CSS), 19

case sensitivity
HTML, 222
URLs, 142

catalogs (WWW)
Excite, 239
Four11, 239
URLs, 12
Web pages, publicizing, 234, 237-241
Yahoo!, 237-238

CD-ROM (enclosed)
audio clips, 199, 267
audio players, 198-199
CoffeeCup, 256
Explorer, 23
files, 268
graphics, 109-110, 267
HotDog Pro, 252
images (viewers), 117
installing, 265
MapTHIS!, 163
reference, 266-268
shareware, 266
templates, 52
video clips, 206, 267
Web pages, uploading, 50

cells (tables), selecting color, 103

censorship (Web providers), 44

<CENTER> tags, 68

CGI (Common Gateway Interface), 26
server-side image maps, 158

characters (special), adding, 81-82

Chrysler Web site, 232

circular image maps, 169

client-side image maps (CSIM), 155, 157-158
creating, 159-167
identifying, 159
server-side image maps, comparing, 158-159

client/server systems (WWW), 16-17

clients (WinSock), 17

clip art, 113

closing tags, 53

Coca-Cola Web site, 37-38

code listings
A Multirow Table, 96
Embedded List Code Listing, 94
HTML code for definition lists, 92
see also HTML

CoffeeCup, 256-257
CD-ROM (enclosed), 256-266
cost, 256
GIFs, 257
JavaScript applets, 257
Web site, 256

Cologne Answer Guy Web site, 216

color
backgrounds (default), 129
hexadecimal coloring, 79-81
named font colors, 78
settings, overriding, 144
tables, selecting, 102-103

COLOR keyword, 78

Colors tab (General Preferences dialog box), 144

COLSPAN keyword (tables), 99

columns (tables), spanning, 99

commands
Edit menu
Paste, 112
Preferences, 122
File menu
New, 163
Save, 166
Save As, 134
Options menu, General Preferences, 144
Tools menu, Options, 253
View menu
Document, 224
Document Source, 221, 225
Page Source, 14
Source, 14, 113

comments
adding, 222, 224
viewing, 224

commercial Web sites, 32-33
Coca-Cola, 37-38
consulting charges (Web providers), 45
ESPN, 37
Forman Interactive, 47

Common Gateway Interface (CGI), 26
server-side image maps, 158

comp.infosystems.www. announce newsgroup, 244-245

CompuServe, 48-49
Home Page Wizard, 48
PNG file format, 116

connections
  ISDN, 17
  modem, 17-18
  Web providers, 43-50
Connectix QuickCam video camera, 208
Connectix Web site, 208
consistency, checking Web page design, 214
construction icons, 128
consulting charges (Web providers), 45
Context Based databases (Excite), 239
CoolEdit audio player, 199
CoolEdit Web site, 199
COORDS keyword (rectangular image maps), 169
copyrights
  audio clips, 200-201
  see also enclosed CD-ROM
cost
  advertising, 248
  CoffeeCup, 256
  counters, 186
  HotDog Pro, 253
  HoTMetaL, 258
  online services, 47
  Submit-it!, 244
  Web providers, 44-45
  Web servers, 49
counters
  adding, 183-186
  advanced, 186
  businesses, 186
  cost, 186
  HTML, 184
  placing, 185
  Web sites, 184-186
Creating Web pages Web site, 138

Crime Scene Web site, 35
CSIM (client-side image maps), 155, 157-158
  creating, 159-167
  identifying, 159
  server-side image maps, comparing, 158-159
CSS (Cascading Style Sheets), 19

D

Daily Wav Web site, 200
databases
  Context Based (Excite), 239
  WAIS, 15
DC Comics Web site, 219
<DD> tags, 91
definition lists, adding, 91-92
designing Web pages
  borrowing concepts, 39, 221
  creeping featurism, 218-221
  hidden links, 219-220
  text length, 214-215
  three-by-three rule, 215
  tips, 214-217
dialog boxes
  Area List, 165
  File Preferences (PaintShop Pro), 134
  Info about this Mapfile, 166
  Make New Image Map, 163
  Open Existing Image File, 163
  Save As, 110

Send Mail/Post News, 245
digital scanners, 115
digits Web site, 185
Dilbert Web site, 110
directories (WWW)
  Excite, 239
  Four11, 239
  URLs, 12
  Web pages, publicizing, 234, 237-241
  Yahoo!, 237-238
<DL> tags, 87
Document command (View menu), 224
Document Source command (View menu), 221, 225
Document Type Definition (DTD), 227
documents, *see* Web pages
domains (URLs), 12
downloading large files, 205
<DT> tags, 91-92
DTD (Document Type Definition), 227
DYNSRC keyword, embedding video clips, 211

E

e-mail, 15
  addresses, adding, 54
  links, adding, 193
  newsgroups, posting messages, 245
  Web pages, publicizing, 247

Edit menu commands
Paste, 112
Preferences, 122

editors (HTML), 42, 251-260
CD-ROM (enclosed), 266
CoffeeCup, 256-257
HotDog Pro, 252-255, 266
HoTMetaL, 257-258
Netscape Composer, 258-259
targets, 147
Web Weaver, 258
WYSIWYG, 252

electronic mail, *see* **e-mail**

<EM> tags, 68

<EMBED> tags
audio clips, adding, 202-204
video clips, adding, 210-211

embedding <FONT> tags, 74-75

ESPN Web site, 37

Excel (Internet Assistants), 259

Excite, 239

Excite Web site, 239

Expert Software (clip art), 113

Explorer (Internet), 21-23
ActiveX, 23
audio clips, embedding, 204
<BLINK> tags, 70
horizontal lines (extensions), 62
images, saving, 111
Netscape, comparing, 23
PNG images, 116
text, formatting, 59

URLs, viewing, 113
video clips, embedding, 211
Web pages, testing, 227
Web site, 22

extended file names, 179

extensions (HTML), 26

F

FACE keywords, 75-76

File Dirs tab (HotDog Pro Options dialog box), 253

file formats
audio clips, 198-199
converting, 199
images, 116-117
video clips, 205-206

File menu commands
New, 163
Save, 166
Save As, 134

file permissions, adding images, 119

File Preferences dialog box (PaintShop Pro), 134

File Transfer Protocol, *see* **FTP**

files
CD-ROM (enclosed), 268
creating HTML, 41
extensions, 41
image maps, 166-167
INDEX.HTML, 142
links, 138
maximum size, 121
naming, 179
saving, 55
size guidelines
image maps, 173
images, 120-121
video clips, 205

uploading, troubleshooting, 141
URLs, 138

<FONT> tags
embedding, 74-75
fonts, configuring, 75-76
hexadecimal coloring, 79-81
relative font sizes, configuring, 73-74
tables, 103
text
coloring, 78
formatting, 72-76
sizing, 73

fonts
configuring, 75-76
testing, 76
viewing (Windows 95), 76

footers, 180
design tips, 214

foreign languages, adding special characters, 81

Forman Interactive Web site, 47

formatting
tables, 97
text, 59-72
blinking, 69-70
bold, 68-69
centering, 68
horizontal rules, 61-65
HotDog Pro, 255
line breaks, 60
paragraphs, 60
preformatted, 66
relative font sizes, 73-74
sizing, 70-71, 73
strikethrough, 70
subscripts, 72
superscripts, 72
underline, 70

forward slashes (/), 53

Four11, 239-240
Web site, 239

FourPalms software Web site, 207

Free Page Site Web site, 46

FTP (File Transfer Protocol), 14
links, adding, 189-190
programs, 50
sites
accessing passwords, 190
anonymous access, 190
HotDog, 190
Web pages, uploading, 50

G

General Preferences command (Options menu), 144

Geocities Web site, 46

GIF Construction Set (graphics tool), 262

GIF Construction Set Web site, 262

GIFs (Graphical Interchange Format), 116
adding, 118
Coffeecup, 257
combining (GIF Construction Set), 262
JPEGs, comparing, 116
PNGs, comparing, 116
transparent, 131-134
browsers, 132-133
creating, 133-134

Gopher, 15
links, 138, 192-193

Graphical Interchange

Format, *see* GIFs

graphics, 108-109
adding (design tips), 214
CD-ROM (enclosed), 109-110, 267
finding, 109-115
GIF Construction Set, 262
PaintShop Pro, 260-262
tables, 101
Web pages, testing, 225
see also images

guestbooks, 186-189
adding links (HTML), 187
Web site, 187, 189

H

<H1> tags
adding, 57
home pages, designing, 214

<HEAD> tags, 52-53, 57

headers (tables), adding, 97

heading tags
adding, 56-58
<HEAD> tags, comparing, 57

HEIGHT keyword, sizing images, 125-126

hexadecimal colors, 79-81
Web sites, 80

HIDDEN keyword, embedding audio clips, 204

hidden links, 219-220

<Hn> tags, 60

Home Page Wizard (CompuServe), 48

home pages, 30

author, 35, 84
business cards, 32
comments, adding, 222
commercial sites, 32-33
Coca-Cola, 37-38
consulting charges (Web providers), 45
ESPN, 37
Forman Interactive, 47
consistency, checking, 214
counters
adding, 183-186
cost, 186
placing, 185
designing
borrowing concepts, 39, 221
creeping featurism, 218-221
text length, 214-215
three-by-three rule, 215
tips, 214-217
guestbooks, adding, 186-189
icons, adding, 126-129
image maps, *see* image maps
images, *see* images
links
adding e-mail, 193
adding FTP, 189-190
adding Gopher, 192-193
adding newsgroups, 191
Magnavox, 156
multimedia, designing, 216
navigating (navigation icons), 128-129
Netscape Home page, 21
organizing, 38-39
personal pages, 31-32
planning, 30-31, 34-39
previewing, 225-227

prototyping, 39
simple, 34-35
sketching, 39
splitting, 176-177, 179-181
tables, 94-97
technical support, 32-33
templates, 52
testing, 225-230
text, *see* text
updating, 216-217
uploading, 50
video clips, adding, 209-211
visitors, tracking, 183-186
Web Consortium's Home page, 25
Web provider, 44
see also Web pages

home sites, planning, 177-179

horizontal rules
extensions (Internet Explorer), 62, 64
formatting, 61-65
shading, 62-63
thickness, 65
width, 63-64

HotDog Pro, 252-255
CD-ROM (enclosed), 252, 266
cost, 253
FTP site, 190
HTML editors, 42
running, 254
text, formatting, 255
Web pages, previewing, 255
Web site, 42, 252, 254
Windows 95, creating shortcuts, 255

HoTMetaL, 257-258
cost, 258
HTML parsers, 258
Web site, 258

<HR> tags, 61
extensions, 62-65

Internet Explorer, 62, 64
SHADE/NOSHADE, 62-63
SIZE, 65
WIDTH, 63-64
replacing with graphics, 127

HREF keyword
anchors, 148-150
audio clips, adding, 201
image maps (rectangular), 169
links, adding, 140-141

.HTM file extension, 41

<HTML> tags, *see* tags

HTML (HyperText Markup Language), 13-14
ASCII, 24
audio clips
adding, 202
embedding, 203
case sensitivity, 222
counters, adding, 184
editors, *see* HTML editors
extensions, 26
files
creating, 41
naming, 179
saving, 55
footers, 180
guestbooks, adding, 187
learning, 51
links, 138-139
adding e-mail, 193
adding Gopher, 192
newsgroups, adding, 191
programming languages, 26
source code
comments, 224
formatting, 222
hiding, 224
structuring, 221-224
viewing, 221

standards, 24, 227
tags, *see* tags
tools, selecting, 252-260
validation tools, 227-230
versions, 25
video clips, embedding, 209
Web sites, 26, 227
WebTechs Validation Service, 228-229
writing, 40-42
WWW future enhancements, 19
see also listings

HTML editors, 42, 251-260
CD-ROM (enclosed), 266
CoffeeCup, 256-257
HotDog Pro, 252-255, 266
HoTMetaL, 257-258
Netscape Composer, 258-259
targets, 147
Web Weaver, 258
WYSIWYG, 252

.HTML file extension, 41

HTML parsers (HoTMetaL), 258

HTML Validator Web site, 230

HTTP (HyperText Transfer Protocol), 14, 138, 189

hypertext links, 11-13, 137-144
adding, 141-142
audio clips, 201-202
default, 171-172
e-mail, 193
FTP, 190
Gopher, 192-193
local Web pages, 140-141
newsgroups, 191
URLs, 142
video clips, 209

anchor tags, 149-150
color, configuring, 144
describing, 153
hidden, 219-220
HTML, 138-139
images, 144-145
keeping current, 153
limiting, 151
organizing lists, 150
testing, 140
text, selecting, 152-153
tips, 151-153
Web pages
    publicizing, 247-248
    testing, 226

HyperText Markup Language, *see* **HTML**
HyperText Transfer Protocol, *see* **HTTP**

I

<I> tags, 69
IBM PCs
    audio clips, creating, 201
    multimedia capabilities, 198
    video clips, viewing, 205
icons
    adding, 126-129
    bars, adding, 127
    bullets, adding, 127
    CD-ROM (enclosed), 109
    construction, 128
    lines, adding, 127
    navigation, 128-129
    New, 128
    see also images
image maps, 145, 155-159
    adding, 162
    CGI, 158
    circular, 169
    client-side, 155, 157-159
    creating, 159-167

designing, 173-174, 219
files, 166-167
images
    mapping, 162-167
    selecting, 159-160, 174
links
    adding default, 171-172
    troubleshooting, 162
MapTHIS! (enclosed CD-ROM), 266
Netscape, 167
planning, 161-162
polygonal, 169-170
rectangular, 168-169
regions, overlapping, 170-171
server-side, 158-159
tags, adding, 167-168
testing, 172, 174
text, providing alternate, 172
URLs, 155
Web sites, 160

images, 108-109, 122-126
adding, 117-119, 162
    background, 130-131
    design tips, 214
aligning, 123-125
bad-image pointer icon, 119
CD-ROM (enclosed), 267
clip art, 113
combining (GIF Construction Set), 262
downloading, 110-113
file formats, 116-117
file permissions, 119
files
    maximum size, 121
    size guidelines, 120-121
finding, 109-115
GIF Construction Set, 262
image maps, selecting,

159-160, 174
Internet Graphics Gallery, 113
linking, 144-145
    legality, 113
    Web sites, 111-113
mapping, 162-167
overlaying, 135-136
PaintShop Pro, 114, 260-262
resizing, 121
saving
    Explorer, 111
    Netscape, 110
scanners, 115
sizing, 125-126
stock images, 113
text, providing alternate, 122-123
thumbnails, 121
viewing
    plug-ins, 117
    viewers, 117
Web pages, testing, 225
see also; graphics; icons
<IMG> tags, 118-119
image maps, adding, 162
images
    linking, 113, 145, 156
    overlaying, 136
    sizing, 126
keywords
    ALIGN, 123-125
    ALT, 123
video clips, embedding, 211

Independence Day Web site, 196
INDEX.HTML file, 142
indexes
    Excite, 239
    Lycos, 242
    Web pages, publicizing, 234
    Yahoo!, 237-238

infi.net Web site, 130

Info about this Mapfile dialog box, 166

installing enclosed CD-ROM, 265

interactivity (WWW), 15
see also multimedia

internal document pointers, adding, 146

Internet, 9
audio clips, finding, 200
e-mail, 193
FTP, 189-190
Gopher, 192-193
multimedia, 10-11
newsgroups, 191
protocols, 14-15
resources, 189-193
URLs, 138
UseNet, 191
video clips, finding, 207
WWW, *see* WWW

Internet Assistants, 259-260
Web site, 260

Internet Explorer, 21-23
ActiveX, 23
audio clips, embedding, 204
<BLINK> tags, 70
horizontal lines (extensions), 62
images, saving, 111
Netscape, comparing, 23
PNG images, 116
text, formatting, 59
URLs, viewing, 113
video clips, embedding, 211
Web pages, testing, 227
Web site, 22

Internet Graphics Gallery, 113

Internet Service

Providers, *see* ISPs

Internet World's What's New Web site, 234

ISDN connections, 17

ISPs (Internet Service Providers)
modem connections, 17
Web providers, comparing, 43

italics, formatting, 69

J

JASC Web site, 160

JavaScript
applets (CoffeeCup), 257
Netscape, 21

JPEG (Joint Photographic Experts Group), 116
GIFs, comparing, 116

K

keywords
ABSMIDDLE (images), 124
ALIGN
adding bullets, 127
<IMG> tags, 123-125
tables, 101
ALINK, changing link color, 144
ALT
images, 123
linking images, 145
AUTOSTART
adding video clips, 210
embedding audio clips, 203
BACKGROUND, 130-131
BGCOLOR, 102-103, 129-130

BORDER (tables), 96
BORDERCOLOR, 103
BORDERCOLORDARK, 103
BORDERCOLORLIGHT, 103
COLOR, 78
COLSPAN (tables), 99
COORDS (rectangular image maps), 169
DYNSRC (embedding video clips), 211
FACE, 75-76
HEIGHT, sizing images, 125-126
HIDDEN, embedding audio clips, 204
HREF
adding audio clips, 201
adding links, 140-141
anchors, 150
creating anchors, 148-149
rectangular image maps, 169
LEFT (images), 125
LINK, changing link color, 144
LOOP
adding video clips, 211
embedding audio clips, 204
Low Resolution, *see* LOWSRC
LOWSRC, 135-136
NAME (anchors), 148-149
NOHREF (image maps), 172
NOSHADE (horizontal lines), 62-63
RIGHT (images), 125
ROWSPAN (tables), 98-99
SEQNUM (numbered lists), 90
SHADE (horizontal lines), 62-63

SHAPE (rectangular image maps), 169
SIZE (horizontal lines), 65
SRC
  adding images, 118
  adding video clips, 210
  embedding audio clips, 203
TEXT, coloring text, 79
TEXTTOP (images), 124
TYPE (numbered lists), 90
USEMAP, adding image maps, 162
VALIGN (tables), 101
VLINK, changing link color, 144
WIDTH
  horizontal lines, 63
  sizing images, 125-126

L

languages, programming
CGI, 26
HTML, 13-14, 26
JavaScript, 21

LEFT keyword (images), 125

legal issues
copyrights (audio clips), 200-201
images, linking, 113
see also CD-ROM (enclosed)

LensCrafters Web site, 33

<LH> tags, 87-88

<LI> tags, 87
links
  ordered, 89
  organizing, 150
  unordered, 88

line breaks, formatting, 60

lines
adding, 127
extensions (Internet Explorer), 62, 64
formatting, 61-65
shading, 62-63
thickness, 65
width, 63-64

LINK keyword, changing link color, 144

links, 11-13, 137-144
adding, 141-142
  audio clips, 201-202
  default, 171-172
  e-mail, 193
  FTP, 190
  Gopher, 192-193
  local Web pages, 140-141
  newsgroups, 191
  URLs, 142
  video clips, 209
anchor tags, 149-150
color, configuring, 144
describing, 153
hidden, 219-220
HTML, 138-139
images, 144-145
keeping current, 153
limiting, 151
organizing lists, 150
testing, 140
text, selecting, 152-153
tips, 151-153
Web pages
  publicizing, 247-248
  testing, 226

listings
A Multirow Table, 96
Embedded List Code Listing, 94
HTML code for definition lists, 92
see also HTML

lists, 84-86
adding, 87-92

 tags, 85
definition, adding, 91-92
embedding
  lists, 93-94
  tables, 100-103
links, organizing, 150
numbered
  changing numbering, 90
  SEQNUM keyword, 90
ordered, adding, 89-90
step-by-step processes, 86
tables, replacing, 104
text, organizing, 84-85
unordered, adding, 88

logical formatting, 68

LOOP keyword
audio clips, embedding, 204
video clips, adding, 211

Lotus white papers, 32

Low Resolution keyword, 135-136

LOWSRC keyword, 135-136

Lycos, 241-242
indexes, 242
Web site, 241

Lynx (table alternatives), 104-105

M

Macintosh
audio clips, creating, 201
HTML editors (Web Weaver), 258
multimedia capabilities, 198
video clips, viewing, 205

Magnavox
home page, 156
Web site, 10

mail, 15
addresses, adding, 54
links, adding, 193
newsgroups, posting
messages, 245
Web pages, publicizing,
247

**maintenance charges
(Web providers), 45**

**Make New Image Map
dialog box, 163**

**managing Web sites,
182-183**

<MAP> tags, 167-168

MapTHIS!
CD-ROM (enclosed), 266
image maps
creating, 163-167
polygonal, 170
Web site, 163

markup tags, *see* **tags**

Microsoft
Internet Assistants,
259-260
Web site, 19

Microsoft Web site, 17

Microsoft Word
fonts, testing, 76
HTML, creating files, 41
Internet Assistants, 259
text (spell-checking), 226

MIDI file format, 199

modems
connections, 17-18
recommendations, 17
Web site, 17

Mosaic
browsers, 18, 23
PNG images, 116
table alternatives, 104-105
Web site, 23

MPEG file format, 206
Web sites, 206-207

mu-law file format, 198

**Multilingual WWW
Publisher Web site, 81**

multimedia, 195-196
audio clips, 198
creating, 201
embedding, 202-204
file formats, 198-199
finding, 199-201
mixing, 211-212
planning, 211-212
stores, 9
tags, 26
video cameras, 208
video clips, 204-208
adding, 209-211
creating, 208
embedding, 210-211
finding, 206-208
Web sites
Buena Vista movies,
196
Independence Day,
196
WWW, 10-11

N

**NAME keyword
(anchors), 148-149**

named font colors, 78

**navigation icons,
128-129**

Navigator, *see*
**Netscape (Netscape
Communicator)**

**NCSA What's New Web
site, 234**

NetCarta Web site, 182

**Netscape (Netscape
Communicator), 21**
audio clips, embedding,
202-204

color settings, overriding,
144
Explorer, comparing, 23
history, 18
image maps, 167
images, saving, 110
PNG images, 116
tables (alternatives),
104-105
text, formating, 59
video clips, embedding,
210-211
Web pages, testing, 227

**Netscape Composer
(HTML editor),
258-259**
Web site, 259

Netscape Home page, 21

**Netscape's What's New?
Web site, 236**

**New command (File
menu), 163**

New icons, 128

newsgroups
comp.infosystems.www.
announce, 244-245
links, 138, 191
posting e-mail messages,
245
UseNet, 14
Web pages, publicizing,
244-246

no break tags, 60

<NOBR> tags, 60

**NOHREF keyword
(image maps), 172**

**NOSHADE keyword
(horizontal line tags),
62**

**Notepad, creating HTML
files, 41**

numbered (ordered) lists
adding, 89-90
numbering, changing, 90
SEQNUM keyword, 90

O

***Official WWW Yellow Pages*, 240-241**
Web site, 240

<OL> tags, 87, 89

online services, 47-49
AOL, 47
CompuServe, 48-49
cost, 47

Open Existing Image File dialog box, 163

Options command (Tools menu), 253

Options menu commands, General Preferences, 144

ordered (numbered) lists
adding, 89-90
numbering, changing, 90
SEQNUM keyword, 90

overlaying images, 135-136

P

<P> tags, 60
Web pages, testing, 225

Page Source command (View menu), 14

pagecount Web site, 185

PaintShop Pro, 114, 260-262
GIFs
creating transparent, 133-134
transparent, 132
image maps, 160
images, resizing, 121
Web site, 114, 133

paragraphs, formatting, 60

parsers (HoTMetaL), 258

passwords, accessing FTP sites, 190

Paste command (Edit menu), 112

PCs (IBM)
audio clips, creating, 201
multimedia capabilities, 198
video clips, viewing, 205

personal pages, 31-32

Photoshop, resizing images, 121

physical formatting, 68

pictures, *see* images

pings, *see* PNGs

plug-ins
images, viewing, 117
Web site, 117

PNGs (Portable Network Graphics)
GIFs, comparing, 116
Web site, 116

Point-to-Point Protocol, *see* PPP

pointers (internal document), adding, 146

polygonal image maps, 169-170

Portable Network Graphics, *see* PNGs

PowerPoint (Internet Assistants), 259

PPP (Point-to-Point Protocol) connections, 17-18

<PRE> tags, 66
tables, replacing, 104

Preferences command (Edit menu), 122

preformatted text, replacing text, 104-105

programming languages
CGI, 26
comments, 222
HTML, 13-14, 26
JavaScript, 21

programs
FTP, 50
Internet Assistants, 259-260
PaintShop Pro, 260-262
shareware, 252
staying current, 263

protocols
HTTP, 189
Internet, 14-15
URLs, 138
WWW, 189

prototyping Web pages, 39

publicizing Web pages, 232
advertising, 248-249
announcement services, 234-236
comp.infosystems.www. announce, 244-245
expectations, 233
indexes, 234
Lycos, 241-242
Submit It!, 243-244
WebCrawler, 242-249
What's New listings, 234-236
WWW directories, 234, 237-241

Q

QT (Quicktime) file format, 206
Web sites, 206-207

Que Web site, 49, 248
QuickCam video camera, 208

R

RA file format (RealAudio), 199
  Web sites, 199
rectangular image maps, 168-169
references (pointers), adding, 146
relative font sizes, configuring, 73-74
resizing images, 121
resolution (scanners), 115
resumes, publicizing Web pages, 247
RIGHT keyword (images), 125
rows (tables)
  adding, 97
  spanning, 98-99
ROWSPAN keyword (tables), 98-99
running HotDog Pro, 254

S

<S> tags, 70
Sausage Software Web site, 252, 254
Save As command (File menu), 134
Save As dialog box, 110
Save command (File menu), 166

saving
  HTML files, 55
  images
    Explorer, 111
    Netscape, 110
scanners (digital), 115
Schedule+ (Internet Assistants), 259
scrolling marquees, 26
search engines (tags), 53
Send Mail/Post News dialog box, 245
SEQNUM keyword (numbered lists), 90
Serial Line Internet Protocol (SLIP) connections, 17-18
server-side image maps
  CGI, 158
  client-side image maps, comparing, 158-159
  identifying, 159
servers, Web, 16-17
  case sensitivity, 142
  cost, 49
  image maps, 157-158
  visitors, tracking, 183
  Web providers, alternatives, 49-50
  Web site, 50
SHADE keyword (horizontal line tags), 62
SHAPE keyword (rectangular image maps), 169
shareware, 252
  CD-ROM (enclosed), 266
  CoffeeCup, 256-257
  HotDog Pro, 252-255
  HoTMetaL, 257-258

shareware Web site, 17
sign-up kits, ordering CompuServe, 49
sites
  FTP
    anonymous access, 190
    HotDog, 190
  Web
    Accent browser, 23
    Accent Software, 81
    Alchemy Mindworks, 262
    Amaya browser, 23
    anchor tags, 146
    Apple Computer, 206
    audio clips, 200
    Audio File Format FAQ, 199
    author, 35, 72
    AVI, 206
    background colors, 130
    BrowserWatch, 23
    budgetweb, 45
    Buena Vista movies, 196
    Chrysler, 232
    Coca-Cola, 37-38
    CoffeeCup, 256
    Cologne Answer Guy, 216
    Connectix, 208
    CoolEdit, 199
    counters, 184-186
    Creating Web pages, 138
    Crime Scene, 35
    Daily Wav, 200
    DC Comics, 219
    digits, 185
    Dilbert, 110
    downloading Winsock client, 17

ESPN, 37
Excite, 239
Explorer, 22
Forman Interactive, 47
Four11, 239
FourPalms software, 207
Free Page Site, 46
Geocities, 46
GIF Construction Set, 262
guestbooks, 187, 189
hexadecimal colors, 80
HotDog Pro, 42, 252, 254
HoTMetaL, 258
HTML, 26
HTML standards, 227
HTML Validator, 230
image maps, 160
Independence Day, 196
infi.net, 130
Internet Assistants, 260
JASC, 160
LensCrafters, 33
Lycos, 241
Magnavox, 10, 156
MapTHIS!, 163
Microsoft, 17, 19
modems, 17
Mosaic, 23
MPEG, 206-207
Multilingual WWW Publisher, 81
NCSA What's New, 234
NetCarta, 182
Netscape Composer, 259
Netscape Home page, 21
Netscape's What's New?, 236

Official WWW Yellow Pages, 240
pagecount, 185
PaintShop Pro, 114, 133-136
plug-ins, 117
PNG, 116
Que, 49, 248
Quicktime, 206-207
RealAudio, 199
Sausage Software, 252, 254
shareware, 17
SoftQuad, Inc, 258
special characters, 82
Star Wars, 195
Submit It!, 243
Toyota, 10
TUCOWS, 263
VRML, 19
Walt Disney, 218
Warner Brothers, 219
Weather Channel, 216
Web Consortium, 19
Web Consortium's Home page, 25
Web Servers, 50
WebCrawler, 242
WebLaunch, 248
Weblint, 230
WebMapper, 182
WebTechs Validation Service, 228-229
Wincam, 208
Worst of the Web, 233
Yahoo!, 237
Yahoo! List, 230

Size 1 headings, adding, 57

SIZE keyword (horizontal lines), 65

skyscraper format (Web sites), 177

slashes (/), 53

SLIP (Serial Line Internet Protocol) connections, 17-18

<SMALL> tags, 70-71

SoftQuad, Inc. Web site, 258

software
CoffeeCup, 256-257
HotDog Pro, 252-255
HoTMetaL, 257-258
MapTHIS!, 163
Netscape Composer, 258-259
staying current, 263
Web Weaver, 258

sound bites, *see audio clips*

source code
comments, 224
formatting, 222
hiding, 224
structuring, 221-224
viewing, 221

Source command (View menu), 14, 113

special characters
adding, 81-82
HTML tags, 81-82
Web site, 82

spell-checking text, 226

SRC keyword
audio clips, embedding, 203
images, adding, 118
video clips, embedding, 210

standard format (Web sites), 177
DTD (Document Type Definition), 227
HTML, 24-25

Star Wars Web site, 195

startup costs (Web providers), 44

startup kits
AOL, ordering, 48
CompuServe, ordering, 49

status bars (browsers), 142

step-by-step processes (lists), 86

stock images, 113

strikethrough text, formatting, 70

<STRONG> tags, 68

<SUB> tags, 72

Submit It!, 243-244
Web site, 243

Submit-it!, cost, 244

<SUP> tags, 72

symbols, adding, 81-82

T

<TABLE> tags, 95-96

tables, 84, 94
adding, 95-97
alternatives, 104-105
cells, 103
color, selecting, 102-103
columns, spanning, 99
formatting, 97
graphics, 101
headers, adding, 97
lists, embedding, 100-103
replacing
lists, 104
preformatted text, 104-105
rows
adding, 97
spanning, 98-99

tags, 95
text
aligning, 101
selecting color, 103
WebTV, 84

tags (HTML), 13, 24, 40, 52-55
<A> (anchor), 138-139, 146-150
adding audio clips, 201
adding links, 140-141
creating anchors, 148-149
HREF keyword, 150
naming anchors, 148-149
placing, 149
Web sites, 146
<ADDRESS>, 53-55
<AREA>
circular image maps, 169
image maps, 168
polygonal image maps, 170
rectangular image maps, 168
<B>, 68-69
<BGSOUND>, adding audio clips, 204
<BIG>, 70-71
<BLINK>, 69-70
<BODY>, 53-54
adding images, 118
coloring text, 79
configuring link color, 144
splitting Web pages, 180

, 60
aligning images, 125
icons, 127
lists, 85
<CAPTION>, 95
<CENTER>, 68

closing, 53
<DD>, 91
<DL>, 87
<DT>, 91-92
<EM>, 68
<EMBED>
adding audio clips, 202-204
adding video clips, 210-211
<FONT>
coloring text, 78
configuring fonts, 75-76
embedding, 74-75
formatting text, 72-76
hexadecimal coloring, 79-81
relative font sizes, 73-74
sizing text, 73
tables, 103
<H1>
adding, 57
designing home pages, 214
<HEAD>, 52-53, 57
<Hn>, 60
<HR>, 61
extensions, 62-65
replacing with graphics, 127
<HTML>, 52-53, 180
<I>, 69
<IMG>, 118-119
adding image maps, 162
adding video clips, 211
ALIGN keyword, 123-125
linking images, 113, 145, 156
overlaying images, 136
sizing images, 126
<LH>, 87-88

<LI>, 87
  ordered lists, 89
  organizing links, 150
  unordered lists, 88
logical (browsers), 69
<MAP>, 167-168
multimedia, 26
<NOBR>, 60
<OL>, 87, 89
<P>, 60, 225
<PRE>, 66, 104
previewing, 225
<S>, 70
search engines, 53
<SMALL>, 70-71
special characters, 81-82
<STRONG>, 68
<SUB>, 72
<SUP>, 72
<TABLE>, 95-96
tables, 95
<TD>, 95, 98
templates, 52
<TH>, 95
<TITLE>
  adding, 55-56
  splitting Web pages,
    180
<TR>, 95
<U>, 70
<UL>, 87-88, 150
viewing, 14
<WBR>, 60
Web pages, splitting, 180
targets, *see anchors*
<TD> tags, 95, 98
technical support
  home pages, 32-33
  Web providers, 44
Telnet, 15
templates
  home pages, 52
  tags, 52

text
  adding, 58
  alternate
    images, 122-123
    image maps, 172
  backgrounds, 129-131
    adding color, 129-130
  coloring, 78-81
    <FONT> tags, 78
    <BODY> tags, 79
    hexadecimal, 79-81
  formatting, 59-72
    <FONT> tags, 72-76
    blinking, 69-70
    bold, 68-69
    centering, 68
    horizontal rules, 61-65
    HotDog Pro, 255
    line breaks, 60
    paragraphs, 60
    preformatted, 66
    relative font sizes,
      73-74
    sizing, 70-71, 73
    strikethrough, 70
    subscripts, 72
    superscripts, 72
    underline, 70
  hypertext, 138
  organizing (lists), 84-85
  preformatted, replacing
    tables, 104-105
  selecting links, 152-153
  special characters,
    adding, 81-82
  spell-checking, 226
  tables, aligning, 101
  tags
    <BODY>, 54
    <PRE>, 66
**TEXT keyword, coloring
  text, 79**
**TEXTTOP keyword
  (images), 124**

<TH> tags, 95
three-by-three rule, 215
**3-D graphics (enclosed
  CD-ROM), 109**
**thumbnails (images),
  121**
<TITLE> tags
  adding, 55-56
  Web pages, splitting, 180
tools, selecting, 252-260
**Tools menu commands,
  Options, 253**
Toyota Web site, 10
<TR> tags, 95
**transparent GIFs,
  131-134**
  browsers, 132-133
  creating, 133-134
troubleshooting
  backgrounds, 131
  files, uploading, 141
  image maps, 172
    designs, 173-174
    links, 162
  links, testing, 140
**TUCOWS Web site (The
  Ultimate Collection of
  Winsock Software), 263**
**TYPE keyword
  (numbered lists), 90**

U

<U> tags, 70
<UL> tags, 87-88, 150
**Ultimate Collection Of
  Winsock Software, The
  (TUCOWS Web site),
  263**
underlining text, 70

uniform resource locators, *see* **URLs**

Unisys (PNG file format), 116

unordered (bulleted) lists, adding, 88

uploading Web pages, 50

URLs (uniform resource locators), 11-12, 138
anchor tags, 147
browsers, 141
business cards, 32
case sensitivity, 142
copying, 142
image maps, 155
links, adding, 142
pasting, 142
viewing (Explorer), 113

USEMAP keyword, adding image maps, 162

UseNet, 14
links, 138, 191
Web pages, publicizing, 244-246

V

validation tools (HTML), 227-230
WebTechs Validation Service, 228-229

VALIGN keyword (tables), 101

video cameras, 208

video clips, 204-208
adding, 209-211
CD-ROM (enclosed), 206, 267
creating, 208
embedding
Explorer, 211
Netscape, 210-211

file formats, 205-206
file size, 205
finding, 206-208
Internet, 207
links, adding, 209

View menu commands
Document, 224
Document Source, 221, 225
Page Source, 14
Source, 14, 113

Virtual Reality Modeling Language, *see* **VRML**

visitors
attracting, 232-233
expectations, 233
guestbooks, 186-189
tracking, 183-186
Web servers, 183

VIVO file format, 206

VLINK keyword, changing link color, 144

VRML (Virtual Reality Modeling Language), 19
Web site, 19

W

WAIS (Wide Area Information Service), 15
links, 138

Walt Disney Web site, 218

Warner Brothers Web site, 219

waterfall model (Web sites), 177

WAV file format, 199

<WBR> tags, 60

Weather Channel Web site, 216

Web browsers, 21-23
Accent, 23
Amaya, 23
comparing, 23
Explorer, 21-23
ActiveX, 23
audio clips, 204
<BLINK> tags, 70
horizontal lines, 62
images, 111
PNG images, 116
text, 59
URLs, 113
video clips, 211
Web site, 22
GIFs (transparent), 132-133
HTML extensions, 26
image maps
client-side, 173
testing, 172
Mosaic, 18, 23
Netscape, 21
audio clips, 202-204
color settings, 144
history, 18
image maps, 167
images, 110
PNG images, 116
tables, 104-105
text, 59
video clips, 210-211
status bars, 142
tags, displaying logical, 69
URLs, 141
Web pages, testing, 227
Web sites, 23

Web Consortium (future WWW enhancements), 19
Home page, 25
Web site, 19

Web pages
addresses, 54
audio clips, adding,
201-204
backgrounds (design
tips), 214
building
GIF Construction Set,
262
PaintShop Pro,
260-262
consistency, checking,
214
cost
advertising, 248
CoffeeCup, 256
counters, 186
HotDog Pro, 253
HoTMetaL, 258
online services, 47
Submit-it!, 244
Web providers, 44-45
Web servers, 49
counters
adding, 183-186
advanced, 186
cost, 186
placing, 185
designing
borrowing concepts,
39, 221
creeping featurism,
218-221
hidden links, 219-220
text length, 214-215
three-by-three rule,
215
tips, 214-217
expanding, 176-183
file size guidelines,
120-121
footers, 180, 214
graphics, 108-109
adding, 214
enclosed CD-ROM,
109-110, 267

finding, 109-115
GIF Construction Set,
262
PaintShop Pro,
260-262
tables, 101
guestbooks, adding,
186-189
headings, adding, 56-58
icons, adding, 126-129
image maps, *see* image
maps
images, *see* images
internal document
pointers, adding, 146
linking, 141-142, 181
creating local, 140-141
keeping current, 153
limiting, 151
selecting text, 152-153
tips, 151-153
testing, 140
lists, *see* lists
multimedia, 195-196
designing, 216
mixing, 211-212
planning, 211-212
navigating (navigation
icons), 128-129
previewing, 225-227
prototyping, 39
publicizing, 232
advertising, 248-249
announcement
services, 234-236
business cards, 247
comp.infosystems.www.
announce, 244-245
e-mail, 247
indexes, 234
links, 247-248
Lycos, 241-242
newsgroups, 244-246
resumes, 247
Submit It!, 243-244
WebCrawler, 242-249

What's New listings,
234-236
WWW catalogs, 234
WWW directories,
237-241
splitting, 176-177, 179-181
tables, 84, 94
adding, 95-97
testing, 225-230
browsers, 227
HTML validation tools,
227-230
text
backgrounds, 129-131
spell-checking, 226
titles, adding, 55-56
updating, 216-217
uploading, 50
URLs, 12
visitors, attracting,
232-233
see also home pages
Web providers
alternatives (Web
servers), 49-50
censorship, 44
comparing, 44
connecting, 43-50
cost, 44-45
home page, 44
ISPs, comparing, 43
listings, viewing, 45-46
online services, 47-49
AOL, 47
CompuServe, 48-49
reliability, 44
technical support, 44
**Web Server (Web
providers), 43**
Web servers, 16-17
case sensitivity, 142
cost, 49
image maps, 157-158
visitors, tracking, 183

Web providers,
  alternatives, 49-50
Web site, 50
Web sites
  Accent browser, 23
  Accent Software, 81
  Alchemy Mindworks, 262
  Amaya browser, 23
  anchor tags, 146
  Apple Computer, 206
  audio clips, 200
  Audio File Format FAQ,
    199
  author, 35, 72, 84
  AVI, 206
  background colors, 130
  BrowserWatch, 23
  budgetweb, 45
  Buena Vista movies, 196
  Chrysler, 232
  Coca-Cola, 37-38
  CoffeeCup, 256
  Cologne Answer Guy,
    216
  Connectix, 208
  CoolEdit, 199
  counters, 184-186
  Creating Web pages, 138
  Crime Scene, 35
  Daily Wav, 200
  DC Comics, 219
  digits, 185
  Dilbert, 110
  ESPN, 37
  Excite, 239
  Explorer, 22
  Forman Interactive, 47
  Four11, 239
  FourPalms software, 207
  Free Page Site, 46
  Geocities, 46
  GIF Construction Set,
    262
  guestbooks, 187, 189
  hexadecimal colors, 80

HotDog Pro, 42, 252, 254
HoTMetaL, 258
HTML, 26
HTML standards, 227
HTML Validator, 230
image maps, 160
images, linking, 111-113
Independence Day, 196
infi.net, 130
Internet Assistants, 260
JASC, 160
LensCrafters, 33
Lycos, 241
Magnavox, 10, 156
managing, 182-183
MapTHIS!, 163
Microsoft, 17, 19
modems, 17
Mosaic, 23
MPEG, 206-207
Multilingual WWW
  Publisher, 81
NCSA What's New, 234
NetCarta, 182
Netscape Composer, 259
Netscape Home page, 21
Netscape's What's New?,
  236
Official WWW Yellow
  Pages, 240
pagecount, 185
PaintShop Pro, 114, 133
planning, 177-179
plug-ins, 117
PNG, 116
Que, 49, 248
Quicktime, 206-207
RealAudio, 199
Sausage Software, 252,
  254
shareware, 17
SoftQuad, Inc, 258
special characters, 82
Star Wars, 195
Submit It!, 243
Toyota, 10

TUCOWS, 263
VRML, 19
Walt Disney, 218
Warner Brothers, 219
Weather Channel, 216
Web Consortium, 19, 25
Web pages
  expanding, 176-183
  linking, 181
Web Servers, 50
WebCrawler, 242
WebLaunch, 248
Weblint, 230
WebMapper, 182
WebTechs Validation
  Service, 228-229
Wincam, 208
Winsock client,
  downloading, 17
Worst of the Web, 233
Yahoo!, 237
Yahoo! List, 230
**Web Weaver (HTML
  editor), 258**
WebCrawler, 242
**WebCrawler Web site,
  242**
**WebLaunch Web site,
  248**
Weblint Web site, 230
**WebMapper Web site,
  182**
**WebTechs Validation
  Service Web site,
  228-229**
WebTV (tables), 84
**What's New listings,
  publicizing Web pages,
  234-236**
white papers (Lotus), 32
**Wide Area Information
  Service (WAIS), 15**
  links, 138

WIDTH keyword
   horizontal lines, 63
   images, sizing, 125-126

WinCam video camera, 208

Wincam Web site, 208

Windows, comparing to WWW, 19

Windows 95
   fonts, viewing, 76
   shortcuts, creating, 255

Winsock (Windows Socket) clients, 17
   downloading, 17

Wizards, Home Page (CompuServe), 48

Word
   fonts, testing, 76
   HTML, creating files, 41
   Internet Assistants, 259
   text (spell-checking), 226

word break tags, 60

WordPro, testing fonts, 76

Worst of the Web site, 233

WWW (World Wide Web), 9-10, 16-19
   browsers, 21-23
      Accent, 23
      Amaya, 23
      Explorer, 21-23
      Mosaic, 23
      Netscape, 21
   client/server, 16-17
   connections (ISDN), 17
   CSS (Cascading Style Sheets), 19
   future enhancements, 19
   history, 18-19
   HTML, 13-14
   hypertext links, 11-13
   interactivity, 15

   multimedia, 10-11
   protocols, 14-15, 189
   search tools
      Lycos, 241-242
      WebCrawler, 242
   searching, 241-242
   Windows, comparing, 19

WWW browsers, *see* **Web browsers**

WWW catalogs, *see* **WWW directories**

WWW directories
   Excite, 239
   Four11, 239
   URLs, 12
   Web pages, publicizing, 234, 237-241
   Yahoo!, 237-238

WWW search engines (tags), 53

WYSIWYG HTML editors, 252

X-Y-Z

Yahoo!, 237-238
   Web site, 237

Yahoo! List Web site, 230

Complete and Return this Card
for a *FREE* Computer Book Catalog

Thank you for purchasing this book! You have purchased a superior computer book written expressly for your needs. To continue to provide the kind of up-to-date, pertinent coverage you've come to expect from us, we need to hear from you. Please take a minute to complete and return this self-addressed, postage-paid form. In return, we'll send you a free catalog of all our computer books on topics ranging from word processing to programming and the internet.

Mr. ☐   Mrs. ☐   Ms. ☐   Dr. ☐

Name (first) ☐☐☐☐☐☐☐☐☐☐☐☐ (M.I.) ☐ (last) ☐☐☐☐☐☐☐☐☐☐☐☐☐☐☐

Address ☐☐☐☐☐☐☐☐☐☐☐☐☐☐☐☐☐☐☐☐☐☐☐☐☐☐☐☐☐

☐☐☐☐☐☐☐☐☐☐☐☐☐☐☐☐☐☐☐☐☐☐☐☐☐☐☐☐☐

City ☐☐☐☐☐☐☐☐☐☐☐☐ State ☐☐ Zip ☐☐☐☐☐ ☐☐☐☐

Phone ☐☐☐ ☐☐☐☐☐☐☐ Fax ☐☐☐ ☐☐☐☐☐☐☐

Company Name ☐☐☐☐☐☐☐☐☐☐☐☐☐☐☐☐☐☐☐☐☐☐☐☐☐

E-mail address ☐☐☐☐☐☐☐☐☐☐☐☐☐☐☐☐☐☐☐☐☐☐☐☐☐

1. Please check at least (3) influencing factors for purchasing this book.

Front or back cover information on book .... ☐
Special approach to the content .... ☐
Completeness of content... ☐
Author's reputation .... ☐
Publisher's reputation .... ☐
Book cover design or layout .... ☐
Index or table of contents of book .... ☐
Price of book... ☐
Special effects, graphics, illustrations .... ☐
Other (Please specify): _____ ☐

2. How did you first learn about this book?

Saw in Macmillan Computer Publishing catalog .... ☐
Recommended by store personnel .... ☐
Saw the book on bookshelf at store .... ☐
Recommended by a friend .... ☐
Received advertisement in the mail .... ☐
Saw an advertisement in: _____ ☐
Read book review in: _____ ☐
Other (Please specify): _____ ☐

3. How many computer books have you purchased in the last six months?

This book only .... ☐   3 to 5 books .... ☐
2 books.................. ☐   More than 5 .... ☐

4. Where did you purchase this book?

Bookstore .... ☐
Computer Store .... ☐
Consumer Electronics Store .... ☐
Department Store .... ☐
Office Club .... ☐
Warehouse Club .... ☐
Mail Order .... ☐
Direct from Publisher .... ☐
Internet site .... ☐
Other (Please specify): _____ ☐

5. How long have you been using a computer?

☐ Less than 6 months   ☐ 6 months to a year
☐ 1 to 3 years   ☐ More than 3 years

6. What is your level of experience with personal computers and with the subject of this book?

	With PCs	With subject of book
New	☐	☐
Casual	☐	☐
Accomplished	☐	☐
Expert	☐	☐

Source Code ISBN: 0-7897-1232-6

7. Which of the following best describes your job title?

- Administrative Assistant ☐
- Coordinator ☐
- Manager/Supervisor ☐
- Director ☐
- Vice President ☐
- President/CEO/COO ☐
- Lawyer/Doctor/Medical Professional ☐
- Teacher/Educator/Trainer ☐
- Engineer/Technician ☐
- Consultant ☐
- Not employed/Student/Retired ☐
- Other (Please specify): _____ ☐

8. Which of the following best describes the area of the company your job title falls under?

- Accounting ☐
- Engineering ☐
- Manufacturing ☐
- Operations ☐
- Marketing ☐
- Sales ☐
- Other (Please specify): _____ ☐

9. What is your age?

- Under 20 ☐
- 21-29 ☐
- 30-39 ☐
- 40-49 ☐
- 50-59 ☐
- 60-over ☐

10. Are you:

- Male ☐
- Female ☐

11. Which computer publications do you read regularly? (Please list)

_____
_____
_____
_____
_____
_____
_____
_____
_____
_____

Comments: _____
_____
_____

Fold here and scotch-tape to mail.

Check out Que® Books
on the World Wide Web
http://www.quecorp.com

As the biggest software release in computer history, Windows 95 continues to redefine the computer industry. Click here for the latest info on our Windows 95 books

Make computing quick and easy with these products designed exclusively for new and casual users

Examine the latest releases in word processing, spreadsheets, operating systems, and suites

The Internet, The World Wide Web, CompuServe®, America Online®, Prodigy® —it's a world of ever-changing information. Don't get left behind!

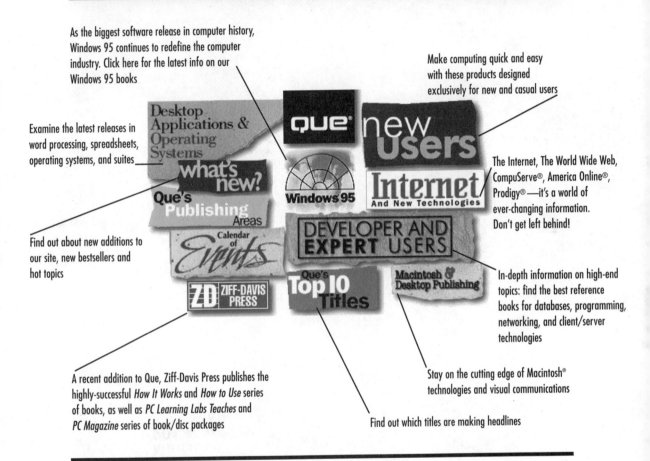

Find out about new additions to our site, new bestsellers and hot topics

In-depth information on high-end topics: find the best reference books for databases, programming, networking, and client/server technologies

A recent addition to Que, Ziff-Davis Press publishes the highly-successful *How It Works* and *How to Use* series of books, as well as *PC Learning Labs Teaches* and *PC Magazine* series of book/disc packages

Stay on the cutting edge of Macintosh® technologies and visual communications

Find out which titles are making headlines

With 6 separate publishing groups, Que develops products for many specific market segments and areas of computer technology. Explore our Web Site and you'll find information on best-selling titles, newly published titles, upcoming products, authors, and much more.

- Stay informed on the latest industry trends and products available

- Visit our online bookstore for the latest information and editions

- Download software from Que's library of the best shareware and freeware

Copyright © 1997, Macmillan Computer Publishing-USA, A Viacom Company